A DEATH IN KENYA

A DEATH IN KENYA

The Murder of Julie Ward

Michael A. Hiltzik

CORGI BOOKS

A DEATH IN KENYA
A BANTAM BOOK 0 553 40357 5

First publication in Great Britain

PRINTING HISTORY
Bantam Books edition published 1991

This book is set in 10/11pt Plantin by
County Typesetters, Margate, Kent

Bantam Books are published by Transworld Publishers Ltd.,
61–63 Uxbridge Road, Ealing, London W5 5SA, in Australia
by Transworld Publishers (Australia) Pty. Ltd., 15–23 Helles
Avenue, Moorebank, NSW 2170, and in New Zealand by
Transworld Publishers (N.Z.) Ltd., Cnr. Moselle and
Waipareira Avenues, Henderson, Auckland.

Made and printed in Great Britain by
Cox & Wyman Ltd., Reading, Berks.

To Deborah and Andrew

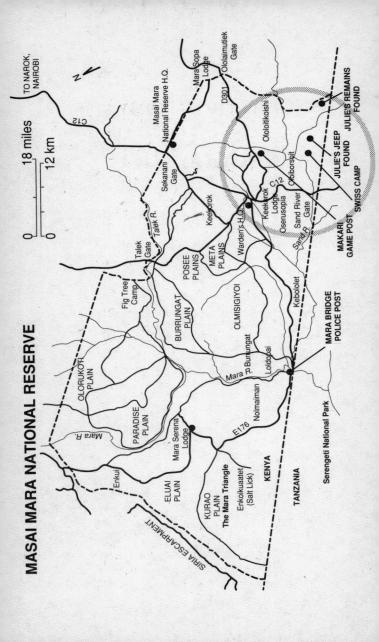

A DEATH IN KENYA

PROLOGUE: Shauri ya Mungu

The day dies fast, so close to the equator. Sunset was already preparing its rapid sweep over the browning savannah one day in early September as two green vehicles loaded with men cut a swath across the knee-high grass a few kilometers north of the Kenya-Tanzania border. Even a distant observer might have gathered from their haste that the vehicles were dashing back to home base before the dark closed in.

What made one of the trucks slow down and stop by an unremarkable clump of bush and tree would become a matter of disagreement in the future. It would not be a small question, for some people in the tiny convoy would find themselves accused of terrible crimes because the explanations they gave later were found wanting.

The issue would never really be resolved, but for now let us accept the version that states that one of the Land Rovers was brought to a halt by a dark shadow spotted off in the middle distance. The shade suddenly quickened and rose, like a resentful spirit disturbed from some malign business, and resolved itself into the forms of two vultures rising in startled haste from a find of partially consumed carrion.

Seven men extracted themselves from the vehicle. Most of them were members of the Masai tribe, which had long guarded its historic protectorate over this place, the Masai Mara Game Reserve, with a ferocious loyalty it reserved only for one other thing: its cattle. One Masai, evidently in charge, was wearing a tan safari suit. Most of the others were dressed in the green issue of the Kenya parks department, although their uniforms had long since worn down to a scruffy tatterdemalion. They may have had the

1

unhappy air of men hauled back to work after thinking they had successfully evaded an unpleasant day's task, which was indeed the case. But there was no avoiding it now.

One man, the lone policeman among the detachment of rangers, entered the thicket. The remains of a campfire made a dark smudge on the ground. At one side was an object that seemed to have attracted the vultures' attention. He touched it, turned it over in his hands, then rose for a look around. Finally he climbed into the vehicle and radioed the second truck to turn back and join his team.

It was getting late. The scene had an air of forlorn isolation that would be more than justified by the baleful shadow it would cast over many people, and this country itself, for the next two years. It was a place so well concealed in the empty miles of African bush that even those who came to know it well would pass by it time and time again, having to double back before spotting the marks of white paint left for identification, as if it remained forever reluctant to give up its secrets. Shown aerial photos of the very spot, they would often fail to recognize it.

The grove's most prominent feature was a great sausage tree. In itself this could be taken for a sour omen. *Kigelia Africanus* is a relative of the jacaranda, but lacking the latter's aromatic grace. The sausage tree is noble only from a distance, where the luxuriant spread of its crown makes it stand out among the flat-topped acacia that punctuate the vista of flat brown grass. Closer in one focuses on the fruit that inspired its name and that hang from its branches on long strands like unappetizingly moldy British bangers. Even its blazing red flowers, which open their blooms for a single day before falling rottenly to the ground to be picked at by bats, lend a distasteful quality to the sausage tree: no-one who describes the plant fails to remark on their foul aroma.

The fire had been set under this tree. Without exception everyone who would then and later come to this spot would make the observation that the blaze had been fierce

2

enough to singe the lowest branches, six and a half feet off the ground.

Inspector George Othiambo, the policeman, resumed his examination of what was clearly the lower jawbone of a primate. Othiambo was a quiet, simple man who would be savagely overmatched by the events his sharp eye had already set in motion. Othiambo was chief of the Mara Bridge police station, the only police detachment located inside the park, but to at least one person who would shortly be joining the clutch of officers around the cold firesite he would give off the impression of having been dropped into an untenable situation without resources or instructions.

That was an accurate enough assessment, as far as it went. But for the moment Othiambo's attention was on the jawbone. It was in two pieces, sliced through so cleanly that a lower tooth had been cleft in half. Othiambo turned it over to show something to some of the other men. Lest there be any doubt what species of animal they were examining, he showed that the line of teeth was stippled in five places with the silvery workmanship of modern dentistry.

Then he turned his attention back to the extinct fire. A shallow path in the loose dirt, like the wake of something dragged over the ground by small animals, led from one side of the fire to a spot a few yards away, where the object that had been tugged over the earth still lay. It was a human leg, cut off at the kneecap, its livid flesh still clad in a denim trouserleg.

The significance of the find was lost on no-one. For two days now the air over the Mara, always busy with regular flights ferrying tourists between Nairobi and the park's four gravel airstrips, had sustained an unusually urgent traffic. Small fixed-wing craft and helicopters ranged all about the park's southern quadrant flying low; earlier on this day the radios at the ranger posts had crackled with the staticky communications of a full-scale search. There was a hum of activity at Keekorok Lodge, the luxury hotel central to this portion of the 700-square-mile park, that

3

could not be mistaken for the cheerful, lazy routine of the tourist trade. Those things alone told the rangers something important had occurred, even before they had been summoned by their boss, the man in the tan safari suit, and packed into two ranger vehicles for a dash across country.

All of them had spent a good many years in this place of primordial natural savagery, where it was as common as sunrise to come across the scattered bones of a victimized gazelle or the grotesque carcass of an elephant with its face chain-sawed off in a poachers' quest for its ivory. Just now was the annual southern migration of the wildebeest, which moved north every April in a vast flood from their dry feeding grounds in the Serengeti, just over the Tanzanian border, and returned home at this time of the year. A great natural spectacle, the migration was an occasion of unexampled violence, as lions, cheetahs, jackals, and hyenas preyed greedily on stragglers and young among the immense herd.

Some of those who stood in the late-afternoon light under the sausage tree had even been on hand on the very rare occasions when a human death occurred in the Masai Mara. Always before, this had been the work of animals, mostly cape buffalo who stampeded a hapless member of a foot party. But it is fair to say that none of the rangers had ever contemplated a sight like this. There was too much about it that seemed beyond the capability of animals.

As the hour drew on, the men shifted uneasily in their places. In early September the light of this time of day could not be mistaken for that of any other place on earth. Except when the heavy clouds of the rainy seasons turn the sky a flinty gray, the sun of equatorial Kenya blazes year round with the intensity of midday at high summer. Its directness struck the region's first white settlers with such a preternatural power that for the first half-century of white settlement it was an article of faith that to take one's hat off, even under the tin roof of a house, was to court sickness, madness, and death. Africans laughed at the *wazungu*, the white men, who in the heat of midday

4

swathed themselves in red flannel under their light outer clothing. But even the Africans knew that the late-afternoon light had a special quality.

As the day nears its end there is a brief passage through that magical hour when the angle of the sun's rays illuminates every feature of the landscape with a golden glow. It is a time when the implacable hunters of the plains see the tracks of their prey etched on the ground in high relief. The modern hunter who shoots with a camera lens is entranced by the splendid radiance of the colors that erupt on the land as if from a divine palette.

Then the elusive glow is abruptly extinguished, the sun falls toward the horizon like a ball rolling off the edge of a table. For a few moments the sky is lit in phosphorescent color, and then with a decisive swiftness that never fails to extract a spiritual gasp of astonishment night closes in like the lid of a casket.

It was nearly that time now. As the hour of four o'clock approached and then passed, the men grew more restive. Wild animals awoke to activity as the sun died, and none of the rangers wished to be motoring on the park's rutted muddy roads after nightfall, when the even the vistas most recognizable in the daylight change into a strange, unfamiliar land into which one could disappear forever.

The Africans wanted to leave. Bones had been found, there was little more to do. Their very expressions silently attested to the words they would have applied to the inexplicable events that had taken place here: 'Shauri ya mungu'. It is a Swahili phrase that refers to the black finality of things beyond man's fathoming. It means 'God's will'.

Suddenly, in the all-encompassing silence of open nature, there was a faint vibration. It grew in strength until it coalesced into the impatient clatter of a helicopter. In the distance, off to the north, the chopper rose into the glimmering sky, seeking altitude so the ranger manning a radio in one of the vehicles could direct it to this hushed place camouflaged in the stippled brown-green topography of the Mara. Coming in the helicopter, they all

5

knew, were two *wazungu*. One was piloting the craft, and his passenger was a man whose daughter had gone missing near here a few days before. They assumed positions of attention. It was late, and there would be much to do before the end of the day.

Part One

Gone Missing

CHAPTER ONE

Nestled neatly between Cambridge and the East Anglian coast, the little town of Bury St Edmunds is perhaps not as unique as it would like to believe. There are dozens of places just like it across England, perhaps hundreds in Europe: towns with pride in having preserved their historic atmosphere and charm amid the bustle of modernity.

The result is as discordant in all those other hamlets as it is in this ancient market town and ecclesiastical center. The invitingly spacious village square, preserved with its rim of timber-beamed houses and bricked shopfronts, is paved and used as a parking lot. The old narrow dimensions of Bury's center-village streets have been carefully preserved, so the traffic is often at a standstill because Hondas and Fords cannot easily negotiate streets that foot traffic and horse carriages once had to themselves. The high street – here called the Cornhill – has a wood-fronted chemist shop like the ones tourists cherish for their atmosphere of having been transported changelessly from the nineteenth century. The old Suffolk Hotel, now run by a modern lodging chain, keeps a tatty grandeur. But these establishments stand cheek by jowl with the Boots drugstores and W. H. Smith booksellers ubiquitous all over Great Britain. At one end of the street a Burger King and a McDonald's stand like sentries.

Bury St Edmunds does have a feature that lends strength to a claim, if not of uniqueness, at least to being a special place. This is the striking ruin of its thirteenth-century abbey, located behind a massive Gothic stone gate and deep within a wide, lovely garden. All that remain of the abbey of St Edmundsbury are its broken columns and foundations of coarse stone and mortar, standing tall and worn like sand castles washed by a gentle wave. They have genuine grace and grandeur, not the least for being all that was left after a townspeople's anticlerical revolt sacked the big church in the sixteenth century.

In a ramshackle office in the shadow of the abbey Ian Rowland and a job applicant regarded each other across a desk one day in September 1979. Rowland Photo Typesetters was a bare-bones operation scarcely nine months old. Its workspace reflected its lack of pretension. The firm had taken a floor of a ramshackle former girl's school that could be described as dilapidated only out of charity. Part of the Rowland suite had been the girls' bathroom; now it was all but filled by a copying-collating machine.

Ian Rowland was a fresh-faced man with a receding line of dark hair and a modest disposition. He gave off a well-scrubbed air, as if still pink from a hot bath; his face fairly shone and his clothes were immaculate. From his side of the desk Rowland regarded the applicant carefully. Julie Anne Ward had recently moved with her parents and brothers to Bury St Edmunds. She had an open, unassuming face under her straight blond hair. Julie had finished school in her old hometown but had chosen not to go on to college; perhaps she was no intellectual, but she was clearly intelligent, with an earnest, confident demeanor. Rowland's firm was still small, with only six employees. It was at a delicate stage where the mix of people on the floor might make a real impact on the business's fortunes. In fact, the job Julie was interviewing for was modest enough: running the big copier in the old girls' cloakroom.

Rowland had many occasions later to congratulate himself on bringing the slight, unassuming girl into his firm. Being crammed into such small, dingy corners was an invitation for people's sharp edges to rub each other raw, but Julie Ward was a person who seemed to have no sharp edges. She was quietly efficient, with a ready smile and a composed approach to crisis, whether it was a monstrously tight deadline or a mechanical problem in the shop. This no doubt derived from her painstaking and

10

methodical nature: her mother later remembered being told that 'if something at work required eight steps to complete it, you could be absolutely certain that Julie would complete each step carefully and correctly.'

Rowland Photo would grow fast in the years Julie worked for the firm. Photo typesetting was the wave of the future in publishing, as the machine age metamorphosed into the computer age and books ceased to be set by printers who arranged metal type into dies, selecting the tiny pieces from drawers. Now a book could be set directly from the keyboard of a computer, which transformed the typescript into pages to be photographed and converted into an ink-taking plate. Business was booming and in mid-1982 Rowland decided he needed a personal assistant. The choice of Julie was obvious. 'I sort of took her under my wing,' Rowland said later.

In part Rowland may have perceived that she had time to contribute to her work. Just coming out of school and having relocated a fair distance from her old friends, Julie had no social life in Bury St Edmunds. Her father would later remark that she seemed caught in some sort of time warp: she still wore her hair in the cute bangs of a schoolgirl although she was already twenty-two. The market squares and lone movie theater of Bury were scarcely enough to keep a teenager occupied for long, much less a young woman. Julie had moved to Bury with the family at an age and in a situation where it was hard to make new friends. There was no longer the easy, accessible social atmosphere of school, and Bury St Edmunds did not exactly have a nightclub quarter. Rowland Photo became her life, a 9 a.m. to 9 p.m. job, with plenty of work left to take home. 'She threw herself body and soul into this job,' Rowland said.

There was no employee more eager to stay late to meet a deadline, none more collected under pressure. She was reserved but not cold, and unfailingly polite and friendly. She was not the type who organized office birthday parties – that would have meant stepping forward in a way that was alien to her personality. But she was the type who would take over someone's job so they could leave early, who provided a calm oasis amid the tension and hubbub of a small office. If she had an idea she would not hesitate to express it, but did so unobtrusively. 'What if we do this?' she would ask quietly, letting the force of the idea sink in without pressure or advocacy. More often than not, it would work.

If Julie's mild disposition was inherited from her mother, Janet, her ability to size up a business problem and develop a solution was the gift of her father. John Ward was that quintessential figure of the Thatcherite revolution in Great Britain: the self-made man.

Ward had been raised in a council house – a quasi-public housing development – in Wealdstone on the outskirts of London. One day, after contemplating the tremendous business being turned over by an elegant coffee house in Knightsbridge, the Harrods district of London, he and a friend borrowed some money from Ward's father to start a similar venture in Muswell Hill. They caught a wave, as cozy bistros became fashionable. The El Toro Expresso Coffee House evolved into a restaurant and then the flagship of a chain of three.

Ward hankered to move into the hotel business and finally came up with some American capital. With a partner he established Saxon Inns; its six hotels were pitched at the businessman's trade, offering bathrooms in every room – a rarity in those postwar days – and locations not far from major motorways and near, but not in, such business centers as Manchester and Newcastle. Ward was a determined executive and a perfectionist. At the opening of Saxon's first hotel in Harlow, when the place was full of traveling liquor salesmen and he was living exhausted out of the office, he noticed the corridors lined with pairs of shoes placed outside for an overnight shine. That night he did the job himself. 'I cleaned every last pair,' he remembered later.

In 1978, at the age of forty-five, Ward sold Saxon Inns upon the death of his partner and made enough to retire to southern California, where he happily contemplated a life of sailing and relaxation. Two years later he was bored with retirement and back in Bury, planning his second chain of hotels. Butterfly Hotels took the Saxon concept a step farther, striving to establish clean and comfortable business hotels all over England, places where a commercial traveler could find a bed and familiar decor at a modest price. Ward may have picked up the idea from the Ramada and Holiday Inns that were so successful in the United States.

By then Ward had already moved his family out of Welwyn Garden City to Bury St Edmunds, where they had a big white house on spacious grounds surrounded by horse farms. Ward later would readily acknowledge that the relocation was probably harder on his daughter than on her two younger brothers. Tim and Robert were still in school, young and active enough to fit into a new crowd without too much difficulty. Boys tend to do so more easily than girls, anyway. Julie had finished school, she was older and more introverted. Her old schoolmates might remember the flashy red car in which she drove around her old haunts, but there was not much in the way of social entrée once the Wards moved into the house in Brockley Green on the outskirts of the old abbey town and Ward established headquarters in an old red brick building just down the street from the great Gothic abbey gate.

There were two sources of companionship for the solitary young woman. One was her family. 'She was my best friend,' her mother remembered later. Julie was the organizer of family projects, the mastermind of Christmas arrangements every year. She never left Brockley Green without methodically scribbling a note for the rest of the family – where she was going, when she would be back, and so on. It was such an ingrained habit that later on, standing in a muddy gully in Africa, John Ward would experience a potent feeling of apprehension when he came upon her trail, and found no note.

The other companions were animals. There were two dogs at the house – Julie and her mother often escorted the huskies to sled-dog events around England – but she went far afield to commune with other animals. There could scarcely be an animal hostel in East Anglia, a place bursting with bird sanctuaries and little private zoos, where she was not known. One was Redwings Horse Sanctuary, a farm in Frettenham that kept old horses, ponies, and mules. Julie felt an instant affinity with a pitiful old horse there named Barney. He was a sickly twenty-year-old swayback with one good eye and had evidently fetched up at Redwings after a lifetime of being mistreated. Julie visited frequently and 'sponsored' Barney's care, as the sanctuary put it, providing regular contributions to keep him in oats and comfort.

It was the same story at the old schoolhouse quarters of Rowland Photo, which housed an old tomcat. No-one knew where he came from or lived; he might have come as a package deal with the building itself. Julie lived the cliché of picking up strays. She named him 'Sniffy' and made sure he got milk and food every day. In 1984, when Rowland Photo was bursting the seams of the schoolhouse and Ian Rowland leased a new space in a gleaming industrial-park complex up the road, he gently informed Julie that Sniffy could not come along. 'What are you going to do about him?' he asked. No problem, she said, she would take him home.

By then the business was a major entity. From the new building they could typeset 1,200 books a year, and the best-selling novels and nonfiction books set in the Rowland shop filled a line of shelves in a windowed, carpeted reception room out front. Rowland acquired a contract to typeset Gideon Bibles. He was a major contractor for important publishers like Penguin and Macmillan. Julie got new responsibilities. She was installed in an office of her own at a big desk in front of a wall-sized chart displaying the typesetting schedule for manuscripts already in or due in and parceled out among the keyboard operators, with everything on color-coded cards. When a rush job came in – 'in the old days we used to have four to six weeks, now the publishers all want the job done in two,' Rowland said – Julie rearranged the cards like a juggler. Rowland was proud of his judgment. The firm could not have grown as it had without her, he said later. She had worked day and night, mastered the complexities of work flow, contributed time and ideas without stint. In seven years she had scarcely taken a day off.

So in 1986 Julie took a vacation. She packed the camera gear she had been learning to use with increasing proficiency, and went off to photograph animals in the best place on earth to see them: Kenya.

The first trip was a relatively short one, a tightly scheduled and closely supervised safari that for most tourists composed the first and last opportunity of their lives to see Africa. When she came back to work a few weeks later, Rowland could not help noticing something different. There was a new glow in her eyes, as if she had discovered a new possibility in life. A year later she took a second trip to Kenya, and this time she seemed entirely changed. 'By the time she came back from that trip,' Rowland said later, 'her heart was there. She had just fallen in love with it.'

CHAPTER TWO

Africa has a way of beckoning, unseen but deep in the spirit, to those given to wanderlust. Even today, so close to the twenty-first century, the continent of Arab and Bantu and Swahili and Zulu offers the risk and excitement not very different from that which more than a hundred years ago tempted adventurers like Mungo Park, David Livingston, and Henry Stanley to land at places like Dakar and Zanzibar on their quests to penetrate the unknown interior.

Jo Jordan heard the beckoning in 1973. It was after she had emerged from the cloistral ordeal of a British solicitor's training, won her license and faced a career that resembled a continuation of her solitary training, stretching toward infinity. Her search for the ultimate vacation pointed her toward Africa.

In popular British magazines of a certain type the classified advertisement sections were full of notices for overland tours through Africa, in which one took potluck with twenty-five or thirty traveling companions and with the vagaries of terrain and bureaucracy to traverse the equator from the Sahara to the Cape of Good Hope. Jordan selected one. The price was 325 pounds sterling, all inclusive, and the routine had long ago been established by a dozen overland firms: They ferried a truck packed with young adventurers across the channel and then the Strait of Gibraltar, and followed a rough-mapped route through the desert, along the equator to East Africa, and then south through what was then Rhodesia toward South Africa.

It was a wide-open experience. One could do a certain amount of material preparation, but the real resources for

16

the trip had to be found deep within oneself. The rain, mud, physical challenge – these all changed unpredictably from trip to trip. Truly, Jordan considered, one could not be farther away from the world of a British solicitor.

This tour was being organized by a young British agronomist named Nick Fisher. He was himself something of a novice in the field. The previous year Fisher had picked a tour group out of the classifieds in *Time Out* or *Private Eye* just as Jordan had, and fell so in love with the experience that he sought out the only way to repeat it at a reasonable cost: organize it himself.

Soon after the trip Jordan and Fisher married each other and decided to continue the business together. They called it Ho-Bo Trans Africa Expeditions and kept it unambitious and modest in scale. Jordan and Fisher could not hope to compete with such big firms as Guerba Expeditions, the leader in the field, and they preferred to keep things personal.

In the first years they led the trips themselves. Jordan worked hard six months of the year as a solicitor so she could take the rest of the year off to see Africa by track and road. In 1981 the couple had a son, but that scarcely slowed them down; when he was two he took his first overland trip to Africa. A few years later Jordan and Fisher tried the bold experiment of taking an 'artic' over the African route – an enormous articulated semi-truck. The baby came along. By the time he was eight or nine, Jordan remembered, 'he was under the impression that everybody's parents went to Africa every year.'

In the late fall of 1987 the preparations were well under way for the annual trip departing the following February. Career and family circumstances had forced Jordan and Fisher to put Ho-Bo on a more professional basis, with hired guides and drivers running the tours while they stayed home.

In a workshop located on a farm a few miles from their home and office in the Suffolk hamlet of Halesworth, Fisher and Jordan and the drivers were beginning to assemble the traveling vehicles. (There would be two simultaneous Ho-Bo groups that year.) The routine was always the same. For each tour they bought two large British Leyland or Mercedes trucks, which provided the best combination of load capacity and efficiency, and stripped them down to the chassis. One would be rebuilt with seats, storage space, an observation deck in front, six spare tires, and room for 150 gallons of drinking water and 600 gallons of gasoline. The second would be cannibalized and its innards hooked and secured to the frame of the first truck. The product was a sturdy, powerful vehicle with bright yellow side panels and a yellow tarpaulin on top, equipped to carry two of nearly everything, including gearbox, engine, rear axle, and radiator. By the end of the trip it would be battered and bruised and so close to worthless that it would hardly fetch a decent price when it would be sold in the inflated vehicle market of Nairobi, where serviceable machines were so scarce, a ten-year-old sedan could go for the price of a new car in Europe.

One day Jordan got a call from a potential client who had picked Ho-Bo's ad out of the classifieds in one of the usual magazines. Julie Ward told Jordan she lived nearby, in Bury St Edmunds. It was only an hour away by car, and she asked to drop by. Halesworth is one of those towns that is a primary destination point on a tertiary road, so it was easy for Julie to find. But Jordan had to give her detailed directions from the center of the village to the secluded cream-colored house from which Ho-Bo conducted its business.

Jordan rarely had much of a chance to size up her clients in person like this. In truth, she never thought there was much point in trying to screen applicants for the trips. 'It's a self-selective process,' she would say. Anyone who had interest enough and the self-challenge to take on the tour, as well as the couple of thousand pounds sterling to pay Ho-Bo's fee and cover expenses along the route, had met the basic entry requirements. Conditions during the five or six months of any overland tour were so indeterminate that Jordan could barely conceive of what an ideal member would look like. 'You need a sense of humor and common sense': That was as close as she could come to it.

Still, she liked Julie and thought she would be a good traveler. The two of them sat over coffee in an ill-lit upstairs room in the Halesworth house. Along the walls and standing in every available space on the floor was a jumble of African artifacts. Statuettes, masks, fetishes – the dusty haul of sixteen years of bumpy African travel. Framed color photographs of sand dunes and market-places hung on the walls and enormous scrapbooks from past tour groups were piled against a musty sofa. On one side stood a bookcase with old, expensively-bound volumes of the great adventurers, including Stanley's multivolumed memoirs and an old classic of West African exploration, Mungo Park's *Travels*.

Jordan was particularly impressed by one thing about Julie. Unlike some Ho-Bo clients who had made earlier trips to Africa, she did not try to show off. Few people around could compete with Jordan's depth of experience on that continent – she lectured widely on her experiences and had recently been invited to give a speech to the Royal Geographic Society – but every so often someone tried, after having endured a cheap safari or two. Julie just seemed eager to learn more.

The tour manager mentally classified her as the type who would be quiet at first but come alive after about six weeks on the road. 'She wasn't confident enough to tackle something like this by herself,' Jordan said later, 'but we're a good group for people like that. We don't organize everything, we let people discover themselves. And often we find that at the end of the trip they've gained the confidence to go off on their own.'

Julie contemplated the Ho-Bo trip for several more weeks. She met Jordan a second time before finally signing up in January and putting down a deposit on the fare of 995 pounds sterling. Starting in Morocco and Algeria and continuing through West and Central Africa, the Ho-Bo travelers could go all the way to Harare, Zimbabwe (and continue on their own to South Africa), or they could end their trip in Nairobi. Julie finally selected the shorter tour, one of the last people to confirm her reservation. That was all right by Jordan and Fisher, for whom the last couple of members on a twenty-six or thirty-person tour often made the difference between turning a profit and breaking even.

Julie told Ian Rowland that she could not say how long the tour would last. Ho-Bo's literature warned group members against buying nonrefundable return air-tickets for dates too close to the scheduled end of the tour, because the travel conditions in Africa were so unpredictable, no-one could really know exactly when they might catch a homeward flight.

'We left things open,' Rowland recalled. In fact, he was convinced that she would never come back to work for him. Since her second trip to Kenya, Julie had often talked excitedly about moving to Africa for good, perhaps even setting up a small business. Rowland thought she really did not know what she wanted to do, but she was entranced by new possibilities. And those were not necessarily in England.

In any event, at Rowland Photo she had done just about all there was to do. It was not a big conglomerate with a career ladder, after all. If she stayed, she would continue to manage manuscript traffic and work late to meet deadlines and help the business grow, but there was no question of getting a title or promotion, because Rowland did not have these things to offer.

'There was no further way for her to advance, but that wasn't really the issue,' Ian Rowland reflected later. 'If you had asked me the day she left here, I would have said she'd got to the point where she wanted to see the world.'

Over the next few months the firm would get a steady stream of postcards from exotic places. Julie's path could be traced from the bubbly messages tacked on to a bulletin board in the machine room. Toward the end of June, when the Leyland truck reached the shore of Lake Victoria at Entebbe, Uganda, she sent out a postcard in her characteristically girlish hand remarking that the group had been stranded by heavy rains in Zaire, but that that had been followed by a high point of the journey.

They had gone into the mountains to see some of the last gorillas extant in Africa.

I spent two hours just 3 ft from a silverback with 3 children, she wrote. *They had to drag me back to camp!!* The crowd at Rowland nodded knowingly at this outburst from Julie, the animal lover. They would get a few more postcards, but nobody there would see her alive again.

CHAPTER THREE

February 7th, Ramsgate. England's abominable winter had set in with a vengeance, and a small group of travelers carrying lightly packed kits for the desert heat and tropical humidity of Africa huddled out of the cold in the only pub still open in the portside town. They began to introduce themselves over beers.

The Ho-Bo truck was late. It drove up to the ferry landing just as the gates were closing on the last boat to the Continent pulling away from the quay at 10.30 p.m. At the moment of greatest anticipation the group, all impatient now to leave England's shores, were becalmed overnight.

One of the clients arrived on the truck itself. Earlier that day Julie Ward's father and mother had driven her up to the cream-colored house in Halesworth to see her off. As Jo Jordan and her husband gave the yellow vehicle a last checkup and had a few words with the two group leaders, David Tree and Nicholas King, parents and daughter kissed each other goodbye.

The next day, a freezing Monday, the truck finally left Ramsgate and made its ferry passage to continental Europe. The twenty-six travelers began sizing each other up and forming the first of a thousand shifting cliques and alliances as they jounced about in its cold, cramped interior. With their offhand system Jordan and Fisher had assembled a varied cast that would have done justice to a Second World War bomber-crew movie. Most of the trekkers were still in their university years or working out a postgraduate wanderlust of some sort; two were taking their last unleashed flings before settling down with fiancées in Britain. Some were escaping family problems or personal tragedies. One of the group later remarked on how many of her companions seemed to have lost their mothers. There was a former military man and a fortyish businessman who had traveled the world but had never seen Africa.

There was the full range of personalities and physical types likely in a randomly chosen if self-selected group: A couple of born leaders, a few loudmouths who wanted to be leaders. One woman was so unfit the others watched with concern as she tried to hoist herself over the high tailgate into the truck. One was an overbearing type whose departure few would regret several months later when she left the group, stricken with hepatitis, from the decrepit river town of Bangui in the Central African Republic.

There were some who made a point of meeting everybody right away – they were the types who tended to pall after a short while, as one of the group later observed. Others took it easy, staying in the background and penetrating the group slowly, taking all the time available on a five-month overland trek to seek out the relationships they wanted.

Julie was in this latter class. It became evident quite early that she had a remarkable ability to stay out of conflicts, neither to provoke them nor participate. 'If you were angry at anyone during the trip, it would never be her,' said one of her companions. During the many periods of crisis and stress over the next five months there would be more than a few outbreaks of backbiting and confrontation, but they never seemed to involve the frail-looking but self-reliant girl from Bury St Edmunds. In this she was assisted by her dreamy manner, which sometimes gave people the impression she was spending a lot of time drifting in her very own world. If she felt ill or depressed or out of sorts during the journey – everybody had a spell of that – you would never know it. But if anyone else fell sick she always seemed to notice and come by a with a spare blanket or some food or aspirin and a consoling expression.

Julie steered a middle course in the informal democracy that emerged among the twenty-six passengers in the rear of the truck. Few among them would have disagreed with Ian Rowland's description of her manner: She did not project herself into the group, but she usually had a workable idea at just the point it was needed. 'In that kind of group – all kinds of people from all walks of life,' remembered one of the travelers, 'some people emerge as leaders, and some are just incapable of making decisions. She was neither.' David Tree, the driver and group leader, began by giving them some vague guidelines on how to organize work details. He made some very general suggestions on maintaining interpersonal relationships in the rolling metal dungeon that was to be their home for five or six months, then more or less withdrew from the scene. Tree was a veteran of fifteen years of hauling young tourists overland twice a year. The experience had given him the ability to project concern and reliability with an air of extreme nonchalance. He was a smallish, wiry man with unkempt thick black hair and a scraggly beard that accentuated the angular contours of his face. He knew enough to let the travelers have their spats alone and keep out of the fray, content to sit up front in the cab with Nick King and map out the route.

The travelers followed Tree's advice and arranged a rotating schedule of chores. Each subgroup was responsible for cooking three meals a day twice a week while another did the dishes and a third handled refuse, and so on.

By then most of them had got over the shock of their first sight of the rebuilt Leyland truck. To get inside, one had to clamber over a layer of packed provisions into a cramped hull with benches lining the sides. 'Our vehicle provides an unusual amount of personal space,' the Ho-Bo brochure said, but at the beginning the twenty-six trekkers were knocking elbows and awkwardly seeking room for their stiffening limbs. As time went on the truck seemed to air out a little, especially as soon as they hit Africa and went off road so some of them could sit on the truck's padded outside ledges and a four-person bench hanging above the cab facing front. As they got to know one another more their elbows stopped chafing so much too.

The next shortcoming they noticed was that the truck was not designed as a cold-weather accommodation. For the two or three days it took to reach the Mediterranean from northern Europe they shivered, despite the close quarters. Nighttime was the worst, as they all laid out their sleeping bags inside, abashed and uncomfortable among strangers in the freezing cold.

Finally, Spain. A few of the group slept outside in the warm Mediterranean breeze and dreamed of the next crossing, as if the adventure could not begin until they had physically put Europe behind them. Of course there was another delay: At Algeciras, the noisy Spanish port on the west side of the bay from the rock of Gibraltar, from where they were to catch a ferry to the Spanish enclave of Ceuta on the Moroccan coast, the harbor was a blanket of fishing pirogues and trawlers, assembled to express some inscrutable fishermen's grievance. At the blocked ferry quay trucks and cars backed up in a vast and chaotic mass, so disorderly one despaired of its ever getting sorted out. Water was going to be the bane of this trip, someone joked: Every time they had to cross water, there was a cock-up. It was truer than he knew.

It was another day before the fishermen's flotilla dispersed and they could get out of Algeciras. On the far side of the Mediterranean there was a further delay while the truck was refitted with new tires for the desert sand and the engine was flushed and tuned up for the searing heat ahead. Some of the group got into the spirit of a nontourist tour right away, slipping behind the edge of the Moroccan markets where baying touts thrust leatherwork and brass and embroidered silk at them, to discover the unspeakable poverty and the grim competition for sustenance that afflicted the life of the people. This was a sight that regular tourists missed amid the gay, knowing banter and blazing variety of the souks.

Cradling her camera, Julie took it all in, snapping pictures of the appalling poverty and the cacophonous markets, absorbing everything with the maturing eye of a training photographer. In the shock of discovery there was an unveiling of personality among her companions; forays like these helped reform the inchoate alliances of the group members into something more substantial. You inclined toward those who saw things like yourself. Some of the travelers reacted to the abject scenes around them with bravado or forced jocularity; Julie took them in with quiet gravity. She took her pictures, but she did not try to camouflage her sympathy, as some others did, with a seen-it-all air of indifference.

As soon as the truck was fitted the group moved east to Algeria, and then turned south into the Sahara. Jordan and Fisher had long since grown disillusioned with the favored cross-Saharan route, the Hoggar, so called because of the mountainous plateau of the same name that punctured the vista of flat sand 900 miles south of Algiers. Modern paving had reduced the crossing from ten days to only two or three. That meant 'the traveler can lose much of the atmosphere of the desert crossing of old,' Jordan advised prospective clients. As an alternative, Ho-Bo preferred a course south through the Tanezrouft Desert, west of the Hoggar.

Four hundred miles inland the travelers were enveloped in a featureless panorama of sand. The vista around them underscored the necessity for self-sufficiency on this crossing, for they were as isolated and alone as if sailing a ketch in the mid-Atlantic. It was fortunate that everything they might need was on the truck, hanging from its underbelly, lining the cabin, or soldered to its frame, for whatever they did not have with them was strictly unobtainable.

At this stage their most useful accessories were ten sand ladders, long metal grates bolted to the side of the truck over the rear wheels. Whenever the truck spun its wheels deep into the sand, teams of people had to dig a rut under the tires and slip the ladders in to give the Leyland traction. There was little point in bolting the ladders back after each use. In another mile they might have to be hauled down again.

At night they left their tents in the truck and unfurled their sleeping bags under the glittering night sky. Months later, after weeks of encounters with African life, human and wild, many would still recall the nights in the serene motionless Sahara as the most affecting of the journey.

Soon they were moving into Africa proper, the sub-Saharan region of black tribes. In traversing the border between Algeria and Mali they were crossing one of the great divides of the African continent, between the Arab Maghreb and the African Sahel. Roiling ethnic tensions affected the vast Sahelian frontier: Arab and African, white and black, Moslem and animist and Christian. Periodically they would erupt, as when the black Senegalese and Arab Mauritanians began shooting at one another over the River Senegal a year after the Ho-Bo truck skirted their lands. But in truth it was hard to establish a border, much less seal it, in the indeterminate wastes of the desert's fringe. The young people on the truck perceived a darkening of the skin of the people they roared past, driving out of the desert into the rocky outcrops of the Mali borderlands. Nomadic Hausa-Fulani tribesmen cast idly curious glances at the yellow truck as it lumbered by their herds of scrawny goats and cattle.

In the first hours in Mali the group got thoroughly lost in the featureless landscape. 'No-one, including David Tree, knew where we were,' one recalled. Finally they were passed by a truck heading toward Mopti, a fishing town and market center constructed on stilts and causeways over the River Niger, and followed it on to their route.

Tree and Nick King steered the truck along the idle wash of the River Niger, 150 miles east of the point where its path passes the fabled city of Timbuktu. Jordan and Fisher had abandoned the idea of side trips to the once-glittering camel depot a few years before, disillusioned again by the encroachment of package tours into their

27

remote world. The alternative took them from Bourem, a tiny village where the south road from Algeria first meets the Niger, east along the course of the river as far as Gao. They would ford the Niger there and take a reasonably serviceable road south-west to Mopti. But on the way they suffered their first real crisis.

The Niger was at its annual low ebb, scarcely more than a string of ponds navigable only by pirogue from Bourem to Gao. It was a shadow of the mighty river whose downstream reaches nourished half of Nigeria and spread into a magnificent delta on the Gulf of Guinea. In some spots the Leyland could speed directly over the dry riverbed. But the Niger's watered portions were treacherous, as the group discovered when the truck forded a sealike reach and suddenly spun sideways, sinking deep into a bottomless river muck and coming to a halt in midriver, tilted over at forty-five degrees.

The travelers eyed the water around them with deep apprehension, terrified to stay in the listing vehicle but panicky at the thought of bilharzia, the parasitic scourge of stagnant African waters. Bilharzia is a worm borne by water snails that afflicts people who bathe in or drink the water of rivers and lakes throughout sub-Saharan Africa. It burrows under the skin and continues its life cycle inside the human body, causing an irritating rash for about a day before disappearing. A month later it provokes an outbreak of pain and bodily catastrophe. The Niger was one of the bilharzia sites mentioned specifically in the Ho-Bo Tour literature – in fact hardly a watercourse in Africa is free of the parasite – and in the first hours some of the trekkers swore they would live on the truck until it was freed.

One of the girls began excavating the layers of provisions under the floor of the cabin to get a look at the underside. She saw that the Leyland was mired in river mud up to its fenders. It would take days to dig out.

There was nothing for it but to disembark. The group stepped gingerly into the water and portaged their tents, sleeping bags, and some provisions to the dry bank.

Nervously they contemplated a village settlement not far in the distance. The tents were pitched in a tight circle and a twenty-four-hour rotation of sentries was established.

In all they spent six days digging the Leyland out of the River Niger, submerging themselves in the water in shifts to clear the sticky mud from under its wheels. In the process they discovered Africa.

From the first the villagers approached the white tourists with wide-eyed curiosity. They seemed to have concluded that the group were all doctors – or perhaps that any such strange-looking white persons had access to inscrutable medical secrets. Several mothers brought ailing children and indicated vaguely that they needed treatment. Stephanie Newell, a Cambridge University student who later wrote movingly of the episode, handed one mother a couple of aspirin tablets, and then had to stand uncomfortably by as the woman fell on her knees to thank her effusively.

In no time the villagers and the tourists reached an entente. The villagers gently infiltrated the Ho-Bo camp, where fears of theft and even violence evaporated in the face of the Malians' gracious dignity. The village women found their white counterparts amusing. They tried to teach the white women some of their folk chants but dissolved in laughter at their pupils' shrill, thin voices.

For the tourists the delay was an opportunity to observe the harshness of rural African life unalloyed. More than before or after on the trip they confronted daily the abyss between their easy affluence and the permanent abjectness of the village. The relative privation to which they were subjecting themselves seemed a joke in the face of this implacable need. One could barely eat a meal without the sensation of gorging oneself arrogantly amid destitution. If someone discarded a finished tin of food, he became a dismayed witness to a squad of ragged children fighting over the empty object. Throw away an exhausted cigarette butt, and the children pounced and fought over it in a squealing cloud.

The travelers tried to engage in earnest debate over

whether and how to distribute a few provisions to the people, but the discussions deteriorated into the most emotional and heated of the trip. There was no answer to the conundrum of ensuring equal distribution of the food to an unfamiliar group of native Africans with recondite customs and social structures.

Amid the strain of the disconcerting stay on the riverbank Julie sometimes seemed the only member of the group maintaining enough equilibrium to stay out of arguments. There was no question how deeply affected she was by the spectacle of African life in the rough spread out around them all, but she could not be drawn into a disagreement. 'She would never seem to take offense,' one friend remembered. No doubt about it, Julie carried deeper reserves of serenity than anyone else on the truck.

She joined in on one of the group's initiatives: trying to ameliorate the chronic eye inflammation that seemed to affect every child in the village. After Stephanie Newell's attempt at aspirin therapy, long queues of village mothers and children had formed outside the Ho-Bo camp. The group had a textbook of tropical diseases and a couple of dozen first-aid kits in hand, as well as the truck's comprehensive emergency store. With that there were enough medical scraps to address a few of the most obvious maladies in the village.

Newell and others arranged a detail to accomplish what appeared to be the most accessible goal, helping to clean the children's eyes of encrusted pus and dirt in an effort to rid them of a tenacious strain of conjunctivitis. It was a process very akin to the Sisyphean challenge taking place around the truck, where no effort of digging seemed to keep the muck from collecting again around the wheels. The Ho-Bo infirmarians would clean a child's eyes one day only to find him back in the queue the next, eyes as deeply burdened as before. Julie joined the detail at first, but even Newell found it a task fit only for the strongest stomachs. In time Julie dropped off the work force and contented herself taking graceful pictures of the villagers.

Out on the river the situation had remained desperate.

A few passing trucks had tried hauling the Leyland out of the mud but had failed. Gerard Evans, a member of the group who spoke French, was assigned to hitchhike to Mopti, a hundred kilometers upriver, to solicit help. He found a mechanic with a hand winch mounted on a four-wheel-drive Mercedes truck who extorted an outrageous price, then showed up at the Ho-Bo truck with a team of incompetent assistants who mishandled the winch for days before admitting failure. He insisted on being paid anyway, provoking an extended argument with Tree. In the end the man, backed up by his friends among the local police, got his money.

Finally, late in the week the group managed to contact a second Ho-Bo tour that was following a parallel route through Mali. On the sixth day it arrived and, at long last, extricated the Leyland from the River Niger with a turbo-winch. Another body of water, another delay. Ahead lay several more rivers and streams, and the rain.

CHAPTER FOUR

From the Niger the tour continued through the Dogon country east of Mopti, an escarpment on which the descendants of these ancient tribes perch their houses like the Indians of the Pueblo south-west. The Ho-Bo truck dashed through Burkina Faso and headed due south to Abidjan, the capital of the Ivory Coast and the travelers' first contact with European civilization in weeks.

Abidjan is a city of glass skyscrapers and flowing freeways, all financed by the country's income as the world's pre-eminent cocoa-producer. A grand modernistic cathedral designed to look like the prow of a fantastic ship stands over the lagoon at the edge of the city's central plateau, and the boulevards are lined with chic French boutiques. The Ivory Coast has poverty every bit as abject as that which the travelers had seen in Mali, but it stays safely out of sight upcountry, far from the city limits of this glittering capital.

The Ho-Bo tour group settled down at a campsite near the ferocious surf of the Ivoirian beachfront and spent hours combating a busy swarm of cockroaches. But for the most part they stuck to the poolsides of the luxury hotels along the strand built to accommodate the country's rich cocoa-trading élite and the stylish French community. The Ivory Coast was a short stop, and presently the Leyland trundled on to the Ghanaian border.

On the route to Ghana they passed a succession of ancient Portuguese and English slaving dungeons littering the coast like forlorn and forgotten sentries. At one an old black curate invited some of the group on a brief tour. 'Come see what it was like,' he said slyly as he locked them in a sweltering dungeon room at the bottom of an air shaft.

Then, standing silhouetted in the bleaching sun, he made an impassioned speech about how the Europeans' grandparents had enslaved his grandparents, just as he had now imprisoned them. A couple of the group felt a frisson of panic at their helpless status. A wave of nervous giggling passed through the cell, but shortly the curate cheerily unlocked the door and they spilled out in a relieved mass.

By the time they all crossed into Cameroon a few days later, the trip was more than half over. Some of the group were feeling the distinct pinch of penury: the 500 pounds sterling that Ho-Bo had recommended as pocket money went surprisingly quickly, especially after the truck reached the Frenchified shores of West Africa where a beer could cost a pound or more and restaurant meals soared beyond the standards of thrift. In Togo, where French colonization had instilled a popular taste for luxury goods and French culture kept alive the market in which to trade them, some people found themselves selling their zoom lenses and Walkmans to augment their dwindling pocket money.

The humid equatorial coast also introduced sickness into the group. Despite the precautions of prophylactic drugs, including an astringently bitter tablet that had to be taken every day, several of the travelers had come down with malaria. At this stage none was afflicted very seriously, but they were reduced to the alternating shivers and sweats of the world's most common parasitic disease.

Much later, they would recall how in the mornings the first voice they would hear and the first face they would see were Julie Ward's. She was like a compound Florence Nightingale and Anne of Green Gables, tirelessly solicitous and generous, offering her feverish companions an extra blanket, a sip of juice.

Many would remark later on Julie's appealing combination of friendliness and quiet reserve. 'She had a quiet aura of gentleness,' one friend said. She talked eagerly of her plans to remain in Kenya after the end of the trip, to photograph wildlife and start some sort of business that would enable her to settle there. 'Her plans weren't very specific,' one of her companions remembered. Although she did have an idea about exporting curios to Europe, she did not have a strong sense of the bureaucratic difficulties a government like Kenya's could impose on people trying to move goods across its borders. Julie talked only vaguely about her life in Britain. Her friends on the truck got the impression that as much as she had done for Ian Rowland, 'it wasn't really what she wanted to do with the rest of her life.' She did not talk much about her family either. People learned that her father was a successful entrepreneur and that she had led a nice comfortable life, but that it was not enough. Most of all, she gave the impression of having that excited glowing receptiveness to possibility that most people get in their first university years. Except she was getting it a little later than most.

Julie was not particularly voluble; there was always something modest, even inaccessible, about her. She was quiet without being withdrawn. One night the group had had a fancy dress party on a Ghanaian beach, what Jo Jordan described as pulling clothes from the bottom of your kit, and they spent a night of relaxed hilarity over tall amber bottles of African beer. Someone snapped a picture of Julie in a small group standing around with unlabeled bottles in their hands. She was dressed as a hula dancer, with brightly-colored garlands in her hair and an African lei around her neck, and she was wearing jeans and a black jersey that seemed to accentuate the spareness of her physique. Everyone in the picture was laughing broadly at someone's remark. Except Julie, who wore a wide grin and had her eyes closed in a sort of reverie, as if paying attention to some different, private joke.

It was during another such party that her traveling companions took the opportunity to show what they thought of her. Whenever someone's birthday came up during the tour, they would hold a celebration and give the guest of honor a little gift – most often handmade, given the scarcity of storebought goods along the route. April 21st was Julie's twenty-eighth birthday, and the group thought they had fashioned something particularly apposite, made from cardboard. It was a halo.

As they moved through Cameroon into the interior of Africa they stopped at an encampment that had been turned into an animal orphanage, mostly for chimpanzees. In the foothills of Cameroon chimps got hunted for their meat in the usual heedless fashion of Africa: The hunters took away mothers and left their infants to die unnurtured in the bush. One of the orphaned chimpanzees was a heartbreakingly tiny thing, smaller than a human infant. Julie picked it up and it clung forlornly to her arms as if still confused at its mother's inexplicable disappearance. As Julie cradled the little baby and tried not to let her expression show the anger she felt at the callowness of the hunters, Lucy Brewer, an Oxford student from the south of England who was her closest friend among the group, snapped a picture. The shot of Julie with her little chimpanzee would soon be on newspaper front pages all over Britain.

They pressed on through the thick brush of the Cameroonian plateau into the Central African Republic, now blissfully rid of its vicious Emperor Bokassa I. A few years earlier the CAR had put Bokassa on trial, inviting the international press to hear long days of testimony about impossibly hideous brutalities in the imperial palace, a caricature of African monstrousness. But now Bokassa's capital, Bangui, had reverted to its sleepy state on a bend of the Oubangui River.

Here among the shaded tree-lined boulevards the tour again flirted with catastrophe. One day they pulled up to a petrol station in town. A few of the travelers disembarked and shambled languidly around in the steamy heat. A few stayed in the truck. Among them was a former army officer named Ron, who suddenly jerked upright in martial alertness and shouted, 'Get out!'

Up the road a driverless truck had slipped its brakes. Now it came careening toward them, gathering speed down the hill. The Leyland's passengers sprang from their seats and vaulted over the tailgate, sprinting away from certain disaster. Lucy Brewer landed awkwardly and crumpled on the ground before limping to safety with a fractured ankle. (A second girl also broke her ankle, but that was not discovered until it was X-rayed later in Nairobi.) As the group watched, flinching, the runaway grazed the Leyland with a crash of metal and came to rest a few yards down the road.

Holding their collective breath, they inspected their truck. Miraculously, it was almost entirely undamaged. At a local clinic Lucy Brewer got her ankle immobilized in a cast as Julie stood by. Another member of the group had come down with a serious case of hepatitis and was going to leave the trip from Bangui, and there was talk of Lucy going home as well. But she refused. She was resolved to finish the trip, she told Julie, broken ankle notwithstanding. At length the group helped her into the yellow truck, and they all headed for Zaire.

After crossing the Oubangui the Leyland pulled into the birthplace of Zaire's rapacious president, Mobutu Sese Seko. Mobutu had lifted the village of Gbadolite from obscurity. It was now one of the glorious presidential follies of Africa, a manicured, modern town buried deep in the Zairean rain forest. At one edge stood Mobutu's presidential palace, filled with marble statuary like an African San Simeon. Gbadolite had strained even the resources of the shameless Mobutu, who had reportedly accumulated a fortune worth millions by appropriating the mineral wealth of his country; it was said that only the first two floors of the multistoried palace were furnished and outfitted, with the rest displaying only a veneer of luxury, like a Hollywood stage set. Even the air of vigor and prosperity on the streets of Gbadolite was a sham, for when Mobutu was not in residence, people said, the electricity was turned off and the water ceased to run.

From Gbadolite they plunged directly into the Zairean jungle, the last significant patch of rain forest remaining in Africa. It was the rainy season and Zaire's decrepit roads were awash in mud. The sand ladders from the desert crossing were unbolted again and put to almost constant use as the Leyland kept sinking into slimy ruts of flowing earth. At Bumba, an entrepôt on the Zaire River, a few of the group disembarked to try to catch one of the famous river rafts of Zaire, arranging to catch up with the truck five days later in Kisangani, the mildewed outpost once known as Stanleyville, after the famous explorer, on a bend of the river made famous in a novel by V. S. Naipaul. The raft never came and the group spent five increasingly tense days in Bumba, eventually being hauled in by the local constabulary for a two-hour interrogation. Finally they managed to catch a bush plane to Kisangani, reboarding the Leyland just as it was about to pull out of town.

But what followed was, they unanimously agreed, the peak of the five-month journey. Reaching the mountain gorillas of Zaire takes a three-hour trek on slippery mud through the permanent crepuscule of the jungle in groups of no more than six persons. Everyone in the Leyland took his or her place, even Lucy Brewer, who marched in pain up the wet mountain in her cast. In time they came upon a gorilla family in a small clearing. They fell into an awed silence broken only by the click of shutters and ratcheting of film, watching the troglodyte family group scarcely an arm's length from their faces. Some of them shrank away, but Julie looked as if she could settle in for hours right among the beasts, taking pictures. Her photographic skills were alive to the opportunity. More than two years later John Ward would screen Julie's slides for the members of the Ho-Bo tour at his house in Bury St Edmunds, and when the pictures of the gorillas went up the guests gasped at their immediacy. Some of the travelers remembered how their own shots of the gorillas were obscured by foliage, with the gorillas reduced to dark indistinguishable shadows against a backdrop of jungle, but hers were not. The faces of the apes filled the screen to its very edges, alive and expressive, as if they were responding to Julie herself.

The group's first view of Kenya was as a distant dark hump of landscape in the distance, across the vast expanse of Lake Victoria from Entebbe, Uganda. It was another week before they arrived. First they trucked south along the lake into Tanzania for a stay at one of nature's great wonders, the Ngorongoro Crater.

Ngorongoro was a world of its own. Wildlife of every description teemed within its 2,000-foot deep bounds as the travelers passed among the herds in Land Rovers. After that they moved on to Tanzania's Serengeti National Park, the wide end of a great funnel pointing north, toward its tip at Masai Mara Game Reserve across the border in Kenya.

It was July. The tour was almost over and a few disagreements arose over how long to stay in the parks. Some were fretting about getting their full money's and five-month's worth but Dave Tree, for one, was impatient to finish. Nick King had left the group a few weeks earlier, having fallen ill, leaving Tree to do all the driving. Tree was quitting Ho-Bo to start his own overland tour company, and he was anxious to finish the trip and start the necessary work on a truck for his first group.

In the second week of July the big Leyland lumbered past Nairobi's downtown, west along a progressively more countrified road. Finally it turned on to a dirt path lined with dwarf spruce and marked by a tiny white sign reading P. WELD DIXON. The truck passed a small cottage with wide windows and a roof of corrugated tin and came around a corner into a great open workshop area. Hulking overland trucks the size of the Leyland lined the edges of the space, some up on blocks and others with their cabs tilted forward with block-and-tackle arrangements supporting their engines. White men and African mechanics clambered over the vehicles and the weighty stink of old oil was everywhere. One could scarcely take a step without treading on a discarded hunk of machined metal. For the Ho-Bo truck this was the end of the line.

Jo Jordan and Nick Fisher long remembered their first meeting with Paul Weld Dixon and his wife, Natasha, the owners of this spread. They had been introduced by a mutual friend who knew that the Weld Dixons often let overland travelers park their rigs and camp out on their twenty-acre estate. 'It was the usual Paul greeting,' Jordan recalled. 'Sixteen dogs ran out, Paul met us with a glass of Scotch, there was Beethoven playing on the hi-fi—'

Jordan exaggerated slightly: There were eight dogs, including an Alsatian and a couple of huge mixed-breeds, one with some Irish wolfhound in it. The dogs were not only protection to the Weld Dixons, but family. Throughout the modest house framed pictures of dogs decorated the bookshelves and mantels.

Weld Dixon had come to Africa in 1965, when a BBC crew for which he was the film editor did a shoot in Uganda. The path home took him through neighboring Kenya, and he fell in love with the place. He never returned to England.

Weld Dixon had mustered out of the British Army in India as a captain. He rarely seemed to tire of relating his experiences on the subcontinent, and it may have been that Kenya seemed to offer him the easy life-style he had had in India, minus that other colony's oppressive crush of humanity and its intractable heat. In India he had had six personal servants, a fellow to sweep up, a 'shaving wallah' who shaved you in bed in the morning for the equivalent of a dime a day, a cook, housekeeper, and so on. He cut back a little in Kenya, but he had a complete household staff and a syce to tend the horses that he and Natasha kept until their own advancing ages forced them to give the horses up.

Paul managed to build a small reputation as a documentary and industrial filmmaker around East Africa. In the 1960s he even garnered a bit of fame making a couple of television films with Jack Paar. The first one built on Paar's style of off-handedly dry, almost imperceptible humor as a travelogue of odd, funny scenes around Kenya. The film featured an outdoor barber stand where customers chose a hairstyle from a sheet of drawings before sitting on a stool in the middle of the bustling sidewalk. There was a man who made shoes out of old automobile tires, a street sign in the expansive, vacant up-country landscape of Eldoret that warned NO PARKING, and so on.

Paar's sojourn at the Weld Dixons' during that production led to the second film, known as the *Donkey Dinner*. Weld Dixon had a tame donkey who, much to Natasha's exasperation, had the run of the house, to the point it would come in through the French doors off the porch and wander into the dining room for handouts. Paar was so tickled by the sight that he got Weld Dixon to stage an elaborate soirée, evening dress required, into which the donkey strolled as the guests sat down to eat in the dark green wood-beamed dining room. No-one batted an eyelid during this display of late-colonial nonchalance, of course. The film was a great, quirky success on American television at the time.

Retirement had since come upon Paul Weld Dixon, but the cottage still projected a combination of English country gentility and Kenyan hospitality. Inside, it had a cozy if somewhat unfinished feel, with floors of unlacquered wood and plaster walls. The high ceilings were peaked like the roof. There were bookcases all around and classical records and discs. Weld Dixon's collection of rare old movie equipment occupied a corner of a bookshelf near the door leading into the dining room. Two magnificent stone lions stood in front of a smallish fireplace, surrounded by some aging but comfortable couches and chairs. A line of trees screened off the mechanics' works Weld Dixon rented out to tour firms.

Paul himself had acquired a reputation around Nairobi as a prickly eccentric. He could be a rough-edged man with sometimes crusty colonial-era opinions and a blunt way of expressing them. He was tall and rotund with a double chin and his skin hung a bit loosely around his girth, as if he had once been much heavier. Weld Dixon was still infinitely gracious to guests and friends, who sometimes found him a tiny bit tiresome, but his long years in India and Kenya seemed to have eroded away a layer of European civilization, so that one of his acquaintances could say, 'He's the type who could never really go back to England, isn't he?'

As Ho-Bo's big Leyland truck pulled into Weld Dixon's estate off the Magadi road the menagerie of dogs put up a howl. Over the next few days a few of the travelers camped out on the property, but in general the group quickly dispersed, with the members heading either directly back to Britain or on their own final exploratory trips to the Kenyan coast or its unexampled network of game parks.

Julie was one who stayed, and it was easy to see how entranced she must have been by her new surroundings. Weld Dixon's twenty acres could have been transplanted from the East Anglian countryside, with the difference that it had been allowed to run a bit wild, in true Kenyan style. A neighbor came over from time to time to cut the long grass, leaving it piled in haystacks he collected later for his cows. Horses from nearby pastures would wander up to graze on the field. Hawks swept overhead and the purple Ngong Hills peeked over the horizon. At night three hired Masai patrolled the property, armed with spears.

'It was the dogs that first brought us together,' Weld Dixon said later. The slight English girl lent a hand in tending the hounds, and the Weld Dixons found her reliable enough to trust with the house and the dogs when they went away on safaris of their own. She pitched her tent on the grounds and became very close to the older couple. When she went away it was clear that she had left a vacuum in their lives. Much later, Paul and Natasha averred that they would not stop the overland tours from staying over on their land, but they would never again befriend one of the young travellers. It was too difficult, too sad, at their late age.

CHAPTER FIVE

It was towards noon on 1 March 1898, that I first found myself entering the narrow and somewhat dangerous harbor of Mombasa, on the East Coast of Africa. The town lies on an island of the same name, separated from the mainland only by a very narrow channel, which forms the harbor . . . Contrary to my anticipation, everything looked fresh and green, and an oriental glamour of enchantment seemed to hang over the island.

This was the first view of what would become Kenya by one of the fledgling colony's founding builders. Colonel J. H. Patterson was assigned to master a hellish engineering problem 200 miles inland, where construction of Britain's Uganda Railway had reached the treacherous Tsavo River gorge, one third of the way to its goal, Lake Victoria. But spanning the gorge would prove to be the lesser of his important tasks in helping the 600-mile railway push into the heart of Britain's young protectorate. As he debarked at the clamorous harbor of Mombasa, a pair of vicious lions were daily decimating the mostly Indian construction crew at Tsavo. It fell to Patterson to dispatch them after a hunt that dragged on for months, all but halting the railway's progress. In their honor he entitled his 1907 memoirs *The Man-Eaters of Tsavo*.

Patterson had been preceded to Africa by a breed of European whose intrepidity has become a byword in history. Livingstone and Stanley, and lesser-known men like Joseph Thomson, the first white man to know the Masai (and who gave his name to the sleek, racing-striped gazelles of the Kenya plains), are heroes even today.

England's interest in Africa stemmed at first from its concern over protecting its sea route to India, the jewel of empire. The British had long realized that India-bound ships rounding the Cape of Good Hope exposed their flanks to Zanizibar, the fabled spice island off Africa's eastern coast.

In time the British arranged a protectorate over the African holdings of the Sultan of Zanizibar (in truth it was forced upon them in 1823 by the headstrong act of a naval officer named Owen, who on his own authority chose to ban the slave trade of Zanizibar and Mombasa). For the balance of the century Britain set about acquiring an African empire in the same fit of absence of mind with which she spread her colors over the rest of the world. British altruism and arrogance fought each other to a standstill as the imperial power strove to justify its gradual encroachment into the interior, first as a countervailing force to the Arabian slave trade (Livingstone was the most obdurate abolitionist among the early explorers), and then by pursuing rumors of matchless wealth to be found and developed in places like Uganda and Rhodesia.

Eventually the rationale of national defense made a return. In 1869 the completion of the Suez Canal gave Britain not only a short route to India but an enduring complex over its security. Eventually this phobia centered on the River Nile itself; once its source was located by the explorer Speke at Lake Victoria the British became convinced that whoever controlled the headwaters could turn the river on and off like a spigot, menacing the canal and the British protectorate of Egypt at whim.

So with visions of Ugandan wealth and the safety of Suez acting as dual magnets, in 1865 work began on the Uganda Railway. For the period it was a breathtaking speculation, an engineering challenge of unknown dimension, and a financial enterprise of questionable return – all factors in its eventual nickname: the 'Lunatic Express.'

The British undertook to build the railway with little comprehension of the landscape it was to bisect. The plains and highlands between the coast and the lake seemed virtually unpopulated. Whatever people the scouting parties and adventurers in the vanguard met seemed savage and unreliable, so the builders imported 32,000 Indians as coolie labor, paying them so scantily and housing them so poorly that strikes were inevitable. Natives who watched the iron road snaking through their territory reacted with alarm, ferocity, and thievery, depending on vagaries of their culture; the Nandi, who occupied land around the western portion of the route, cherished the steel of the railway for weapons and the copper wires of its telegraph lines for jewelry.

This was the railway that, in the words of an early territorial governor, 'literally created a country.' But for the period of its construction and for years afterward the region that would become known as Kenya was lightly regarded only as the place that had to be gotten through before reaching the genuine El Dorado of Uganda.

The very name of the line showed how little attention was devoted to the territory banking its length, as opposed to what beckoned from the terminus. More than a little peevishly Sir Charles Eliot, the key man among the early governors of the 'East Africa Protectorate', complained that 'it is perhaps not superfluous to repeat that the Uganda Railway is not in Uganda at all but entirely in the East Africa protectorate, the whole breadth of which from the sea to Lake Victoria it traverses. It is as if the line from Charing Cross to Dover were called the French Railway.'

In mid-1899 the railhead had reached an expanse of spongy ground 327 miles inland and a mile above sea level known by the Masai words *Uasu Nyrobe*, 'place of cold water'. There was an old oxen depot in the middle of the swamp, and as the last level land on the route before the railway's climb toward and into the Great Rift Valley, it was selected as a headquarters camp.

Nairobi's location had been chosen more for administrative convenience than physical allure, drainage, or hygiene, in all of which it was deficient. For years after its founding the hollow in the highlands selected by the railway engineers would be roundly cursed by those forced

44

to live within its boundaries. The settlement's real purpose was underscored by its coldly functional appearance: The first photographs of the town show nothing but row upon row of military tents, arranged in bivouac pattern across a horizonless plain. Well into the new century the city's proliferating establishments retained an ephemeral, Wild West flavor. Carriages splashed down muddy, rutted roads while pedestrians tried as best they could to keep their trouser legs unsoiled by staying to the wooden sidewalks.

Fresh from his successful exploits against the Tsavo man-eaters and the river gorge, Colonel Patterson won the responsibility for forging the encampment into an operating administrative center that was, he complained, '327 miles from the nearest place where even a nail could be purchased.' He arranged construction of a water supply, quarters, roads, and bridges while keeping a weather eye on the willy-nilly evolution of the Indians' bazaar. This latter caused him an early administrative crisis when plague broke out within its boundaries. He solved it in characteristically decisive fashion.

'I gave the natives and Indians who inhabited it an hour's notice to clear out, and on my own responsibility promptly burned it to the ground. For this somewhat arbitrary proceeding I was mildly called over the coals, as I expected; but all the same it effectually stamped out the plague, which did not reappear during the time I was in the country.'

Among those who detested Nairobi was Sir Charles Eliot. 'Nairobi is built just at the point where the railway enters the hills,' he wrote in his memoirs. 'The situation is unfortunate from a sanitary point of view, owing to the extreme difficulty of drainage; and it is regrettable that after the visitation of the plague in 1902, when many sites were moved, the whole settlement and railway station were not transferred a few miles higher up the line.'

At the time he was writing (1905), the administrative capital was still not much more than a handful of bungalows occupying the high ground along a modest ridge, the Indian bazaar, a couple of 'European' shops and a Japanese bordello, and the railway depot that was the focal point of the whole affair.

Eliot found much similarity between Nairobi and the other renowned frontier in the English-speaking world: 'Nearly all the houses are constructed of white tin, and somewhat resemble a mining town in the Western States of America. It must be confessed that the result is not artistically satisfactory, and that the beauty of a view in Nairobi depends on the more or less thorough elimination of the town from the landscape.'

When that could be accomplished, he acknowledged, 'the effect is superb, and not spoilt by the spectacle of a distant train slowly crawling like an ant across the gray-green expanse.'

Still, in writing his memoirs of the East African Protectorate, Eliot was pursuing a lifelong campaign to popularize the emergent settler colony of Kenya, and he praised the region's prospects.

'Meat, milk, and butter are plentiful, cheap, and really excellent,' he wrote. 'The mutton can compare with that of Wales. Fowls, though common at the coast, are neither plentiful nor stout up-country, but there is no reason why these deficiencies should not be remedied by the larger introduction of foreign birds, which have been found to thrive. European vegetables, particularly potatoes, flourish in such profusion and excellence that it has been hoped that they will form one of the staple exports of the Protectorate.'

By Eliot's time European contact with the Kenyan tribes had begun to settle into something resembling routine, if not exactly familiarity. The Masai were among the first to lose their ferocious reputation. Eliot called them 'perhaps the most interesting and important race in the country,' although he added that 'they have not the qualities which offer much promise of progress and increase in the future' and remarked that they 'were long the terror and scourge of all their neighbors.'

The first explorers who encountered the Masai *moran*,

or warriors, would find little to recognize of the old tribesmen in the picturesque herdsmen of today's color magazines and Sunday supplements. Current fashion in the West bemoans the destruction of their proud and inscrutable way of life by the encroachment of civilization even to their remote grazing lands, but the nineteenth-century adventurers opening Masai land to white habitation had an entirely different view. To them the Masai warrior was the most ferocious obstacle in their way. The Masai wasted countless caravans – many of them slaving parties – thus forcing trade routes from the coast to make long detours around the tribal lands. The reach of their looting parties was known to stretch almost to the gates of Mombasa itself.

The Masai range extended from the Serengeti plains south of Mount Kilimanjaro into the arid north of Kenya. As it happened, this included part of one of the more delectable belts of pasture and farmland in East Africa, and one of the few places where climate and cultivability invited white settlement. As British settlers, in part at Eliot's urging, discovered the potential of this great land the Masai were herded into a southern reserve in a confused sequence of dispossessions and migrations imposed by white settlers and acceded to by their own elders. The reserve included a region of varied grass and woodland called today by the Masai word for *spotted*, referring to the stippled appearance of the plains broken by trees and bush: the Mara.

The Masai recognized only two things as worthy of their attention, Eliot wrote: 'cattle and warfare'. Intra-tribal wars designed as much to give youthful warriors training as to settle real grievances had resulted in the extinction of at least one clan, he noted, and he observed with disapproval the tribe's practice of allowing warriors to cohabit with 'immature unmarried girls.'

The governor's appraisal of Masai dress and physique betrayed the usual mix of fascination and repulsion with which 'civilized' Europeans regarded the natives: 'A Masai warrior is rather a fine looking creature, though generally so smeared with oil and red clay that it is better to interview him out of doors and at a slight distance.' Eliot commended the polygamous Masai for taking only two or three wives on average, as opposed to the 'connubial extravagancies of other tribes', but he professed himself mystified at the source of sexual attraction.

'The women have a pleasant expression, but are rendered hideous according to the ordinary ideas of beauty [that is, European ideas] by shaving their heads. When one sees these shaven heads, leather garments, and masses of burdensome and totally unornamental metal, one can only wonder at the trouble the good ladies take to make themselves hideous.'

Eliot observed that the more feral habits of the Masai had been tamed not only by the advent of European influence but by smallpox and cattle plagues, which weakened them enough to be victimized by competing tribes. He concluded by likening them to beasts of prey in their grace and dignity but warned, 'It can hardly be denied that they have hitherto done no good in the world that anyone knows of; they have lived by robbery and devastation, and made no use themselves of what they have taken from others.'

Gradually the whites – known as 'Europeans' whatever their origin, just as Indians, Pakistanis, and Goans were known as 'Asians' – cemented their hold on the country. Year by year they overcame tropical disease and the plagues that afflicted their cattle and the shoots of coffee and tea imported to make their fortunes. British laws governed the tribes of Kenya, and if the settlers had to fight continually with London over whether the land was being governed for the settlers' benefit or in some sort of trust for the indigenous tribesmen, an issue known as 'paramountcy', by the early part of the twentieth century there was no irony in the common sobriquet for a land they had tamed and begun to make rich: In contrast to other colonies that were seen as the 'white man's burden', Kenya, it was said, was 'White Man's Country'.

The settlers liked to see themselves as paternal masters

of their African charges, but they taxed them, required them to carry passes, and barred them from most profitable trades. Farm labor, the only work left, was compensated at slave wages. The settlers often treated Africans just as their stereotypes warranted: *lazy*, *childish* and *dishonest* were some of the less pejorative terms used to describe a typical African laborer.

After the Second World War this state of affairs could not last. Resentment had been building for years, particularly among the Kikuyu, heavily concentrated in the area of the white highlands. In 1950 a British district commissioner had already warned of 'a secret society known as Mau Mau'.

Two years later a wave of Mau Mau violence had sufficiently alarmed the whites to provoke the colonial government into declaring a state of emergency. In October 1952 British troops arrested 187 men thought to be the group's leaders, including a British-educated Kikuyu leader named Jomo Kenyatta, who was not. The Mau Mau continued to engage in sensational murders of isolated settlers, and the British continued to kill African protestors with scarcely noticed abandon.

The Mau Mau campaign lasted another five years, with thousands of Africans killed and detained and scores of Europeans murdered. There were atrocities on both sides, including many committed by British soldiers frustrated and fearful of fighting Mau Mau detachments in the deep forests of the highlands. By 1957 thousands of alleged Mau Mau warriors and sympathizers were interned in a network of detention camps throughout Kenya. One would come to symbolize the endgame of British rule.

The Hola detention camp was nothing less than a concentration camp for eleven hundred of the colony's most obdurate Mau Maus on a detested plot of land on the edge of the coastal desert near the often-flooded Tana River. In the guise of 'rehabilitation' and under a blanketing cloud of mosquitoes in the unforgiving sun, these men were forced to scrape an irrigation scheme out of the land. A thousand of Kenya's most fearsome warriors interned in one place begged the question of how harsh the warders should be. The incessant discussion in British councils over the difference between 'compelling force', which was permitted, and 'overwhelming force', which was not, could have little meaning to the exiles of Hola.

For years there had been reports of unacceptable treatment of the Hola detainees, but these were ignored by the settlers and their nominal rulers in London. Finally, on 3 March, all the pretense came apart. Hola's British supervisors were to test a new plan to force the hard-core detainees to work. This involved assembling an intimidating force of armed warders to coerce the detainees into violating their Mau Mau oath, which required them to resist working under the British. Originally one hundred African warders were to oversee twenty prisoners, bringing them to their knees by brute force if necessary. In the event, the camp commandant assembled a work detail of not twenty, but eighty-five prisoners. When they and their armed guards arrived at the work site, someone blew a whistle.

Perhaps the African guards misunderstood the instructions they had been given in crude Swahili. They set upon the prisoners savagely. When a second whistle blew, at least one prisoner was dead. Then a third shrill blast was heard, and the beatings began anew. This time they raged out of control for as long as ten minutes. By the end of the ferocious day eleven prisoners were dead and twenty seriously injured.

Hola was to Kenya what the British massacre at Amritsar was to India, an act of unthinking atrocity that instantly redefined the terms of colonial debate. Hola exposed what had been the underlying but unexpressed inevitability of British colonial policy: In Africa the empire was nearing extinction. With its colonial secretary besieged by calls for his resignation, the government of Harold Macmillan acceded to a call for a formal inquiry. That summer the tribunal commenced in Nairobi.

The targets of the inquiry were Hola's commander, Superintendent Gerald Sullivan, and his second-in-command, A. C. Coutts. For their defense counsel they chose from Nairobi's small corps of élite British-trained lawyers a young Tanganyikan native of Cypriot descent, whose parents had started one of the colony's first tobacco plantations before selling out to British American Tobacco.

Byron Georgiadis was short and stocky, with close-cropped wavy black hair and a pair of arresting black eyebrows over his skeptical blue eyes. Three decades later, the hair a glistening silver but the eyebrows still raven black, the skepticism of Georgiadis's eyes had hardened into mocking despair at the deteriorating rule of law in his adopted country. By then he was much closer to the end of his career than he was to the start of it in 1959. As his last case before taking retirement Georgiadis would agree to represent John Ward in his quest to establish what had led to the death of his only daughter.

The two Hola commanders would prove to be challenging clients. As a defendant Sullivan, in particular, was unprepossessing. Among the more charitable judgments of this stalwart British colonialist in the twilight of his career were that he was 'a bit thick' and 'not a clear thinker'. Judging from his actions and his version of the events on 3 March, these were breathtaking understatements. Reaching camp at midday, at a point when the work-detail melee had been in full swing, Sullivan had replied to a query about how things were going with the comment that there had been 'the odd spot of trouble', but overall things were 'satisfactory'.

Late in the day of 3 March, Sullivan's nominal superior, the provincial commissioner, asked the commandant for an explanation of the deaths. Standing next to a rank of broken bodies lying on the sand, Sullivan replied that the men had been drinking contaminated water. As it happened, there was a witness at hand: a local engineer named Peters who had brought the water tank to the site. Peters contradicted Sullivan on the spot. He gave the PC an eyewitness account of Sullivan's guards attacking the detainees without provocation. Nevertheless, when a

Kenya government team arrived to investigate, they repeated Sullivan's canard with a minor alteration: The detainees died not from drinking contaminated water, but from drinking too much water in the heat.

Byron Georgiadis would later consider his Hola defense a touchstone of his career, giving it pride of place among the scrapbooks he kept in his Nairobi home and hauled out for visiting reporters during the Ward inquest. And on the face of things he served his clients well.

On 24 March 1959, the *East African Standard* relegated to a bottom corner of its front page the latest report on a story that had been occupying its readers for days, the health of Queen Elizabeth II during her ongoing state visit to Canada. The queen had laughed off an episode of discomfort earlier in the trip, the newspaper reported. But most of the rest of page one was devoted to the British government's Hola report, released the previous evening. Sullivan was responsible for the disaster, the report found. But the investigators recommended only that he be retired, with full pension rights in place. Coutts was completely cleared.

The text of the report ran on page five in disquieting detail. For one thing, between the lines Sullivan was condemned as a rank liar. His testimony was literally incredible, said the commissioners, who explicitly weighed it against not only Peter's but that of his native assistant, and gave the latter two the palm. Still, with one of his clients cleared and the other permitted to retire with honor, Georgiadis could feel that he had won.

But it was scarcely lost on the world outside that Hola marked the end of an era. By some accounts, the desperate behavior of the colonial administrators in Nairobi inspired the Macmillan government to accelerate the African colonies' march toward independence.

In 1960 the government invited settler and African delegations to a conference at Lancaster House, London, where a constitution awarding universal suffrage to Kenyans was drafted. As the settlers watched in dismay, the government released Jomo Kenyatta from detention the following year. The old man, nearly seventy, moved quickly into the forefront of African politics in Kenya and on 1 July 1963, after his Kenya African National Union won an election under British monitoring, he became Kenya's first prime minister.

The new leader took immediate pains to pacify jittery whites and stem the enormous drain of capital and resources out of the country. Six weeks after the election he stepped to the lectern to address his first all-white settler audience in the farming center of Nakuru. Full independence was only four months away.

The fearsome devil of settler legend proclaimed, 'Let me tell you Jomo Kenyatta has no intention of retaliating or looking backwards. Many of you are as Kenyan as myself. Let us join hands and work for the benefit of Kenya, not for the benefit of one particular community. We want you to stay and farm well in this country: that is the policy of this government. We can all work together to make this country great and to show other countries in the world that different racial groups can live and work together.'

He left to a standing ovation. The evolution of the old man – 'Mzee' was his revered title – in the regard of the British settler was evident in this story related by a white native Kenyan in Nairobi not long after Julie Ward's arrival in the country.

'I remember an old farmer I knew telling me one day that as soon as Jomo Kenyatta was released from prison he would leave the country. Years later I saw him again, and he said that as soon as Kenyatta died, he would leave. He's still here.'

CHAPTER SIX

There is a photograph dating from 1959, when Jomo Kenyatta had not yet been freed from British detention. The future president is in jail in a place called Lodwar. It is a remote and despicable site of oppressive heat and big insects, but he is among his fellows and is allowed visitors. One day a young schoolteacher comes to have his picture taken with the old hero. Jomo Kenyatta rests his arm on the shoulder of Daniel Toroitich arap Moi a little uncomfortably, because Moi is nearly a head taller than he is. The five men standing around Moi and Jomo Kenyatta all wear the sullen expressions of imprisoned warriors, glaring at the lens as if down the barrel of a gun. Among their strong angry faces the one that stands out is Moi's, wearing a shy smile.

Nearly twenty years after that picture Daniel arap Moi succeeded to the presidency of Kenya upon Jomo Kenyatta's death. Almost no-one thought he would last. Even in 1988 when Moi, now stout and gravel-voiced, confidently celebrated the tenth anniversary of his regime, Kenyatta's erstwhile colleagues still thought of the new president as the slender, taciturn, modest Kalenjin teacher who as vice-president was relegated to the far end of the cabinet table and made the butt of Kenyatta's nasty jokes.

In his first days in office Moi did little to change anyone's mind. To most observers of Kenyan politics it was apparent he had been installed as a caretaker until the kingmakers of Kikuyu nationalism could place one of their own back in the president's chair. Foremost among them was a squat Kikuyu lawyer named Charles Njonjo, one of the most disliked, but also powerful, men of nascent Kenya.

Moi spent the beginning of his term in undisguised fear of Njonjo, who strode through the presidential quarters as if they were his by right. The haughty Kikuyu extracted a certain amount of fealty from the shy schoolteacher-president for having quashed an attempt to forestall Moi's succession – a move that pitted Njonjo against some fellow Kikuyus – but many people thought Njonjo's real goal was to become president himself.

One magazine editor of that period remembered a telling display of presidential faintheartedness. The magazine had been one of the few Kenyan publications to editorially support Moi's right to a full term as president. One day Moi called the editor to his office, ostensibly to thank him personally for a gracious remembrance the magazine had run about the late president. Along with a photographer laden with equipment the editor was shown into Moi's chambers. Suddenly a buzzer rang on the president's desk. He took the call from a secretary with increasing consternation, and when he put the phone down in near panic it was to urge his guests to pack up their things and leave out a side door. It was too late; within moments the main door swung open and Njonjo swaggered in. Nervously, Moi introduced the two newsmen. 'I was just thanking them for their tribute to Mzee,' he said bashfully. Then they were unceremoniously pushed out.

Njonjo was not to keep this domineering position long. Already behind the scenes Moi may have been plotting against him. The boom fell in 1983. By then Moi had already survived the greatest crisis of his regime, a 1982 coup attempt by air force officers, and had responded by rewriting the constitution to concentrate more power in his own hands.

Njonjo's Achilles heel would prove to be his Anglophilia, always a sensitive issue among the former colonial subjects. Behind his back people called him 'Lord Charles'. There were snickers about his three-piece pinstriped suits. One day he was caught at the airport bringing in suitcases full of oranges purchased in England, as if Kenyan oranges weren't good enough for Lord Charles. Finally, Moi kicked Njonjo out of parliament and the party, and convened a judicial inquiry into his affairs. The old kingmaker was reduced to living out his years on his Nairobi estate, surfacing from time to time at dog shows, where he and his daughters put their Rhodesian ridgeback hounds on display. For a time at least, Moi was the undisputed political king of Kenya.

When Julie Ward got to Kenya its government was firmly under Moi's thumb. There was little in the economy in which he did not have a strong role. Take a ride in one of Nairobi's new London taxis (imported duty-free); rent space in any of dozens of downtown Nairobi office buildings; buy an item at a boutique in the new surburban shopping mall called the Yaya Center; buy a Kenya-made Eveready battery or Firestone tire; ship some transit goods by truck from Mombasa to Uganda; bank at the Commercial Bank of Africa or buy a life policy from the local unit of Alico insurance; or purchase or service a car at the local Peugeot dealership; and businessmen said to be directly or indirectly associated with Moi would earn a profit from the transaction.

He had fastened his grip on the civil service the same way. Moi was acutely sensitive to the need for delicate tribal balances in the Kenyan government, so top jobs, including the leadership of the various military branches, were painstakingly apportioned among the leading tribes like the Luo and Kikuyu or handed over to one of the country's nonpolitical ethnic groups, like the Somalis. But in the bureaucratic strata just below the top men, where lay the semivisible positions of important influence, members of Moi's minority Kalenjin tribal group were heavily over-represented. They were the permanent secretaries and deputy chiefs of the armed services, district and provincial commissioners. The minister of finance (who was also vice-president) was a Masai, but the head of the Central Bank was Kalenjin.

No-one who displeased the president could last long in the party or government. Instead he would be subjected to a Njonjo-style ordeal of vilification and public humiliation, followed by exile to his home region. If lucky, sometimes the miscreant would be permitted to keep his land and businesses, living out the years in a Kenyan nonpersonhood.

For all that, modern-day Nairobi still had the capacity to elicit delighted surprise from travelers entering Kenya from other African countries. It bustled in a way that no other African city could match. Nairobi might not have Abidjan's sweeping super highways and chic French boutiques. It lacked the smooth race relations of Harare, Zimbabwe, and the Muslim graciousness of the people of Dakar, Senegal. Addis Ababa, Ethiopia, had an efficiency and tidy cleanliness that Nairobi had long forgotten.

But none of these places combined as many good qualities as Nairobi. The old administrative bivouac in the Kenyan highlands had a much better climate than Abidjan's energy-sapping steam heat; there was much more to do and better airline connections to Europe and the African continent than in Harare; and the telephones and electricity worked better than almost everywhere else south of the Sahara (except South Africa, a special case). There was so much business activity, so much traffic on the roads, and so many smokestacks spewing forth the waste products of industrial development, that it was hard to believe that Kenya was still, like every other country in its region, on the international dole.

But Jomo Kenyatta's dream of a multiethnic, multiracial Kenya had been undermined in twenty-five years of independence. In part this was the special legacy of British rule. After importing 30,000 Indian coolies to build their railroad the British had barred them, as well as the Africans, from owning land in the coveted white highlands. The 'Asians' were herded into petty commerce and trading and the Africans into sharecropping on vast white farms. The grand clubs and hotels that barred blacks from their doors were no more receptive to Asians.

By the time of Julie Ward's arrival the racial strata of Kenya reflected distinct class differences. By any measure the top of the pyramid of everyday Kenyan life, particularly in Nairobi and its suburbs, were the whites, the least numerous group as well as the most privileged. At the bottom were the great mass of Africans, more than twenty million people dividing among themselves the country's relatively meager national output. Occupying a gray middle were the Asians, the widely resented merchant class viewed as clannish and arrogant shopkeepers.

Most Europeans knew they were the beneficiaries of the greatest respect. They were the least likely to be stopped on the road for an arbitrary traffic check, the first to be served among a mob of customers at a bank or shop or streetcorner restaurant. Travelers coming into Jomo Kenyatta Airport without a visa often knew that from the distant end of a queue of passengers off a just-landed Air India flight they could wave a British or American passport with a ten-dollar fee and be taken directly to the front of the visa line. It was not because they were the richest people in country; they were not. Most white expatriates were salary earners assigned to Kenya for three- or four-year tours. They might have been enormously well paid by African standards but the real money was held by the Asians, who had their own businesses. The whites motored around in late-model four-wheel-drive cars, but these were generally owned by their employers. Asians drove Mercedes sedans, bought with their own money.

Whites were also comfortable in highlands Kenya because they knew they were privileged by their own society's standards. They were favored visitors here: The stereotypical European settler matron pronouncing kitchen Swahili in an upper-class accent was disappearing by the nineteen-eighties, and carousing Brits had relinquished their place at the bar of the exclusive Muthaiga Club to rich Kikuyu farmers. In the new community of European expatriates there were few who could expect after their African assignments to return home to houses as big as their Nairobi mansions or to grounds as spacious and green. In Kenya they hired ayahs to watch their

58

children, shamba-men to tend their gardens and lawns, and housekeepers to sweep up and cook. They could afford to entertain frequently and in lavish style. And within reasonable limits they felt physically safe. There were frequent house break-ins but only very rarely physical attacks. In 1982, when the coup attempt provoked widespread looting around Nairobi, the mobs bent on destruction entirely bypassed the big homes occupied by white executives. But no neighborhoods were as thoroughly despoiled as those of the Asians, whose homes and shops were ransacked.

Still, an undercurrent of resentment against the whites of Kenya sometimes surged into the open, most frequently when they strayed out of place by voicing political opinions. When this happened the Kenya government displayed a strain of racial xenophobia, even as it relied increasingly on foreign aid to balance its budget, that was not hard to trace back to the independent country's difficult origins. Having shed British rule after seven years of bloody insurgency, Kenya's new leaders greeted with indignation any overt hint that they needed help – particularly white help – to run their young country.

African politicians kept a weather eye out for any suggestion that the British had run things better, or that Europeans had any useful lessons for Africans to learn. One day John Ward, Julie's father, would have occasion to suggest that some British police officers might be able to assist the Kenya Police with their inquiries into his daughter's mysterious disappearance and death in the Masai Mara. He got his reply through the Foreign Office in Whitehall, which was succinctly informed from Nairobi that the assistance would not be appreciated. Kenya, didn't the British know, was a sovereign country. It could manage an affair like this by itself.

CHAPTER SEVEN

Several miles from downtown, on a road that today carries drivers past Nairobi's municipal stadium, Wilson Airport, a couple of military messes, and a monument to the war dead bearing a curious similarity to the Iwo Jima memorial, the old European settlers had perfected Sir Charles Eliot's ideal of more or less thoroughly eliminating Nairobi from the landscape.

In Langata the flame trees and bougainvillea lining the quiet streets recall not only the English rural countryside but the genteel life-style of the pre-independence White Man's Country. Some of the transplanted institutions of the British settlers still thrive on this side of town. At Ngong Racecourse's weekly Sunday meetings one can wander under the shade trees from paddock to white-washed clubhouse, speculate with the hugely fat Asians who take bets from implausibly tiny stools, and take a late lunch at the Indian restaurant on the grounds. Down the road, in a corner of what is now Jamhuri Park, the East African Kennel Club still strives to maintain British breeding standards at regular terrier and hound shows on its grounds.

Yet one cannot find a place around Nairobi more different from the landscapes of rural England. Next to the supernaturally wide vistas of Langata and its sister suburb of Karen, the groomed fields and straight hedgerows of England are claustrophobic in their compact tidiness. There is one great natural feature that contributes powerfully to this feeling; to the east every view is dominated by the topographical feature made famous by Karen Blixen's elegantly spare prose, the Ngong Hills, their four dark peaks lowering over the horizon as if some great god had molded the Earth with his knuckled fist.

No-one coming upon them for the first time can question why Blixen chose to open the Kenya memoir she published under the name Isak Dinesen, *Out of Africa*, with this ruggedly romantic description of the Ngong Hills: 'In the evening, when it was getting dark, it would first look, as you gazed at them, as if in the sky a thin silver line was drawn all along the silhouette of the dark mountain; then, as night fell, the four peaks seemed to be flattened and smoothened out, as if the mountain was stretching and spreading itself.'

The landscape she described is still essentially unchanged from the perspective of a Langata or Karen estate more than sixty years later. The quality of light and the inspiring breadth of the great blue sky makes an unforgettable impression. 'Everything that you saw made for greatness and freedom', she had written, 'and unequaled nobility.'

Langata and Karen, which was developed on the old farm where Karen Blixen grew coffee and watched her servants hunt lion, attract a particular kind of resident. It is easy to forget the smoky traffic and cramped humanity of the urban downtown barely five miles away; the wide fields are the ideal counterpoint to the breathtaking blue skies of the Kenyan highlands. Artists and photographers and successful craftsmen establish studios on this side of town, where they are surrounded by indigenous shrubs in fiery colors. Secluded religious retreats nestle among great private estates.

The pace and outlook of life always seem different for the Langata set from those of busy businessmen's and diplomats' neighborhoods like Muthaiga and Lavington. Closer to downtown Nairobi the whitewashed homes in the latter quarters are ringed by spiked fences and gates, wired with elaborate alarm systems, guarded day and night by askaris uniformed in blue and gray. In contrast wild game still wander over the unfenced property lines of Langata and Karen. There is even a neighborhood weekly newspaper, the *Karen'gata Gazette*, whose gossipy style reinforces the insular aura. To be fair, sometimes the locally printed weekly simultaneously undermines that feeling in stressing on its pages the frequency of burglaries on the exposed estates.

Inconveniently far out of town for most day-working expatriates, Langata also attracts people whose long years in Kenya provoke them to seek a gentility and space beyond that which Americans or Britons, coming from life in cramped, noisy cities, find in the busy suburban neighborhoods. Homesteaders who leave Kenya and pine to come back to stay do not tend to dream of life in Muthaiga, any more than a businessman hankering after retirement envisions nirvana as a cramped apartment in New York. Ex-Kenyans, when they close their eyes, dream of a place like Langata.

One who did so was Doug Morey. Morey was an American whose graying walrus moustache gave his face an expression of good humor and capability even in repose. He had first come to Kenya more than fifteen years earlier to pilot passenger planes for East African Airways, then a commercial line jointly run by the governments of Kenya, Uganda, and Tanzania in the era of good feeling and limitless African potential immediately following independence. But the African curse of internecine squabbling, aggravated by Kenya's economic dominance of the region, did not take long to assert itself. While these three countries inevitably tied together by geography, economic necessity, and colonial history, fought over trade and politics, their regional economic initiatives collapsed. East African Air splintered into Kenya Airways, Uganda Airways, and Air Tanzania, none of which was a money-making proposition, and Morey moved back to the United States. He took a job with a small carrier flying out of Kennedy Airport in New York.

Morey had expressed his love for this country by purchasing a piece of land with a small one-bedroom house in Langata during his flying days. For ten years he left Kenya behind, but presciently he kept title to his beautiful retreat.

By 1986 he was back. Piloting commercial flights into the big American airports, congested as the airspace might be, maintained its novelty and charm for the pilot about as long as it does for the frequent flyer. When Morey was ready to return to Kenya he signed on as a pilot with AirKenya Aviation, a private outfit flying DC-3's and deHavilland Twin Otters from Nairobi's old Wilson Airport, where charter flights originate, to the beaches of the coast and the airstrips of Masai Mara.

This was a job that never felt routine. The most unpredictable weather of a northeastern American winter could not compare to the capricious meteorology of what weathermen and pilots called the 'itsy', the ITZ, the intertropical zone girdling Africa with a belt of roiling clouds. The itsy accounted simultaneously for Africa's uncertain harvests and its high toll of small aircraft. It was no irony that the bush pilots who flew their planes into mountains or got lost forever in the sinister weather of this region were almost invariably described as the best around; it took the best to survive for any length of time in the pressing charter schedules and eccentric air currents of the stormy belt.

That the air-traffic equipment of Africa was not exactly world class did not help. The best-equipped regional airport might get a weather-radar photo transmission every half hour. Planes and lives could be lost by an experienced pilot taking off for an airstrip peeking out from a clearing in the cloud cover in the 10.30 radar map, but invisible in fog and cloud and unreachable by radio twenty minutes later. By then even the route home could be blocked by vicious weather closing in like a jungle reclaiming an abandoned trail.

At Wilson Airport there were pilots for the Flying Doctor Service who could be called to a bush rescue anywhere in three or four thinly charted countries. Some fliers ferried food to starving villages in war-torn southern Sudan. Morey's job was more regular, but from his veranda in Langata he could expound from personal experience on how a pilot could believe he knew the route from Nairobi to coastal Lamu like he knew the layout of his own house, but in a shift in the flickering light of a Kenyan afternoon or under the shadow of a cloud, the familiar topography below could suddenly become as strange and forbidding as a moonscape.

Tourists tend to remark on the unchanging sameness of the African bush as seen from the air, like a featureless flat lake of brownish green. Experienced pilots like Morey see something else, a richly diverse land where landmarks like mountains and rivers can vanish or transmute themselves in the slanting rays and chiaroscuro of the sun and clouds. No matter how many times he flew between Nairobi and Lamu, or to the four gravel airstrips of the Masai Mara serviced by his airline, Morey would never be headstrong enough to believe he could have perfect knowledge of the ground passing under his wings.

He was satisfied to make one postage stamp of Kenyan land his own. Contracting out the masonry but doing the woodwork with his own hands, Morey had erected a gracious two-story bungalow next door to the tiny house that once stood alone on his Langata parcel. There was a comfortable living room and serviceable kitchen on the ground floor, where a windowed corner looked out on the yard. The second-floor veranda opened on a majestic view: the Ngong peaks outlined sharply in the magical light and perfectly framed by the trees reaching up toward the etched ridge of the hills as if to cradle them in their branches.

In midsummer 1988 Morey was trying to let out the old bungalow that was the original dwelling. Normally it was occupied by a longterm tenant, a Finnish television producer who used Nairobi as a base from which to travel around the region. That summer the Finn informed Morey that he would be away for two months. The house would be available, he said, if Morey could find someone to take it over for the duration.

Not far from Morey's house stood the social center of Langata and Karen. The *duka*, or market, consisted of a general store, dry cleaner, gas station, and a courtyard bordered by an elegant restaurant and a couple of expensive shops. Morey posted a notice at the *duka* advertising the guesthouse for rent. Almost simultaneously Julie Ward, tiring of camping out at the Weld Dixons, posted a note seeking something a little more formal. The arrangement was so self-evidently ideal that their letters crossed in the mail. Paul Weld Dixon was an old acquaintance of Morey's, it turned out; their properties almost adjoined each others', although going from gate to gate involved a roundabout trek of a mile or two. Weld Dixon escorted Julie over to Morey's one day in early August to look over the guesthouse.

It was a hit almost from the first. The guesthouse was perfectly scaled for Julie. From the two houses' common dirt drive she entered a tiny foyer facing a small kitchen. The living room extended down to the left as one came through the door, toward a stone riser along the left-hand wall, where a fireplace faced two sofas upholstered in gray corduroy. Opposite the hearth the living room opened on to a porch giving out on to a typical Langata vista. At the far end of the room a door led to the bedroom. The main room was compact enough to give its occupant the pleasant impression of having everything conveniently to hand. That the differing chores of the pieces of the day could be performed in discrete parts of one room rather than in separate rooms gave the little house a generous air, in the way of the best Kenya homes.

By now Julie Ward had settled into the unassuming social life of Nairobi's community of rootless young expatriates. Telephones were scarce among the largely transient population, and the preferred mode of communication for the shifting community of casual friends was found instead at an open-air restaurant in a courtyard at the corner of Jomo Kenyatta Avenue and Kimathi Street (reflecting the postcolonial government's ambivalence about the largely Kikuyu insurgency that had helped drive the British away, this is the only street in downtown Nairobi named after a Mau Mau warrior).

The Thorn Tree Café is part of the adjoining New Stanley Hotel, a musty old pile among Nairobi's tourist hotels. At the center of its patio floor stands the eponymous tree, around which are nailed four great bulletin boards. Businessmen in suits and tourists in scruffy khaki sit over cups of bitter coffee while people post messages and ads and scan the boards in search of their own names. Julie came often to make and meet friends and scan the bulletin boards.

She also fell easily into the young Langata set. The atmosphere in this group resembled that of a college dormitory. Friends were made easily, living arrangements were informal. For Julie Ward the solitary life and homely routine of Bury St Edmunds were receding, and the confidence and self-reliance built up during the Ho-Bo tour took root. David Tree spotted her from time to time in the Weld Dixon compound, where he was spending hours in greasy overalls working on an overland truck for his first tour. He knew she was planning to stay in the country, and he introduced her to some of his own acquaintances around town.

People who met her during this period could later remark on how she had acquired a familiar infatuation with the unaffected and casual East African life-style. Langata was full of pleasant young Europeans just like Julie, many of them fresh out of school or college, surviving on a stipend from their parents like old-time remittance men or looking for enough part-time work to support an inexpensive existence living in groups in old Langata guesthouses and taking camping trips into the Kenyan and Tanzanian game parks. The abler among them might find work as tour guides or newspaper stringers or academic researchers; most of the others hung around for a while and finally, when their money or the fun ran out, returned home to England or America, only to be replaced by a new arrival very much the same.

Julie had never lived such a relaxed and carefree life. Her letters home began to mention new friends. John Ward was struck by how bright and full of fun they were.

As August drew to a close and her departure time from Kenya neared, it seemed she was really settling in. She talked as if her return to Britain would be only temporary. The easy sojourn in Nairobi had made her even more intent on coming back to stay.

Morey found Julie an easygoing, quiet tenant. She would occasionally visit with him next door and join in the regular Saturday afternoon open-house parties Morey gave to play volleyball in his yard, a Langata social institution. She had a few visitors, mostly fellow campers from the Ho-Bo overland tour or friends acquired among the shifting trade of the Thorn Tree, but her social life was nothing out of the ordinary. Once she brought a friend to the volleyball game, an Australian scientist named Glen Burns, who made very little impression on Morey.

Burns was a lodger with the Weld Dixons. Julie had introduced him there herself, after meeting him through a group of Australian acquaintances. A PhD in zoology, Burns had spent the eighteen months before he met Julie in picaresque wandering. He had left Australia in March 1987 for a long sabbatical. Over the next year he toured the South Pacific and southern Asia, stopping in Indonesia for four months, Malaysia for three, and Thailand and Sri Lanka for another four. In mid-July he finally made it to Kenya and traipsed around the country for a while. When he first met Julie he had been staying in a tourist-grade hotel in Nairobi. The next day she offered him a ride and an introduction to the Weld Dixons, and he got permission to pitch camp in the spacious grounds on Magadi Road.

Julie herself was still visiting the house frequently, dropping in 'Kenya-style', as Paul Weld Dixon recalled: 'She would come in around nine or ten in the morning and ask for coffee.'

Julie behaved like a confident expatriate resident of Nairobi. She spent about $2500 on a rattletrap of a car, a beige Suzuki jeep with four-wheel-drive, built on a short wheelbase that made for a decidedly bumpy ride. Like many Suzukis on the Kenya roads it had an unadorned interior of painted metal, a rolling version of an unfurnished room. Typically, the vehicle was overpriced by the Kenyan market in scarce used cars, especially four-wheel-drives and off-road vehicles. But it was good enough as an urban runabout, and reasonably serviceable for some of the game parks closest to Nairobi. There were two seats in the front of the boxy jeep and space in the back for cargo and provisions.

One day she brought it by to show Paul Weld Dixon, who regarded it skeptically. Months later, asked to describe the vehicle in a courtroom full of strangers gathered to contemplate Julie's mysterious end, he struggled for a matter of minutes before giving out a remark that reflected all of his contempt for a car he forever identified with her unhappy fate. 'It was the color of vomit,' he said.

CHAPTER EIGHT

Every August and September the Kenya-Tanzania border is witness to one of the most extraordinary sights on Earth: the migration of the wildebeest.

These members of the antelope family are impressive chiefly in the aggregate, for no-one could say that as individuals they are among Nature's most graceful creatures. From their long bisonlike faces crowned by a pair of crescent oxlike horns and bearded with a sand-colored neck mane, to their thick shoulders and paltry hindquarters, the wildebeest look like three or four different animals stitched unbecomingly together. The effect is reinforced by their spindly, too-long legs which give them a heavy limping gait that looks ludicrous compared to the elegant bounding dance of the Mara's gazelles.

The wildebeest spend the year in a circular trek within the Serengeti–Masai Mara ecosystem. In April and May they head north from Tanzania into the Masai Mara in search of water, returning south in late summer. The great treks often degenerate into wild stampedes and exceptional carnage. Lions watch from the edge of the herd with the timeless patience of predators, prepared to bring down the stragglers, wounded, or young falling behind the main body of the migration. They feed richly and vultures and hideous marabou cranes fatten up on the leftover carrion. The broad plains of the reserve come to be littered with skeletons, stripped rib cages reaching for the sky like bleached white blades sprouting from the grass. At the wildebeest crossings the Mara River becomes clogged with carcasses lying livid black and red in the rushing water, picked apart by scavengers.

There can be few times of the year anywhere in which

69

nature presents such an unalloyed spectacle of life and death. Before she left Kenya, Julie was intent on photographing the great event.

It was the beginning of September, and she had very little time left in Kenya, although she was not especially in a hurry to get back to England. She had booked an airline ticket for 10 September but her route back was almost an aerial repetition of the Ho-Bo tour, in reverse. It began with a cross-continental leg starting from the Ethiopian capital of Addis Ababa (poverty-stricken Marxist Addis is the hub of the African airline with the best service and route system, Ethiopian Airlines), followed by a series of hops up the steamy West African coast. Julie was going to undertake one final outburst of touring before returning home and planning a radical change in her life.

As for the last Mara trip, there had been some difficulties in the program. At first Julie planned to make the seven-hour drive in the Suzuki with two girlfriends, but they both withdrew as the date approached. About that time, as it happened, Burns resurfaced at the Weld Dixons after a week in Mombasa on the Kenya coast. Julie asked some of their mutual acquaintances if he was 'safe' to travel with and, satisfied with the answers, invited him to join her. Their destination would be the southern Mara, where they could camp out near where the herds would be best viewed. It was to be a quick trip, leaving Friday and returning late Sunday. They arranged to leave together in her Suzuki early on the morning of 2 September.

The Weld Dixons were already beginning to regret the departure of their onetime lodger and frequent visitor. In the last week before the departure for the park, Natasha offered her a lift to the airport for her flight on the eleventh. The final arrangement was that Julie would stop by the night before, cook dinner for the Weld Dixons at their house, and fly off the next day.

Early that Friday morning Julie loaded down the Suzuki with a jumble of provisions and equipment – a couple of cartons of food, tent and sleeping bag, a rudimentary cooking stove, and some light clothes. She packed her camera, an Olympus with a good 300-mm lens for close-up shots of game. A little while later she pulled up at the Weld Dixons to pick up Burns. He crammed his tent, sleeping bag, and a valise of clothing into the back on top of her own and clambered into the rolling tin can.

Burns never said much about the car that brought him and Julie to the Masai Mara. It was sturdy in its no-frills way like an army jeep; built not to resist punishment so much as to ignore it. The Suzuki's short wheelbase took every pothole big, producing a rocky ride over the decrepit route, which deteriorated sharply on the way to the Mara after passing Narok, the last major town.

Four-wheel-drive vehicles were the emblems of the European expatriates in Nairobi, who imported Range Rovers and Toyota Land Cruisers and Mitsubishi Pajeros equipped to survive the rugged Paris–Dakar rally, only to drive them around Nairobi with their children strapped into baby seats. ('Pajero' became a popular nickname for the newly introduced Kenyan 500-shilling bill, which was a larger denomination than most Africans ever used but common currency among the rich whites.) But the tiny Suzuki was a dinghy in a fleet of four-wheel-drive yachts, and it rode harshly over the choppy roads and trails of Kenya.

Julie's approach to maintenance had been expedient at best, perhaps because good care and spare parts were expensive commodities in Africa. Tires were costly, too, and anything better than retreads hard to find at all. The Suzuki's were worn almost bald, not a promising condition in which to challenge the Mara's muddy paths and slippery ruts, which often bested even the powerful engines and all-terrain tires of the Mara hotel fleets, leaving tourists stranded with their well-tipped drivers out on an isolated plain of the park. One day not long before the Mara trip the Suzuki began clanking with an unfamiliar noise under the chassis. Julie's mechanic diagnosed the problem as a broken differential linkage between the front and rear wheels. Fixing it with a new part could cost almost as much as the car was worth. Instead he simply disconnected the link, converting the car from four-wheel-drive to two. That was perfectly adequate for tooling around Nairobi. Anything rougher – that was a different story.

Morey, for his part, had paid little attention to the plans of his quiet tenant. It was his busy season; he was flying to the Mara and back twice a day, sandwiching flights to Lamu on the northern coast in between. Friday morning he slept through her departure and awoke to find that she had left him a farewell note on lined paper in her clear girlish hand.

It was cheery and familiar, as her notes always were, addressed partially to his two dogs. But no writer of Grand Guignol thrillers could have contrived a message so full of innocent foreboding. It read as follows:

> Good morning! Hope I didn't wake you, with my early departure.
> Gone down to the Mara for a couple of days – be back Sunday evening sometime. If you fly over a little Suzuki stuck in the mud down there – give us a wave! Please tell Chumley & Dale – I'll be back soon & give them a cuddle for me.
> See you soon
> Julie.

72

CHAPTER NINE

For all its fame the Mara is not exactly the best place to contemplate nature in an atmosphere of serenity. The songs of hundreds of species of birds are often drowned out by the engine drone of aircraft; one thing that makes Wilson Airport in Nairobi one of Africa's busiest is its full schedule of tourist flights to the Mara's four tarmac airstrips. In 1988 the park had seven lodges and tented camps capable of housing thousands of tourists; now there are even more. In its bustling maturity the country's tourist business has been criticized for overcrowding the game parks: The Masai Mara is the epitome of a place where a visitor is as likely to spot a pride of Land Rovers as of lions.

It might even be true that some of the romance of seeing the animals in their natural habitat has been drained away by the Mara animals' easy familiarity with humans and their green tour vehicles. A game guide might respectfully halt his Land Rover in the shadow of an elephant occupying the rutted trail ahead, but by then he would already have driven his customers almost close enough to the beast to touch its leathery skin, and he would drive off only when the beast lifted its trunk and blared a warning. Lions lie indolently in shaded glens, yawning uninterestedly at the fleets of tourist vans that pull up alongside. Terrapins thrive in the pools which collect in the tread tracks of the hundreds of four-wheel-drives that criss-cross the savannah, leaving the characteristic muddy trails which help make the park easy to identify from the air.

Still, there are few places on Earth with such a great and varied concentration of wildlife. Elephant and black rhinoceros share the plains with Masai giraffe and zebra. Thomson's and Grant's gazelles gambol in herds with impala, as jackals and hyenas slink guiltily around them in the dark grass. In the evening, just as the sun is setting, a knowledgeable driver can sometimes find leopards and cheetahs trotting purposefully through the thick brush, almost invisible in the gray twilight.

Julie and Glen Burns reached the park's Sekenani Gate at about 4 p.m. after a long bone-jarring ride. As was customary, the Suzuki's license number was recorded in the gate book, along with the time and date of arrival, the number of passengers, and the driver's name. Julie signed the register, the pair paid the park and vehicle charges, and they headed south toward a spot near the Tanzanian border marked as the Sand River Gate, which had an adjacent public campsite.

Halfway through the park they drove under the peaked gate of Keekorok Lodge, a busy tourist hotel, for a late lunch. By the time they could order, eat a couple of fruit salads, and pay their bill, two hours had passed. When they arrived at Sand River, another half hour's ride, it was nearly dark. They crested a hill and stopped the Suzuki next to Sand River Gate, a dun-colored set of twin stucco arches spanning the road, which continues through into Tanzania.

Sand River Gate at this time had a certain unsavory reputation. Scarcely one kilometer from Tanzania, uniquely among the six official entrances to the park it also served as a border post. Authorities on both sides of the border nominally discouraged crossings at Sand River, preferring traffic to use better-staffed posts at Namanga, near Mount Kilimanjaro, or Nyabikaye, fifty kilometers from Lake Victoria. But as Tanzania is a socialist country with a strict regime of price controls for most commodities, and Kenya a capitalist one where free-market prices are higher, quiet Sand River had inevitably attracted an active smuggling trade.

One party of Western tourists who stopped at Sand River about a week before Julie's arrival found the atmosphere there sordid. 'It was a den of thieves,' they recalled bluntly. Immigration officers and a plainclothes policeman lounged around, seemingly oblivious to the prostitutes who had made the place a headquarters from which to service illicit tradesmen. The dual gates under the stucco arches were kept locked, but there was an understanding that they could be opened for a fee. The gatehouse itself was situated out of sight of most Kenya-side approaches, although a short stroll along the river-bank, which crossed the road and meandered parallel to the border on the Kenyan side, afforded a fair view of the park campsite, which extended off the road on both sides of the river, a fraction of a kilometer inside the park.

This campsite was Julie's and Burns's destination, and at the gatehouse they registered and paid the fee to pitch two tents for one night. The campsite is built on rocky, undulating ground next to the riverbed. Burns and Julie drove through the gate to the Tanzania side of the river, selected a suitable spot, and pitched their tents.

On Saturday, 3 September, they both awoke before dawn. The Mara birds had begun to chatter and among their neighboring tents one could hear the stirrings of game watchers eager to move out on to the Mara plains for what could be the best spotting of the day. The park fairly bustled with moving game in the purple light of daybreak, as the animals converged on den and lair from their nocturnal wanderings. Mist nestled among the hillocks and hollows and the silence was unbroken except for the grunts of hippos escorting their young back to ponds carpeted with lily pads.

Burns and Julie planned to keep camp for another day. They loaded their removable items into the back of the Suzuki and drove north up the graded road back to Keekorok to fuel the jeep.

The fuel pumps at the entrance to Keekorok Lodge were dry. Julie pulled out a map of the park. They had enough fuel to cross the park as far as the Mara Serena Lodge, about fifty kilometers away. It would take just over an hour. They could fill up there, make another game drive, and return to the campsite by evening.

The route across the park, on a graded and well-tended road that is one of the Mara's best, took them through herds of grunting wildebeest. Occasionally the animals stampeded across their path. Halfway to the Serena they crossed the Mara River over a dual bridge, the product of a construction project that had opened fully half of the reserve to tourism by spanning the river. The original bridge, a low concrete affair, was still in use, but Serena Lodges – they owned the only permanent lodge in the park west of the river – had built a new one, sitting high off the water and supported by a gleaming galvanized steel girder. As they crossed the bridge a powerful stench of rotting flesh rose from the river and they could spot the humps of decomposing wildebeest carcasses breaking the surface of the water.

They got to the Mara Serena early in the afternoon. Burns later recalled their spending a couple of hours sunning by its teardrop-shaped pool, looking north over a vast wedge of the Mara plains bisected by the streak of red clay road up which they had come. A line of stumpy trees in the distance marked the course of the Mara River. Between that and the foot of the Serena's hill herds of wildebeest and zebra could be made out grazing around a pond. At one end of the same broad field was a spot where the grass had been worn away; this was where the lodge's balloon pilots set up their tourist balloons every morning before dawn. The plains seemed to stretch infinitely into the distance, toward the dark shapes of the northern escarpments dimly visible at the horizon.

By 2.30 or so Julie and Burns had got the Suzuki filled with fuel and set off again for their camp. This time they decided to turn off the Serena access road to take another route back to the main trail. This northwestern portion of the Masai Mara is crisscrossed by a network of unmarked roads and trails, each an indistinguishable meandering path in the grassy plain. In no time at all they were lost. Convinced they would never be able to find the way back to Sand River, they decided to backtrack and start again from the Serena.

The trouble came upon them slowly in the pitching ride of the jeep, until suddenly they realized that its cantankerous ride had a cause other than its tight suspension and short wheelbase. Something serious was wrong. The engine sputtered and coughed and suddenly choked to a stop. Julie tried to rev the engine a couple of times, but the jeep would not start. Burns calculated that they were about ten kilometers short of the Serena. It was much too far to go on foot for help, in a place where a chance encounter with an animal in the bush could be fatal.

Burns could barely hide his irritation. He was planning to attend a scientific conclave in Nairobi the next day, and he was impatient about the unexpected foul-up. The Mara teemed with tourist vehicles, but they were like policemen in the adage: You could never be sure of finding one when you needed it. Suddenly a van filled with twenty Europeans appeared over a hill.

At the wheel, sitting next to a hired Mara guide, was a young Englishman named Stephen Watson. Watson had curly dark hair and an innocent, boyish air about him, but he had accumulated years of experience conducting groups around Kenya and Tanzania for Guerba Expeditions, a big British tour company that arranged overland trips like Ho-Bo's as well as game drives and luxury safaris.

Watson had led his group into the Mara that very morning, stopping at noon at the Mara Serena Lodge. They established a camp on the outskirts of the lodge property and had lunch. Watson hired a game tracker from the ranger's office nearby, left his co-driver by the Serena pool for a morning off, and headed out with his nineteen European and American clients at 3.30 that afternoon. About ten minutes later they came upon a tan Suzuki stopped in the road. A blond girl and an Australian came over and explained that the jeep had seized up.

'It looks like the fuel pump,' the Australian said.

It was part of the ethos of tour guides in the Mara that one stopped to offer assistance – 'Someday it could be you out there,' Watson said later. He told them to wait to see if anyone else passed, but assured them he would pick them

77

up later if they were still stuck. 'We're just heading out now,' he said, 'but we'll come back this way. If you're still here, we can give you a tow back to the Serena.'

When they returned more than an hour later the Suzuki was still there. Watson had not formed any impression of the pair on his first pass – in fact, he did not expect to see them again – but now he was getting a fix on a Glen Burns nettled and peeved by his forced inactivity on the Mara plain. The Australian walked around agitatedly as Watson got a rope to tie to the Suzuki's axle, and muttered about meeting a tight schedule.

'Which one of you wants to get behind the wheel?' Watson asked when the tow line was secure.

'She can drive,' Burns snapped, as Watson recalled later. 'It's her damn car.' Watson glanced at the girl, who seemed detached and unperturbed at her companion's behavior. She had barely said a word during the entire encounter. The young tour conductor gave a mental shrug at the man's pointless display of annoyance.

Watson towed the Suzuki up to the Serena parking lot and untied the rope. By then the swift equatorial darkness had fallen. The Serena kept an African mechanic employed to tend its small fleet of bright orange Land Cruisers, and the pair told him they would have him take a look.

That evening Watson again came upon the two stranded tourists at dinner. Burns, somewhat more engagingly, came over to invite him to have a drink.

The two travelers informed Watson that they were stuck for accommodation that night. They had left their tents at Sand River Camp, to which they expected to return that day. Agreeably, Watson invited them to use one of Guerba's spare tents and to pitch it at the firm's campsite, down the hill within the Serena grounds.

'We must have two or three extra,' he said. 'Some of my clients are going to stay the night inside here instead of camping. Come on down and you can have one.' After dinner Julie and Burns followed him to the campsite and pitched a single tent.

The next morning the two of them placed a radio call from the Mara Serena to Paul Weld Dixon in Nairobi. Amid the obscuring static Weld Dixon gleaned that Julie's Suzuki had broken down and needed a new fuel pump. Julie came on to ask him if he could buy one in Nairobi and send it down to the Serena by plane.

'I'll take care of it tomorrow morning,' Weld Dixon replied.

Burns continued to fret about his schedule. He wanted to catch part of an anthropological conference at the Kenya National Museum in Nairobi, but it ended the next day, which was Monday. Even if Weld Dixon got a replacement pump first thing in the morning and had it flown down on the first morning flight, by the time it got fitted and they could retrieve their tents it would be too late to return home. He could never get back to Nairobi in time to make the end of the conference.

'Why don't you just fly back to Nairobi? You can leave from here,' Julie said. 'I can collect the tents myself, and I'll see you tomorrow night. You can take the fuel pump up to show Paul.'

It was the selfless Julie again, more concerned for Burns's schedule than herself. Moreover, she treated the prospect of driving around the Mara as an unaccompanied woman with absolute composure. Even from the relative security of a big Land Cruiser, the sight of the powerful predators of the Mara plains is often enough to give a visitor chills. But as Burns later observed, Julie had no fear of the park's wild animals, flimsy as her jeep was.

It may have been because of Julie's composure, but Burns finally acceded to the plan to leave her to pull down the tents and drive back to Nairobi alone. The mechanic unbolted the apparently faulty pump from the Suzuki so Burns could show it to Weld Dixon for comparison and the two stranded visitors hitched a ride in a Serena van to the nearest airstrip. Carrying the pump, Burns caught the Sunday-morning flight back to Wilson Airport. As the plane taxied down the airstrip and took off, he could see Julie waving him off through his window.

Watson had taken his group out on a morning game drive, and when he arrived back at the Serena at 11.30 that morning he was surprised to find Julie still there, alone. He let his co-driver manage the afternoon game run for the clients, and stayed by the pool to do paperwork and write letters. Julie was relaxing with a couple of Watson's clients who had passed up the game drive, and he joined the small group.

Now, away from the angry presence of Glen Burns, he found Julie Ward to be a pleasantly appealing girl. Over the five months of the Ho-Bo tour and the following weeks in Nairobi she had shed some of her habitual reserve, and Watson found it easy to draw her out about the overland trip and her plans to stay in Africa. They had considerable experience of African travel in common, and Watson could nod knowingly at her descriptions of the landscapes she saw and people with whom she had traveled. He intuited quickly that she had found the trip a liberating experience, and as a trained Africa hand he sensed himself, as he put it later, 'that she had caught the bug and wanted to stay.'

'I got the impression that she'd been very busy in England and hadn't had much of a social life,' he said. 'But now she had quite a bit to look forward to.' Watson was also taken with another quality Julie projected: her calm self-assurance. 'I thought she could handle herself in situations,' he said.

That night they met again. Julie had taken a room in the Serena to await the new fuel pump, and as Watson recalled later she offered him her spare bed. The young tour guide later remembered spending hours in conversation about her old job in England and her plans for the future. She talked about setting up her own business, and someday, she wanted to have children.

But it was the immediate future that concerned Watson. He wanted to see her again, but she was scheduled to fly out of Nairobi the following Sunday. Watson was committed to shepherding his tour group around the Kenyan countryside until late that day, but after that he would have a free week in Nairobi.

'Why don't you stay another week,' he asked. 'Put off your flight.'

But Julie was adamant about her final aerial tour of Africa. 'She was very keen to fly away,' Watson remembered.

'I'll be back in November or December,' she told him. 'I'll see you then.'

Watson frowned. At that time of the year he would be out of the country with another tour. He would not be back in Nairobi until January. He pressed to see her once more before she left. 'We're going from here up to Naivasha,' he said. Naivasha was a lovely lake deep in the recesses of the Great Rift Valley, not an hour's drive from Nairobi. 'Why don't you think about meeting me up there?'

Julie said she would try. She had a few things to settle in Nairobi before her flight – visas to Ethiopia and Ghana, among other things. If she could get everything done by midweek, she would see him in Naivasha, she said.

Doug Morey arrived back at his house in Langata that same night from a flight to Lamu, an ancient Arabic tourist trap on the Kenyan coast south of the Somalia border. He was not home long before Paul Weld Dixon called.

'Julie's car broke down in the Mara and I'm getting a new fuel pump for it tomorrow,' Weld Dixon said. 'Can you send it down on a flight?'

'Sure,' Morey replied. 'Send it over to Wilson, put my name on it, and I'll see that it goes down.'

On Monday Watson ate lunch with Julie and listened as she made a radio call to Weld Dixon to confirm that the new pump was coming on the afternoon flight from Nairobi. Then he and his group left the Serena to make

81

one last game run in the park before heading north to Naivasha.

Julie was standing by the Serena Lodge reception desk later that day when David Weston walked past. Weston was an easygoing American with a shock of striking black hair and a dark moustache who piloted hot air balloons on game-watching flights from the field below the Serena. The good-looking blond girl seemed to be alone. Weston was a sociable guy, so he said hello and introduced himself.

'What brings you up here?' he asked. 'Is everything OK?'

'Not really,' she said with a little smile, explaining her travails with the Suzuki and its fuel pump. 'The mechanics are checking it now.'

'Let me take a look,' Weston said. 'Maybe I can help.'

Weston found there was not much he could do. Outside by the fuel pumps the Suzuki, hood upright, was surrounded by a crowd as a mechanic tried to fit the new fuel pump. At last he got it attached. Julie climbed into the driver's seat and turned the key. Nothing.

With the crowd mumbling suggestions the mechanic fiddled around the engine again. 'Try it now,' someone said. The engine did not even turn over. There was a long period of consultation in Swahili and further manipulation of the insides, until one of the mechanics discovered the real cause of the jeep's failure: it was just a loose wire to the starter motor. The fuel pump, it seemed, had not been the problem after all. The Suzuki sprang to life.

But Julie had wasted another day. The quickening darkness was already closing in, so she was bound to stay overnight again in the Serena. Weston seized the opportunity to invite her to dinner.

That night they spent a pleasant evening. Like Watson, the balloon pilot was taken with the slight, strong-minded Julie, but his face darkened at the story of Burns's flight to Nairobi. Weston fashioned himself a gallant, and he thought Burns's behavior in leaving her alone in a bad situation violated a code. 'I thought he was jerk,' he remarked bluntly, later. After dinner they listened to some music and had a couple of beers in his room, and he escorted her back to her room and bade good night at the door. But he arranged to take her up the next morning in a balloon before she left the park.

Early-morning game-watchers in the Masai Mara are often enthralled by the sight of the multicolored balloons rising lazily over the treetops and sailing over the plains at seven or eight o'clock in the morning. Eight passengers ride in the wicker baskets suspended underneath, spotting whatever wildlife is ranging below the arbitrary path on which Nature sends the balloons. They come to earth a couple of hours later, bumping roughly over the ground until a ground crew can anchor the balloon, to be met by a convoy packing a champagne breakfast. They toast each other in the instant camaraderie of people united in a strange and unusual experience, and then they are driven back to their camps and lodges.

In the dry season, with the grass short, the conditions were ideal for aerial game viewing. Julie and Weston returned to the Serena at about 9.30, Weston recalled, after an exhilarating flight they shared with four French tourists and Weston's co-pilot. Julie's plan was to check out, drive back to the Sand River camp to retrieve the two tents, and continue on to Nairobi.

Weston instantly tried to dissuade her from heading off by herself. 'I was concerned,' he later explained. 'A woman driving alone in the bush, it's dangerous.'

He told her, 'If you're short of cash I'll give you the money for the airfare.'

Julie looked amused and brushed off the suggestion. She had traveled overland for five months, been stuck in a river, slogged through the Zairean rain forest. Julie had been a textbook Ho-Bo client, the tour adding an adventuresome streak to the solitary self-confidence she had brought to the journey. After that it was as if Africa harbored very few further mysteries.

'I'll be fine,' she said.

'If you hang on here a little bit there'll be lots of people driving back to Nairobi in their cars,' Weston said. 'You can go in convoy.'

'I can't,' she said. 'I have to stop off at Sand River first to collect the tents. Don't worry. I can manage.'

Weston unhappily escorted her back to the Suzuki and gave it a sour inspection. He eyed its four bald tires and reflected uneasily on what she had told him about its broken four-wheel-drive. He gave a last glance at the disorderly load of gear in the back. *Looks like a junkyard in there*, he thought.

Julie padded over to the driver's side in a pair of red rubber flip-flops. Dressed in jeans and a shirt she smiled unconcernedly at Weston, gave him a wave, and roared off down the Serena driveway.

This visit to the Mara had to be judged less than a success. Given the Suzuki's mechanical problems and the two-day stranding at the Serena, Julie had found very little time for game watching and taking pictures. In this park the best viewing was always found off the main roads, amid the faint serpentine trails etched over the plains by experienced Masai drivers in heavy Land Cruisers. Julie had been so rushed in finding fuel for the jeep that there had been no time to head up into the rolling hills.

Early in the afternoon she arrived at Sand River Camp. A few sets of eyes followed the tan jeep as it pulled through the gatehouse and up next to two tents. The blond girl got out and, without ceremony, took down the tents and stuffed them into the back of the jeep.

She pulled out of the campsite, over the small bridge spanning the river, and into the gate. David Nchoko, the Masai revenue clerk there, pointed at the tents in the rear of the vehicle: They had been left there for two extra days, bringing the additional charge Julie owed to 200 shillings. She settled the bill. Then she restarted her Suzuki and drove north toward Keekorok. Nchoko noted the time in a logbook: 2.37 p.m.

It might have been a small detail to be buried like so

many other formalities in the overgrown bureaucratic paperwork of Kenyan officialdom. But it turned out to be important, because no-one else ever admitted to seeing Julie Ward alive after that day.

CHAPTER TEN

Glen Burns attended his conference on Monday and returned to the Weld Dixons' house to wait for Julie. He was again displaying impatience, for he had signed on for a month-long overland trip to Tanzania, Rwanda, Zaire, and Uganda leaving at the end of the week, and she had his luggage in her jeep.

Judging from what Burns had said, Weld Dixon expected her back in Nairobi by late Tuesday. When she did not show up, he called Morey in a fretful state.

'I'm worried about her,' he said over the telephone.

Morey all but chuckled to himself. Paul could be an old lady sometimes. It just seemed to be in his character to worry. Morey tried to calm him down. After all, Julie was a young kid with a lot of friends. Maybe she had met some young people in the park and hooked up with them. But the older man would not relax.

'Look, I'll ask some of the pilots down there to check around, all right?' he told Weld Dixon.

One of Morey's friends in the Mara was an African-born Swedish balloonist and helicopter pilot named Sebastian Tham who kept a safari headquarters at Keekorok. 'She's missing,' Morey told Tham the next day. 'If you get a chance, check around and let me know if she's been seen, would you?'

Tham responded quickly; that very afternoon he got a message to Morey saying Julie had signed out of the park at Keekorok with a large group of people. Morey was satisfied. He thought it stood to reason that she might have met another group of young campers and joined them for more game watching.

'She's probably gone to Nakuru or something,' he told

Weld Dixon, mentioning a wooded lake and game reserve a few hours north of Nairobi. The great attraction of Nakuru was the flock of millions of flamingos that went there to breed and lined the lakeshore in a spectacular fringe of pink.

Weld Dixon refused to be pacified. 'But she's leaving for Europe,' he told Morey. 'She's supposed to be here to cook dinner and then we're taking her to the airport. It's definite.'

At this Morey was slightly taken aback. Julie had not mentioned to him that she was leaving Kenya so soon. But still he could not imagine why Weld Dixon was so concerned.

'Paul, you've just got it wrong. What's the big deal? There's a flight leaving here for London every night. So she'll take a different one.'

But Friday night and again Saturday morning Weld Dixon was back on the line like a clucking mother hen. He was driving Morey crazy. 'She is not the kind of girl not to call,' Weld Dixon repeated frantically. 'Something must be wrong.'

Finally Morey mollified Weld Dixon by checking the guesthouse. Maybe he could find a clue to Julie's plans inside.

On the table Julie had left a note to herself. Morey frowned when he read the roll of things to do listed in her precise hand. She had tightly scheduled all of the week just past, getting visas, making last-minute purchases, and so on. Her plans seemed to be much firmer than Morey had known.

He rummaged around the house and at length came up with an airline ticket. To his further surprise it was not a simple British Airways passage to London, but a complicated itinerary involving connecting flights in out-of-the-way places like Addis Ababa and Abidjan. Three or four African airlines were involved, some of which flew these routes no more than once a week. And indeed, she was scheduled to leave on Sunday. Tomorrow.

When he left the house Morey found himself agreeing

with Paul Weld Dixon. There was cause to be worried, in a big way.

That morning he piloted AirKenya's regular morning flight to the Mara. When he landed at Keekorok he tracked down his friend Sebastian Tham. 'We're all worried,' he told the balloonist, asking that he reconfirm at Keekorok Gate that Julie had signed out of the park with a group. Later in the day Tham reached Morey by radio. The earlier information had been mistaken, he said. In fact, Keekorok, as an interior post, did not even keep track of people entering or leaving the park. Morey reported this unhappily to Weld Dixon when he landed. Now, it seemed, there was genuine reason to wonder what had become of Julie.

Stephen Watson had waited in vain for Julie to show up in Naivasha on Wednesday and Thursday. He absorbed the disappointment philosophically. He had thought the chances were good that she would come, but he reflected that when one was so early in a relationship you never could tell, even when the girl said she wanted to see you again.

There was still one slim chance he might see Julie before she flew off. That Saturday night – the evening she was to cook dinner for the Weld Dixons – he had a party for his clients at the Carnivore, a nearby open-air restaurant. It was a customary end-of-tour do, and the group was scheduled to fly home from Nairobi the next day. Watson had invited Julie to come over when her own dinner was finished, but he figured she would not.

The person he did see was Paul Weld Dixon. The old filmmaker had learned from a friend who allowed Watson's firm to keep its tour vehicles on his property that Watson had met Julie in the Mara. Weld Dixon came searching for Watson at the Carnivore that night. When he discovered Julie was not with him, Weld Dixon let his panic show. He was clearly sick with worry, as if it were his own daughter missing.

'Where is she?' he asked. 'She wouldn't fly out without letting us know.'

The next morning Watson delivered his passengers to Jomo Kenyatta International Airport and made a fruitless run around its parking lots to see if he could spot the tan Suzuki. He stopped at the Ethiopian Airlines counter to check its passenger list for that morning's flight to Addis Ababa, the one she had booked. Julie's name was there, all right, but she had not called to reconfirm or cancel her reservation.

Watson was apprehensive as he walked out of the office on to the open terminal plaza. Next to him the passengers were already queuing up for the flight to Addis and its connections to flights all over the world. Something was definitely wrong, he thought.

The day before, the same sense of apprehension had reached Bury St Edmunds. John Ward was spending a noisy morning coaxing his sclerotic garden tractor over the wet grass of his secluded property when he let his mind wander and he thought of Julie. Wasn't it about time for her to be heading home? Impulse, he said later, drove him to give his machine a break and to call Nairobi.

It was lunchtime at the Weld Dixons'. John Ward got Natasha on the phone. She tried to keep her softly-accented voice nonchalant even as she allowed that she and Paul were a little concerned. 'She was meant to be back by now,' she said. 'We're trying to locate her.'

CHAPTER ELEVEN

In Kenya, as in many parts of Africa, one of the first images that occurs to people keeping a vigil for stragglers is of the horrifying carnage of the road. Ferocious might be the wild game of Africa, bloody its wars and virulent its diseases, but the continent's roads and drivers comprise its deadliest combination.

In Kenya the road is the great leveler. One might read one morning of a bush taxi, known locally as a *matatu*, sideswiping a truck or plunging into a ravine, killing several dozen riders. The next day the traffic toll will include a cabinet minister or a member of parliament in a Mercedes, and the day after that a European businessman in a Toyota. Photographs of disembodied limbs and scenes of even greater carnage are daily features of the newspapers.

Vehicular mayhem is widely judged one of the country's principal threats to health and security. In its handbook for newly arriving diplomats and their families the American embassy in Nairobi warns of 'local driving habits involving speed, ignoring traffic controls, and a tendency to take chances.' That is a diplomatic way of referring to the Kenyan practice of careening down the wrong side of the highway, flirting constantly with disaster and heedlessly menacing everyone on the tarmac.

A major problem is the decrepit condition of even major thoroughfares. Government penury compounded by a general African disinclination toward maintenance has turned the national road system, once unparalleled in Africa, into a network of potholes connected by thin strands of eroded pavement. In part this is a legacy of colonial-era road building; there are few competent roadbeds anywhere in Kenya, and during the rainy seasons each year the pavement flakes away and red soil bubbles up through the cracks like stew on a hard simmer.

The rolling stock is a further hazard. The roads are a sea of unworthy vehicles. Africans have a marvelous ability to keep cars and trucks running long after any other user would have consigned them to the junkyard, but the result is a fleet of bizarrely patched-up vehicles held together with wire and string, car bodies riding along on sprung suspensions at a precarious list. Chugging sedans with windshields cracked to the point of opacity and tires misaligned in four different directions are as common as giraffes in the game parks. Naturally the mends have a way of coming apart at exactly the most inopportune places and times, so that drivers along major roadways must stomp on the brakes to avoid hitting a truck or bus immobilized in the traffic lane or left abandoned without any warning for oncoming drivers except a few tree branches laid across the pavement a hundred yards up the road. Every commercial truck or van bears a rear tag giving its maximum allowable speed, usually sixty-five kilometers an hour. This is a running joke: Either these vehicles are found straining their way sclerotically up hills, cars backed up behind them for a mile with drivers coughing at the carpet of metallic soot the ill-tuned trucks laid down over the pavement, dense enough to turn day into night, or they are careening hair-raisingly down the other side on two wheels. They never seem to be going at the rated speed.

But it all comes down to the drivers. People joke that the road is the only place where Kenyans ever seem to be in a hurry. They swing out into oncoming traffic to pass a single vehicle, flashing their headlamps in warning and grinning at the thrill. They roar over shoulders and bounce over speed bumps, playing a nerve-wracking game of chicken on residential streets and four-lane highways alike. The routes are littered with the twisted remains of buses and trucks rolled over on their sides in positions that flatly defy all the laws of Newtonian physics except whichever natural forces govern a shoddy vehicle taking a sharp curve at a ludicrous rate of speed, with vegetables, furniture, and other freight piled high enough on its roof to give it the center of gravity of a twelve-story building. Trucks careen over the roads with a full load of workmen loaded into the back, sitting on the gunwales and holding on for dear life, jouncing around like figures in a cartoon.

More fearsome are *matatus*, the up-country buses that provide an indispensible supplement to the meager mass transit of the country. These are often no more than pickup trucks fitted with cabins in the back, painted gaily like circus wagons with bright stripes and Kikuyu slogans attesting to the driver's trust in God. Some have horns that can play anything from 'Colonel Bogey's March' to a tribal folk-song at the press of a button. Colored lights arranged over the windshield give them an eerie presence on the dark roads of Kenya at night. The *matatu* drivers and their 'touts', who lean perilously out the doors to buttonhole passengers like barkers at a carnival, are paid by the passenger and the number of round trips made. This is a further incentive to speed maniacally down the road, passengers crammed inside to a density that would be unacceptable at rush hour on a Tokyo subway.

When John Ward first called, Paul Weld Dixon had been consumed with these very images. The road was so unpredictable. He spent hours visiting and telephoning the local hospitals and morgues and agencies like the Flying Doctor Service, a fleet of airborne medics who treated and airlifted the injured out of inaccessible spots all over East Africa.

But so far all his inquiries had turned up negative. *Now what?* he asked himself. Late that afternoon, as darkness was already falling, he decided to call a neighbor.

Perez Olindo was one of Kenya's more accomplished technicians and bureaucrats. By September 1988 he had already been director of the country's national parks, and director of the private African Wildlife Foundation. His name was on the covers of countless scientific tracts about the ecology of East Africa, including a groundbreaking study of the decline of the ecosystem of Lake Victoria,

92

Africa's greatest lake, whose political misfortune it is to form the boundary waters of the eternally squabbling Kenya, Uganda, and Tanzania.

Now Olindo was director of the Department of Wildlife Conservation and Management. The filmmaker knew the bureaucrat socially because their properties nearly abutted each other in Langata. Over the telephone Weld Dixon explained to Olindo that Julie was a tourist who had spent at least three days in the Mara but had now evidently gone missing. He needed information from the park about when and if she had left, and in what direction she might have been going.

Olindo recalled later that when he first heard Weld Dixon's alarmed voice come over the telephone it was already too late to reach the Masai Mara by departmental radio. The network shut down at 6.30 p.m. and would not open again until around 8.30 Sunday morning. But Olindo could offer other help: his private plane was moored at Wilson Airport, five minutes' drive away, and he could fly Weld Dixon down to Keekorok himself the next morning for a few hours' reconaissance.

Later that evening the Weld Dixons got a second call from John Ward. This time Paul, constitutionally unable to suppress his panic, took the phone. Julie was seriously overdue, he said, admitting he was extremely worried and that he would fly down to the Mara himself to look around. His voice fairly vibrated with trepidation.

Weld Dixon's hysteria may have provoked Ward to seek out calmer counsel, for almost immediately he called Morey.

'What do you think?' he asked.

From the laconic pilot he got the same degree of concern, expressed in chillingly rational tones. 'I wasn't worried before,' Morey said, 'but now I am. It seems a little unusual that she would disappear like this without letting anybody know.'

The next morning Olindo piloted his Cessna 182 four-seater to the Keekorok airstrip with Weld Dixon as his only passenger.

At Keekorok Lodge, Olindo got a briefing from the chief game warden of the Mara, a short, pudgy Masai named Simon ole Makallah. Makallah had checked the gate registers of the park and determined that Julie and a companion had signed in at about 4 p.m., 2 September, at Sekenani Gate, the most convenient entry for a driver coming from Nairobi. Her destination was Sand River Camp.

Sand River had informed Makallah that the tourist had left camp the morning of 3 September for a game drive. From the Mara Serena he had learned that she had spent two nights there, leaving on the sixth. Sand River further reported that Julie had returned to the campsite that same day, packed her tents, and left via the Keekorok road.

'The police have been informed,' Makallah said.

'The police?' Olindo repeated. Well, he thought, the matter seems to be well in hand.

The four of them – Weld Dixon, Tham, Olindo, and Makallah – piled into a park vehicle and sped down the blacktop to Sand River. Olindo himself checked the vehicle register and the receipt book from which the revenue clerk at Sand River Gate had checked Julie's Suzuki out of the campsite. Curious, he flipped the pages of the receipt book. The time entries of the departing vehicles were out of order: The clerk seemed to have skipped two pages.

'What happened here?' he asked, showing the clerk the discrepancy.

'It was just a mistake,' the clerk said. For the moment Olindo let the matter drop.

On their way back to Nairobi, Olindo and Weld Dixon made a pass by air over the browning Mara landscape. From 300 feet aloft they followed the Keekorok road as far as Sand River Gate and Camp, circled east to follow the meandering river until it intersected with the park boundary about twenty kilometers away, then turned back and traced their route a second time. They spotted nothing. That evening, just as Weld Dixon got home, the telephone rang with a third call from John Ward. He was phoning from Heathrow Airport to say he would be landing in Nairobi in the morning.

CHAPTER TWELVE

Ward's commercial flight arrived on schedule the next morning at 5.30, in solid darkness. By the time he had wended his way through passport formalities daylight was streaming into the airport baggage hall. Ward filled out the obligatory currency declaration on flimsy newsprint (the Kenya government required travelers to get it stamped every time they changed their money into Kenya shillings), got waved through customs, and was greeted as he emerged into the chaotic airport waiting area by Paul and Natasha Weld Dixon.

On the way to Langata, Paul told Ward all he could about Julie's mysterious disappearance. He mentioned the Suzuki's breakdown and Burns's return to Nairobi, and filled the father in on what was known of her arrival and apparent departure from the game reserve. The Weld Dixons offered him lodging at their house in Langata. Ward took a look around the modest quarters and reflected on the long drive in from the airport, and told them he would prefer to take a hotel downtown. By then they had sat down to breakfast, where Ward first met Doug Morey.

Morey impressed him with his professional grasp of the situation. 'What you need for an aerial search like this is a single-engine plane that can fly low and slow,' he said. Apologetically he explained that he could not take part in a search that day because he was flying for AirKenya, but he could help Ward hire a pilot and plane from among the large general aviation community at Wilson Airport. The search flight was soon set for that afternoon at one o'clock.

After breakfast Ward checked into the Norfolk Hotel on the edge of Nairobi's downtown and took a taxi to the

British High Commission. The embassy offices were a few blocks away on four floors of a concrete high-rise office building. There was a wood double door off the hallway and a reception desk, where Ward gave his name to be sent through. At one side people were queued up to have their bags and persons searched before they could be admitted.

Stephen Watson had reached the front of the line and had just explained that he had come to have his six-month cholera booster shot at the embassy's medical clinic. A Kenyan guard was searching his bag when Watson heard a British voice inquire of someone from behind the barrier: 'Are you Mr Ward? Come right this way.'

A tall stocky gray-haired man with a pleasant face drawn tight with anxiety was being directed through the gate. Watson interrupted him.

'Are you Julie Ward's father?' The man nodded yes.

Watson explained that he had met Julie in the Mara, where he had been leading a tour, and that like Weld Dixon he was concerned about her disappearance. He offered to do anything he could to help find her.

'Why don't you meet me tonight? You can tell me all about it,' Ward replied.

Ward continued through into the high commission offices, where he met Jenny Jenkins, a petite blond consular assistant who would become his factotum and all-around girl Friday on embassy matters in the coming months. Jenkins and the other consular assistants helped Ward get copies made at a nearby shop of a photograph of Julie to post around the park.

At 1 p.m. Ward squeezed into the co-pilot's seat of a two-seater plane next to Glen Slater, a local pilot, and they took off for Keekorok. The British businessman stared out the window at the majesty of the African landscape. From Wilson Airport the route to the Mara took him over the immense gash in the earth known as the Great Rift Valley and the imposing escarpments that lined its sides. Two glowering extinct volcanoes rose blackly from a green valley checkered with farms and pastures.

Soon the neat arrangement of crops gave way to open

97

fields of brownish green. Slater kept the plane low so Ward's eyes could follow the roads below and pick out anything that might look like a stranded car. From time to time they made a second pass, low, to examine some bit of twisted wreckage along the side of a strip of pavement.

Then the rolling topography ceded to a rocky landscape tortured by nature into a series of ridges. It was sheer desolation as far as the eye could see, Ward thought to himself, and that was about twice as far as the eye could see anywhere in England. The last ridge was the great Oloololo escarpment cresting the Mara's northwestern edge like a great frozen wave of green, and then they were flying over plains crisscrossed by muddy tracks and dotted with the flat crowns of acacia trees. Ward could pick out giraffe and elephant from the air, standing in still-life poses. They looked a little lost out there alone, he thought, lost like his own daughter. There were great long trails of wildebeest beginning their trek south to the Serengeti – the very thing Julie had come down here to photograph. Seeing the vastness of the landscape Ward reflected with a shudder that at this moment, five or six days since she had disappeared, he was conducting the first real search for her.

In another minute Slater touched bumpily down on the airstrip at Keekorok. Slater got the plane refueled and quickly they were off again, cruising over herds of wildebeest and elephants massed in their introverted social units. They retraced the route taken the day before by Olindo and Weld Dixon over the Sand River and along the Keekorok road. Here and there Ward noticed clusters of metal huts, glinting in the sun's reflection and arranged in rough circles. He recalled later being struck by a single hut off by itself, not far from one of the circular encampments.

But there was no trace of a stranded jeep. If Ward had harbored expectations of spotting Julie waving happily at her rescuers from the crest of a hill, he put them aside at the sight of Africa's inscrutable immensity laid out like a vast carpet below the little plane. When the two-man search partly landed that night at Wilson after eight hours aloft, they were exhausted and Ward was dejected. Morey landed at about the same time from a training flight in AirKenya's new deHavilland Twin Otter. He took off shortly to do some night circuits in the unfamiliar plane, but arranged to join Ward as soon as he was finished.

The planning session for the following day took place on the verandah of the Norfolk Hotel's Delamere Bar. Ward, Morey, and Stephen Watson were surrounded by history on the stained-wood terrace of the hotel once called the 'House of Lords' for the nobility of its clientele, but which now looked out on a street choked with rattling taxis and belching trucks.

Morey judged that a full-scale search of the Mara would require up to a half-dozen airplanes, each one with three observers. They would divide the Mara into square patches and cruise them in succession, starting from Wilson at 9 a.m. Morey was flying AirKenya's shuttle to the Mara, so he would not be able to join in the search. But he would keep in touch by radio.

Meanwhile the Weld Dixons had mustered a large search party – too large, as it turned out. Ward got to Wilson Airport the next morning to find nearly fifty people milling around, ready to climb aboard five hired planes as observers. They only had room for fifteen, and Ward thanked the others gratefully as he turned them away. Spotting Watson in the crowd, he asked him to come along as one of the few people present who might recognize the Suzuki. As they all crossed the apron he noticed a gray hangar labeled KENYA POLICE AIR WING. The doors stood partway open. Ward's feeling that he was operating on his own was underscored by the shadowy sight of the police fleet standing idle within, as he and his friends set forth to find his missing daughter.

It was a beautiful day. A cool breeze blew over the airfield under a crystalline blue sky with the lightest flecks of cloud. At nine o'clock the tiny flotilla took off. An hour later Morey guided a DC-3 laden with tourists over the runway and followed their route to the Mara.

Forty-five minutes later he had just begun his final

approach into Keekorok when he heard the sputter of air-to-air communications on his radio. In his search plane Ward heard the same thing on a ground relay from Keekorok.

The message came from Andy Stepanowich, the pilot of a government game-counting plane that was not a part of the Wilson search group. Like other pilots in the area, however, Stepanowich had been asked to keep an eye out for anything unusual. Now he radioed that he had spotted a tan jeep just five or six miles east, in a gully located along the path Ward had traversed the previous day. In mud on the roof was scrawled the legend: SOS.

As he cruised down toward Keekorok, Morey looked out his window toward the east. Not very far away he could see the spotter plane circling over the site.

A couple of the search planes flew east to take a look. Ward asked his pilot to set him down at Keekorok, where Sebastian Tham managed to scare up a jeep to take the two of them to the gully. Tham had been on the radio to the spotters to get a fix on the location.

'It doesn't seem to be on an established road,' he told Ward, 'but the planes will keep over it and guide us in.'

Tham and Ward set off in the jeep, heading between the humps of two hillocks toward the course of the Sand River. They followed the muddy river for a few more kilometers over the rough and dry land of the Mara's south-east corner, so different from the flat swampy plains of the rest of the park. At length they came under the circling planes.

A moderately deep gully ran north off the main Sand River, like a tributary. Muddy sand filled its bottom and ran along both sides, although there seemed to be a dry ford a few yards farther up.

Just as they came up to the edge of the gully, they spotted it. At the bottom, sunk down to the wells of three of its bald tires with the fourth one hanging uselessly in the air, was a sand-colored Suzuki, license plate KTS 597. Some of the mud from the SOS on the roof had run in rivulets down the side, as if a light rain had started to wash it away. The sides of the jeep were dark with a dried crust of mud thrown up by the spinning wheels. As the planes overhead turned and departed, complete silence fell on the scene.

Some twenty-five miles away Doug Morey was just taking off from Kichwa Tembo, an airstrip on the northwest border of the park, when he heard the radio say the search party had reached the jeep. Morey tried to envision the scene. If Julie had left the stuck jeep and was wandering the Mara on foot, he thought, they wouldn't need planes any more. They wouldn't be able to find a walking person from a plane, no matter how low it was flying. They'd need helicopters.

Tham had a helicopter at Keekorok, but the searchers might need more. As Morey banked his DC-3 under the Oloololo escarpment, he began to think of how to find some.

CHAPTER THIRTEEN

It was 11.30 in the morning. Ward swatted the occasional fly and tried to keep his emotions under control as he considered the strange sight of a jeep half stuck in a muddy ravine. With anticipation and suspense he clambered down the side of the gully with Tham and they tried the doors. Both were locked. Ward put his hand over his eyebrows and peered through the dusty windows into the jeep. It was a mess. There seemed to be a couple of tents rolled up sloppily, a sleeping bag, and a jumble of clothes and other things. He looked up from the jeep. No-one seemed to be around.

'She might be in the back there, under that stuff,' he said to Tham. 'We'd better look inside.'

Tham hefted a rock and braced himself on the ground, then brought it down on the passenger's window. He reached through the smashed glass and pulled up the door lock.

Ward called: 'Julie?' There was not a sound or a stirring from beneath the pile of camp goods.

He rummaged frantically among the dirty papers and cans stowed behind the seats and scanned the dashboard. 'She must have left a note,' he said. 'Julie never went anywhere without leaving a note.'

But there was no note. This was so unlike her. Ward looked along the muddy sides of the gully. Perhaps she had scraped an arrow or sign into the dirt to show which way she headed. Nothing. He could see no footprints around in the soft dirt, other than his and Tham's. That was another strange thing. *How did the jeep even get here?* he asked himself.

The father made a mental inventory of the packed jeep.

Two tents, a sleeping bag. He noticed a camp stove and a pair of binoculars and two maps. One showed the Masai Mara and the second a map of Kenya. *Now*, Ward asked himself, *where would she go without a map?* He picked up a pair of sneakers. There was an unopened bottle of beer and a couple of bars of chocolate, softened from the heat. There was no sign of Julie's camera. That was something; obviously she would not go anywhere without it.

Ward stepped away for a moment. It had never occurred to him that he might find the jeep, yet no sign of Julie. Find the car and you find the girl, he figured. Now he was struck by the absence of any evidence of a week's human habitation. There was not a cigarette butt or a piece of discarded refuse. The only thing was that at the ridge of the gully someone had lit a small fire, too small to burn much or cook anything. A strip of plastic lay in the ashes. Ward tore off a corner of the strip and felt in his pocket for a matchbox to put it in. He walked down to the main branch of the river and looked around.

At his side rose a small hill, and he climbed up to the top, calling out Julie's name. The surrounding land was low, with a few groves of trees, and in the hazy distance he could see the peaked roof of Keekorok Lodge and dark straight line of the airstrip. Except for that the place was desolate.

Suddenly there was a vibration in the air and the heavy grumble of engines. Ward trotted down to the foot of the hill just as a pair of green Land Rovers with faded and illegible white lettering on their sides hove into view.

Ten men in civilian dress and one in a police-type uniform got out of the two cars, landing heavily on the soft earth. They nodded at Ward and Tham, who watched silently as they tramped curiously and unsystematically around the jeep, talking among themselves in some African language. They went down to the river as Ward had done and came back. Ward was mystified, but he stood quietly by as the group collected most of what had been inside the truck. Two men carried off the sleeping bag, holding it by the corners. Ward held the maps and

Julie's binoculars in his hand, and he kept them. After a short time the two vehicles drove off.

Ward wanted to do some more reconnaissance, but Tham was uneasy. 'We shouldn't spend much more time here alone,' he remarked. 'This place is full of wild animals.'

Dismayed, Ward asked, 'What would you do if you were in her position, Sebastian?'

Tham considered the question for a moment. 'Well, either of two things,' he said. 'I would walk along the Sand River back the way I had come, which would bring me right back to the campsite. Or I would just walk to the top of this hill and get my bearings to Keekorok.'

Clearly, Julie had done neither or she would not be missing. So where was she?

After spending about an hour by the jeep Tham and Ward drove back to Keekorok.

'I'll take my helicopter up and search along the river,' Tham suggested. 'You can go up in one of the planes and look around the hills.' Ward assented to this plan, and by 2 p.m. they were both back in the air. Ward had his pilot fly over the jeep again, where he could see another group of people, evidently rangers, around the vehicle.

They stayed in the air for another two hours, until the pilot got another radio message. He glanced over at Ward. It was 4 p.m.

'Something's been found,' the pilot reported as he banked back to Keekorok. 'They've found a body.'

Keekorok was swarming with people. The search pilots and their spotters had gathered at the airstrip, anxious to get back to Nairobi before nightfall. But they waited for Ward with the news.

'I don't want to go back to Nairobi,' he said. 'I want someone to bring me out to this body.'

Watson detached himself from the crowd and went off to find a Keekorok ranger he knew who could drive Ward in a jeep down to where a detachment of rangers was standing by. Watson, Ward, and two rangers got in and sped off toward Sand River.

Meanwhile Doug Morey had devoted most of the afternoon to rounding up a helicopter at Wilson Airport. He had tried to stay in touch with the search pilots at Keekorok by radio call, but when the calls went through they had been patched through so many connections that screaming and shouting was the closest they could come to communicating with one another.

Morey had a friend who ran an air service out of Wilson with a chopper, but the friend's license was not fully certified. Finally, after emergency calls to the department of civil aviation, they got permission to take the aircraft to Keekorok. Morey handed off his afternoon flight assignment to another AirKenya pilot, and he returned by helicopter to the Mara.

The afternoon light was already fading. Morey was struck for the thousandth time by how unfamiliar the landscape could look at this hour. He had flown exactly this route earlier in the day, and now he could not recognize it in the sharpening angle of the sun.

At 5 p.m. they set the chopper down on the gravel airstrip in front of the lodge. Morey sensed immediately that something had happened from the way people were standing around staring at the tips of their shoes. It took a couple of minutes to learn that a body, or rather part of a body, had been found.

Things were not going well in the jeep carrying Watson and Ward. Even to a novice Africa hand like Ward it was obvious that they were lost. The driver kept pulling up short, conferring with the second ranger, and looking out over the featureless grass. When the vehicle came through a stand of trees and stopped at a ravine it clearly could not cross Ward angrily halted the maneuvering and insisted on retracing the route to Keekorok.

'This is ridiculous. I can take a helicopter from there.'

One of the rangers turned around. 'There is a ranger post near here. We can radio from there and the helicopter can come and get you.'

Uneasily eying the sky Ward assented. In a few

minutes the Land Rover pulled up at a cluster of metallic huts like those he had spotted from the plane. Ward commandeered their radio, a two-way unit powered by an old car battery. Ward got through to ranger headquarters at Keekorok, from where he ordered the chopper.

'What's the name of this place?' he asked aloud.

'Makari, sir.'

'Makari,' Ward repeated into the microphone. 'Makari ranger post.'

They were not very far from Keekorok. Not far from the Suzuki, for that matter. As he awaited the chopper, Ward wandered around the small outpost. It was filthy. Trash littered the ground behind the tin huts, which looked unkempt and foul inside. Dusty scrub and a campfire occupied the cleared compound between the huts.

As he strolled around, he noticed something glinting in the dirt and stooped to pick it up. It was a shiny yellow Kenyan ten-cent piece. Atop the coin someone had placed a tiny button battery, the kind that powers a wristwatch or an automatic camera.

Ward's scrutiny was cut short by a radio call from Keekorok. He put the coin and battery back on the ground. There was more news from the crew of rangers who had made the discovery: It was in fact not a body. It was just a leg, and it had been burned.

Ward felt despair on despair. He had started the day optimistically, gathered with eager well-wishers at Wilson Airport. Even the discovery of the vacant jeep stirred hope. Then had come the word of the body. The father was trying not to lose all composure at this latest bizarre detail when a roar overhead told him the helicopter had come. Sebastian Tham's two-seater landed with the balloonist in the pilot's seat. Steve Watson stayed behind with the two rangers as Ward and Tham took off.

Over the clatter of the chopper blades Tham managed to tell his passenger that he did not know where the site was. 'We'll lift up until the ground party can see us from the site,' he shouted, 'and they'll guide us in by radio.'

They went high aloft, and then the helicopter moved resolutely forward as Tham followed the radioed instructions. They went south about eight kilometers, passing over the jeep and the Sand River, landing at a place not more than one or two kilometers from the border with Tanzania. Ward opened the door on his side. Crouching under the blades, he ran toward a tall man in a police uniform, who saluted.

They seemed to be in the middle of nowhere. A tall tree dominated the scene, surrounded by bushes and low grass. There were no obvious trails or paths – little enough to even show the direction from which the two Land Rovers parked in the glade had come. A handful of rangers or policemen, dressed uniformly in official tatters, leaned against the vehicles. One man in a safari suit stood at one side, a short, pudgy man with a Masai's distended earlobe. No-one spoke until the tall policeman said, 'Come. This is what we have found.'

Ward followed him until suddenly he spotted the lower part of a leg lying on the ground, still partially clothed in denim. Four or five yards away, gleaming eerily white in the grass, lay half a lower jawbone, cleft down the middle, with the second half nearby.

Ward felt horror as he took in the entire scene. Objects were strewn about. Under the tree were the remains of a campfire, and in the ash Ward made out a pair of red flip-flops.

At the fire he dropped to his knees, mumbling to himself in a low voice. To the man in the safari suit it sounded like Ward was praying. He watched silently as Ward plunged his hands into the ashes, sifting them. The cloying sweet stench of burnt flesh rose up as Ward stirred the ashes with his hands and picked out some hard metal objects. There were a couple of D-rings, like those on a handbag or safari jacket. Some 35-mm film cassettes, blackened from the flames. A singed piece of fabric with a metal zipper attached.

Ward was making a conscious effort to control himself in front of the strangers gathered in the clearing. He rose and looked around again. No-one was speaking. Around the thicket he picked out a little bottle of shampoo and a charred pair of sunglasses. And near them his fingers picked from the grass a lock of light hair.

His eyes took in the utter isolation of the place. The clearing was deeply shrouded from trails or paths by vegetation. The man in the safari suit looked to be in charge. With genuine curiosity Ward asked him, 'How did you ever find this place?'

The man said something about following footprints from the jeep, then spying vultures scattering into the air from a spot in the distance. Ward wondered how they could have spotted footprints to track from that silent gully. But implausible as it sounded he could not think of a better explanation. To find this spot without footprints and vultures as guides, Ward would later reflect, one would almost have to know where to look.

Tham had stepped out of the helicopter and padded over to a tall tree where he had spotted a flash of bright color. His hand came down with a strip of orange terry and an opened, half-consumed can of food. Around the side of the can someone had written in marking pen: PILCHARDS.

Ward stared at them disconsolately. They had a set of orange towels just like that at home. He turned the tin can over and thought the block lettering looked like Julie's.

There was a stirring in the thicket. Ward looked up to see the African men climbing back into their Land Rovers. The sun was setting, casting a red-gold glow over the miles of grassland.

'What are you doing? You're not going to leave all this here, are you?' he asked the tall man who had first saluted him. The man hesitated.

'Well, if you are I'm not,' Ward said. Gingerly, he began to collect all the pieces together. He looked around. 'Do you have anything to put this in?'

The man shook his head. 'Hold on,' said Tham, who trotted over to the helicopter. He unzipped a plastic cover from one seat and brought it over. He held it open as Ward placed the leg and jawbone inside, along with the pathetic collection of objects from the fire.

At this moment the tall man stepped forward on the safari-suited man's prompting. He said he would take charge of the bag. Ward responded sharply.

'First you didn't want anything to do with it. Now you want to take it?'

'I must show them to my superior.'

The man in the safari suit spoke up. 'Tell him who you are,' he said to the tall man. 'Write down your name and address.'

The tall man did so on a scrap of paper. *Kenya Police Inspector George Othiambo, Mara Bridge Police Post, Narok*, it read.

'And who are you?' Ward asked the other man.

'I am Simon Makallah,' he responded.

'He's the chief game warden here,' said Tham.

Tham revved the helicopter to take off. From the air Ward stared back at the thicket, already hard to spot in the deepening dusk.

'Sebastian, could you find this place again?'

Tham turned the craft back and took some bearings. 'Yes, I can find it again,' he said.

Most of the planes and spotters had already left Keekorok in order to beat the nightfall back to Nairobi. Natasha Weld Dixon had gone back in Morey's helicopter, leaving the American pilot as the only one on the airstrip who knew Ward. Morey felt somewhat responsible for Ward now.

He watched the helicopter approach from the south and come down. The engine was cut, and the passenger door came open. From the edge of the airstrip Morey saw Ward step down into the gloomy twilight. As the pilot walked out on to the gravel he stared curiously at Ward's hands. They looked black, as if Ward were wearing gloves. But he came closer and saw with a shock they were covered with black ash.

When they got close together Ward suddenly threw his

arms around the big American pilot and broke into tears. He could barely speak.

'She's just cut up in pieces,' he sobbed. 'There are only a couple of pieces left and she's all burned up.'

'Are you sure it's her?' Morey asked.

'I'm sure,' Ward cried. 'A father knows his own daughter's leg.'

CHAPTER FOURTEEN

That night a room was vacated at Keekorok Lodge to make space for John Ward. Morey saw him to the door of his bungalow and left him alone. Ward sat on his open verandah and let the African night close in tight around him. In private, away from the prying eyes of the African rangers, he allowed himself to break down in grief.

Stephen Watson was waiting for Morey in the lobby. 'He just wants to be left alone,' Morey told him. Then he headed for the bar.

Sebastian Tham was already there. Together, the bewildered pilots tried to figure out what could have happened to Julie. The only thing that seemed to make sense, strange as it might be, was that she had committed suicide.

'She must have got completely freaked out or something,' Morey suggested.

News of the discovery in the bush had penetrated the Keekorok Lodge clientele, and the two pilots could hear the murmur of discussion behind them. Tham quietly described the scene for Morey.

'That fire wasn't big enough to do more than barbecue a steak,' he said. 'But you know, it singed the branches overhead.'

That night Morey later described as one of the strangest of his life. The wildebeest massing for their migration south to the Serengeti were everywhere. Anyone who has been among them knows of their eerie sound, an other-worldly call-and-response of guttural brays and snorts that fills the air like a great number of voices in a conversation too distant to make out. Morey could barely imagine what it would be like for an English tourist stranded in the wilderness, stuck up in a tree on a long night, amid the alien call of these weird ungainly animals. Truly, he thought, one might lose one's mind.

Ward, too, heard the strange calls as he sat numbly on the verandah with a glass of whiskey. For a while the sound was punctuated by the thrum of a native dance troupe entertaining the diners at the lodge restaurant, the beating of their drums and their rhythmic chants pounding through the darkness. Finally the show ended, and Ward fell asleep.

The next morning Morey arranged a flight back to Nairobi for himself and Ward. He found Ward sitting over a breakfast tray in his room. Ward made arrangements to give his daughter's Suzuki to Tham in payment for all his help the day before, for which Tham had asked nothing. Tham would have to haul the Suzuki out of the muck and tow it to Keekorok, but it might be of some use.

As they waited for the plane to Nairobi, Morey and Ward strolled around the Keekorok Lodge compound. Ward was curious about Kenya, as if trying to understand what had made his daughter love it so much that she would come back again and again and think about staying on. He asked Morey why he stayed. As he tried to explain, Morey thought he was bidding farewell to John Ward. The body had been found, it was all over, a terrible misadventure.

In Nairobi Ward called Bury St Edmunds to break the news to his family. Stephen Watson called to ask him if he could keep company with him on that final evening. But when Watson got to the Norfolk that night, he found that John Ward had already gone home. Ward had left him a letter, apologizing for that missed appointment and saying he had changed his mind about staying another night. He felt he needed to be home to be with his wife and sons.

Around the same time Aris Grammaticas arrived back in the Masai Mara from a tour of Botswana. He was more than a little put out by what had been happening in the park.

Grammaticas was a tall and powerfully built man with a

bald dome of a head and strong friendly features. He had a booming voice and the garrulous presence of a successful businessman and tour operator. For years he had been an influential and well-known figure around the Mara, and not just because his Governor's Camp was one of the largest and best-run tourist operations within its boundaries. One other reason was that his partner in the venture was William ole Ntimama, a Masai politician who was Kenya's minister for local government. In the patchy network of tribal quasi-ownership that governed the Mara, Ntimama's clan controlled the land on which Governor's was built. Also, Ntimama's political clique had recently taken over the Narok County Council, a prize it had sought for years in a long rumble with an opposing group headed by another powerful tribal politician, Justus ole Tipis. Under Kenyan law the council governed the Masai Mara.

Governor's Camp is justly famous among the tourist establishments of Kenya. In fact it consists of four camps, situated in the north-west corner of the Mara not far from the Mara Serena Lodge, in an area once reserved for the private use of the colonial governors of the East Africa Protectorate. Main Governor's has been erected on the lip of a curving gorge of the Mara River with its tents oriented so guests can sit on their tiny verandahs after lunch watching baboons cavorting in the overgrown woods on the opposite bank and crocodiles sliding around wallowing hippos in the muddy river below. Little Governor's, which many tourists prefer for its intimacy, is upstream a bit and on the other side of the river. Nearby are two camps available for rent by large private groups.

Governor's is the quintessential luxury tented camp in the Masai Mara. Each green canvas tent erected on a solid slab of concrete comfortably sleeps two and is equipped with lamps and an adjoining bathroom and shower with hot and cold running water. A fleet of open-topped Land Rovers manned by experienced Masai guides stands ready to take clients on game drives three times a day. At 5.30 or 6 a.m, when the sky is just turning purple with the dawn, the place comes to life with the chatter of the guides comparing notes on where each had spotted game the day before. The tourists straggle into the cars before sunrise so they can be out to catch the last nocturnal movements of hippos and other animals. They return to camp in time for a huge breakfast laid out beneath a cluster of trees by the river, digest it for an hour or two, and head out for the second drive before noon. Another huge meal follows of curries and roast meats, and then a third drive late in the day. At night the guests flash their lanterns from their tents to summon guards armed with spears to escort them to dinner under a long mess tent. If they choose they can end the evening at a towering bonfire, watching a group of Masai performers dance and sing.

The prominence of Governor's and Grammaticas's potent connections gave him a significant input into policy decisions of the Mara management. He had his differences with some of the rules and practices, including the tradition that most if not all Mara rangers and staff were Masai. Grammaticas thought this created a security problem, as it was difficult to make Masai come down hard on relatives they found poaching or behaving badly. For Governor's itself he imported guards from the Samburu or other remote nomadic tribes – he described them as 'wild men' – to patrol the grounds as part of a private thirty-six-man force.

But he had a good relationship with Simon Makallah, the chief warden, who often acceded compliantly to Grammaticas's suggestions on park management. One time the rangers found a den of cheetah cubs who had lost their mother, possibly to hunters or poachers. Makallah at first wanted to have the cubs shot or taken away, on the grounds that they would have little chance of surviving in the wild for very long. Grammaticas opposed the idea. He persuaded Makallah to leave the cubs to be raised in the park; by the time they were full grown they were thoroughly acclimatized to humans and were known to tamely hitch rides on the tops of tourist vehicles around the Mara, delighting the visitors.

Grammaticas considered Makallah something of a devious character, but over the years he had developed a certain sympathy for the warden's difficult position in the park. For one thing, Makallah had little real authority over the rangers nominally under his command. Their hiring and firing, and consequently their discipline, was entirely in the hands of the Narok County Council, which based its rulings largely on the requirements of nepotism and tribal solidarity. Once when Grammaticas complained to the warden that a number of rangers, at least one of whom was drunk, had raided Governor's Camp, Makallah had thrown up his hands.

'I can't control them', he had said. 'I send them to the council to be fired, and ten out of ten come back with a note telling me to give them another chance.'

At the time of Julie Ward's disappearance Makallah was in a deep hole. He had long been allied with Justus ole Tipis's political clique, now ousted by Ntimama's cadre, and the new people seemed out to get him. They were preparing a list of charges of malfeasance, including things like misusing park vehicles on personal business and illegally collecting fees from visitors to establish private campsites. In real terms, Grammaticas felt, these were all simple misdemeanors, but given the political weather in Narok they might be enough to get Makallah sacked.

But that was still a few months off when Grammaticas returned from Botswana. As he drove up to Governor's he found Makallah passing the time with the Governor's manager, a burly African named Jonas.

'What's going on here with you?' Grammaticas complained to Makallah. 'I'm getting calls from all over the world about a dead tourist found in the park. What's all this talk about wild animals killing her?'

Makallah gave a little smirk. 'That wasn't wild animals,' he said. 'That fire where she was found? Somebody set it with petrol.'

CHAPTER FIFTEEN

The flight from Nairobi to Heathrow is never easy, no matter the condition or state of mind in which one flies. It amounts to eight hours of enforced idleness invariably beginning a few minutes after midnight. The enervated passengers are treated in the glare of cabin lighting to hours of superfluous meal service and duty-free hawking lasting into the tiny hours of the night, when one might catch a few hours of exhausted sleep before being awakened in the wan twilight of the sky over London.

After such a flight a heavily burdened Ward arrived at Heathrow the morning of 15 September and made the ninety-minute trip north to his home in Bury St Edmunds to grieve with his family.

Ward was still in the air when Paul Weld Dixon looked out his window in Langata at a police car pulling into the yard. An officer came up the dirt path to his house. A postmortem was to take place in the city mortuary, the officer said, and Mr Weld Dixon was asked to witness it on the family's behalf.

Paul collected a notebook and called to his wife. Together with the officer they drove to the mortuary, which was located off a busy roundabout across from the teeming public hospital of Nairobi.

The examining room was a tiny, noisome warren with barely enough space for himself, his wife, two police constables, and the pathologist. As he shouldered his way into the room Weld Dixon's eye fell on a table with Julie's remains and the few artifacts collected two days earlier from the fire. He fought off revulsion at the sight of the dear girl reduced before him to a couple of scraps of flesh

116

and bone. Punctiliously he took out his notebook.

The police pathologist, Adel Youssef Shaker, put on his gloves and picked up the jawbone to begin. Youssef's manner of directing his remarks toward his visitors gave the scene the strange air of a stage performance. Examining the two pieces of bone, he pronounced: 'The jawbone has been anatomically dissected.'

Then he turned to the limb. At length he said, 'This seems to have been severed by a sharp instrument.'

'Do you mean a panga?' Weld Dixon interrupted, thinking of the machetelike blades as long as a man's forearm carried by African handymen and gardeners.

'No,' the pathologist replied carefully. 'I mean a sharp instrument.' Weld Dixon took it down.

'Judging by the condition of the leg,' Youssef said, 'I would estimate that death occurred no more than thirty-six to forty-eight hours ago.' So Julie was most likely still alive on 12 September, when her father was just arriving in Nairobi to take on the search. She might have been murdered just as he was flying over the Masai Mara.

Finally Youssef noted that the limb seemed to have been burned subsequent to being cut. The significance of this detail evaded Weld Dixon for a moment, but Youssef's next remark left no room for question.

'That makes this a case of murder,' he said.

In Bury St Edmunds the family scarcely knew how to deal with its grief. Julie had been so much a part of daily life in the house that her loss created a void everywhere. There would be no-one to organize Christmas celebrations or to take the huskies to sled-dog competitions with her mother. Without her chatty notes left around the premises it was as if an audible voice filling the house was stilled.

One day Jo Jordan came by to express her condolences with Nick King, the driver who had fallen ill and left the overland trip early. Julie's mother plied them with questions about Africa, as if she were trying to plumb the allure of the place for her dead daughter, just as John Ward had interrogated Doug Morey at Keekorok Lodge.

'She was just trying to understand,' Jordan remembered later.

Not long after his dispiriting return from Nairobi John Ward was interrupted by a phone call from Whitehall. The caller identified himself as Nigel Wicks of the Foreign Office. He sounded hesitant as he told Ward he was passing on some information from John Ferguson in Nairobi. Ward recognized the name as that of the High Commission's first secretary. Wicks tried to be as diplomatic as he could, but the message was blunt: A postmortem on the remains from the Masai Mara had established that Julie was murdered.

Amid the overwhelming shock of Julie's death the significance of the message did not much sink in. *Murder. Well, that explains a few things*, Ward thought. *But we already knew she was dead, and dead is dead.*

Ward was inclined, however, to call Ferguson directly for more details. The diplomat relayed what a distraught Weld Dixon had told him the previous afternoon about Youssef's autopsy. Ferguson explained that he had immediately tried to reach Youssef for confirmation and finally ran him to earth at 5 p.m. Youssef was cordial, if a little uneasy, over the telephone. He confirmed Weld Dixon's account, and agreed to allow Ward to view the remains if he again came to Nairobi. Ferguson had remarked to Youssef that the police officers at the scene seemed to regard the case as one of suicide.

'Is that possible?' he asked.

Youssef was concise. 'No, suicide is not in question in this case,' he said.

Over the telephone Ferguson cautioned Ward that the pathologist would have to submit his report in writing before his conclusions were deemed official, although there seemed to be little enough room for doubt. With the case transformed into one of murder, however, a formal identification of Julie's remains was a legal prerequisite to a police investigation. Ward arranged to have Julie's dental charts telefaxed to Nairobi.

★

Few experiences available to the resident of a civilized place can match the spectacle of the British press in full cry. Ever since the discovery of Julie's remains in the park the Ward estate in Bury St Edmunds had sustained a full-scale siege from the massed forces of tabloid and quality press. The family was virtually paralyzed in its state of shock, and the pain was magnified by the chore of keeping reporters out of the house itself and maintaining the family's refusal to comment on the case. Ward hired a security firm to post men and vans in front of the house and on a fence post out front he tacked up a handwritten notice politely warning against traspassers; deprived of direct contact with the grieving family, the newspapers ran pictures of the vans and the fluttering piece of paper.

Meanwhile, Ward waited for some word of how the Kenya authorities meant to investigate Julie's murder. Within a few days he began to get an answer. The Kenya Police, it seemed, were denying it was murder at all.

With growing confusion Ward read the reports from Nairobi in the British papers. 'Murder has not been ruled out,' one said. Ruled out? Ward figured that the post-mortem had confirmed it. But the scenarios seemed to be getting more bizarre. The newspaper articles quoted police officials speculating about Julie's having walked away from her jeep in search of help after miring it in the gully and then getting attacked by wild animals. Or she might have lit the fire and collapsed into it, overwhelmed by poisonous fumes. Or she might have committed suicide.

English girl devoured by man-eating beasts: The British papers were in a transport of ghoulish excitement. They certified Julie's stature as a newsmaker by posthumously dubbing her the 'Lion Girl' and the 'Safari Girl'. Julie smiled out at the readers from a photo showing her cradling a baby chimp, the picture snapped during the Ho-Bo stop in Cameroon. Ward was getting increasingly offended by newspaper stories talking about how dumb his daughter must have been, walking off like that from her stranded jeep. Julie was not stupid, Ward knew. But here were tabloid reporters, no great brains themselves, serenely remonstrating with the dead girl for having gone wandering out in the bush. 'People with years of experience in Africa' told one newspaper it was just not done.

Ward waited two or three days for the newspapers, or the police, to get things right. But the question of murder seemed to be receding, if anything. As the days passed he felt a rising determination to get to the bottom of things. Unhappily, he realized the task would be impossible to accomplish from where he was sitting. As unpleasant as the thought might be, he knew he would have to return to Nairobi. It was less than a week since he had left a place he thought he would never want to see again. He had departed Nairobi in a hurry then, impelled by the need to be at home to share the unbelievable grief of Julie's death with his stricken wife and the two boys. Now he had to leave them behind again. John Ward might not have realized it at that moment, but he was embarking on a solitary journey that would be his way of dealing with an inconsolable personal loss. All he could admit to at the time was a quest to get to the bottom of a case of factual confusion. As he told friends before his departure, 'I need to learn what the hell is going on.'

Jenny Jenkins met him on his arrival at Kenyatta airport and escorted him to see John Ferguson at the High Commission office in Bruce House.

Two days earlier, Ferguson said, he had brought the faxed copy of Julie's dental records to the city mortuary for Youssef to compare with the jawbone. Youssef had disappeared for a few minutes, then re-emerged into his office to confirm that the jaw was Julie's. Youssef had been in an expansive vein. He'd nattered on about his findings, as if elated to be associated with such an interesting and important case. Ferguson had let him talk, not realizing that the pathologist was pitching himself into a political abyss.

'It's clear from my examination that the girl was killed,' Youssef had told the diplomat. 'But not by any animal.'

Ferguson had asked him when his written report would be ready, and Youssef had volunteered that he would be personally responsible for typing the document. Youssef continued to nourish a peculiar taste for unprovoked portentousness. He ended his conversation with this remark: 'I will stick by this report no matter what.'

So in essence they were faced with a perplexing discrepancy. The pathologist was still contending Julie had been murdered, but the official police statements were still saying she had been killed by wild animals. Ferguson and Ward drove out to the city mortuary so the father could take Youssef's measure for himself.

Ward's first meeting with the pathologist took place at 11.30 that morning. To Ward, Adel Youssef Shaker was not somebody who cut a professional figure. Unprepossessing in his sloppy and soiled clothes, he merged in gray dimness with the verminous atmosphere of the mortuary, which was a confusing compound of several buildings with crowds of idlers hanging around. Youssef was a pear-shaped man with thinning black hair and an aura of sweaty profuseness reminiscent of Dickens's Mr Chadband. Ward thought the pathologist looked to be almost fifty. In fact he was twenty-eight years old.

The habitual look of nervousness that contributed so much to Youssef's premature aging was understandable. For he was living in the country purely on Kenyan sufferance as a refugee. A member of the Egyptian Christian Coptic sect, Youssef was a victim of the Egyptians' periodic harassment of Copts, who were often barred from businesses and professions and saw their churches become the targets of violent mobs; they had scarcely more political security in Egypt than the Asians did in Kenya, and much less money.

Ward would never cease considering Youssef a thin reed to lean on in his campaign for a murder ruling. The pathologist would later be described, justifiably, as a man lacking backbone but with an impulse to tell the truth. For

121

his part, Youssef would be shamelessly manipulated by all sides in the case. He left the impression of a man perpetually on the point of breaking down, cornered and abject, a victim of the events he set in motion himself by his heedlessly confident utterance of the word *murder* to Paul Weld Dixon.

Youssef's presentation was a strange mix of forthrightness and fidgety evasion. To Ward and Ferguson he reiterated his postmortem findings. Ward then got an introduction to the clinical unemotionalism of the pathology laboratory. Youssef showed him Julie's leg, now a rubbery and livid blue. He pointed out the sharpness of the wound and the scorch marks on the cut end of the bone, clearly indicating that the bone had been cut first and burned subsequently.

He showed Ward how the two halves of the jawbone fitted together along the clean line of the break like pieces of a plastic model. And he explained why these injuries and the sequence of events – first the cuts, then the burning – mandated a conclusion of murder: Someone had thrown pieces of the body on the fire. If it had been suicide or even an accident, Julie's entire body would have been burned first, and the cutting, whoever or whatever did it, would have followed. If it were animals, the cut would have been jagged from the tearing motion of teeth.

Ferguson reminded Youssef that he had agreed to give him a copy of his written report. The Egyptian was reassuring. Because the office was short a typist, he said, he would type the report himself that very afternoon.

Ferguson was experienced enough in the ambiguities of African promises to insist on nailing Youssef down to a specific delivery time.

'Will it be possible to have a copy later today?' he pressed. Youssef agreed, and further offered to prepare a plaster cast of the jaw for the father. He told his guests to return at 4.30 that afternoon. 'I will stand by the report,' he repeated sententiously.

Ward and Ferguson left for their next meeting. It was to be Ward's first session with Police Commissioner Philip

Kilonzo. As they walked down the steps from the mortuary building Ferguson brushed past an African man coming up the way in civilian clothes. There were people wandering all over the compound on myriad errands, and at the time he thought nothing of it.

At the time of John Ward's first return to Nairobi two trends were developing in Kenyan society. One was the growth of an African middle class. Not only were the Kikuyu farmers who had moved back on to the old white highlands after independence growing rich, but Kenya's comparatively strong industrial sector was making a lot of other Africans affluent. There were more Kenyan doctors and lawyers than ever before, driving Mercedes around town and building big houses in the formerly white neighborhoods of the suburbs.

As would happen in any society, this increasingly well-educated layer of people was more and more discontented by the dearth of means for political expression in the Kenya of KANU and President Moi. Given KANU's monopoly of politics after opposition parties were outlawed in 1982, the politically sophisticated middle class had almost no voice in molding the Kenya of the future. Under the surface – still quite deep, to be sure – this was giving rise to considerable social tension.

The second trend arose from KANU's ponderous domination of the political scene and its increasing paranoia about opposition: This was a progressively more cowed civil service. Among bureaucrats and government officials it had become the rule not to speak out, not to stick one's neck out, not to volunteer. Everybody thought he knew what was expected of him, and that thing was caution.

John Ward was about to spend a year in an encounter with this paralyzed bureaucracy. And the man he was about to meet was nothing if not a very experienced bureaucrat.

CHAPTER SIXTEEN

There was a division of opinion among present and former police officers about Police Commissioner Philip Kilonzo. He was widely regarded as a thorough professional, a career officer who had never done anything to blot his record and was even responsible for a handful of valuable reforms in the deteriorating force. If he were given a free hand, it was sometimes said, he could make the police department an efficient one.

But in present-day Kenya there was no free hand for the police; its responsibilities were too political. And many saw the real power in the Kenya Police residing not in the commissioner's office, but in that of his nominal subordinate, Noah arap Too, head of the Criminal Investigation Department.

In part this was the reflection of tribal politics. Kilonzo was a Kamba, a minority tribe from south-east Kenya. In President Moi's Kenya this was not as threatening as being a Kikuyu, the dominant tribe in the country and one that Moi constantly suspected and feared for its capacity for disloyalty. But it meant that a counterforce was necessary: someone like Too, a member of Moi's own Kalenjin tribe.

Kilonzo also faced difficulties in office because of the way he had been promoted: jumped ahead of four more senior men when former commissioner Benjamin Gethi had retired. At the time Kilonzo was a relatively low-ranking Nairobi provincial police chief, and the choice mystified many. But he had won some modest prominence in a politically sensitive area. As Nairobi chief he had been responsible for the custody of scores of political detainees eventually released by Moi in the late nineteen-seventies. To a man they praised Kilonzo's fairness and humanity.

'It may have been his way of showing the world that he could promote someone who had been praised by political dissidents,' one observer of Kenya politics later remarked. In any event, Kilonzo's rapid promotion deprived him of the long-earned loyalties of a solid cadre of subordinates.

Some thought Kilonzo prone to vacillation and regarded him as a weak leader, although he had his defenders among former colleagues in the ranks. The more charitable saw him as smart and polished. After a rare public scandal over police torture of criminal suspects, he had managed to eliminate torture from police procedure – at least in nonpolitical cases. In any event, who would not be overmatched in the job of supervising a force that was steadily being enfeebled, like all African institutions, by the tripartite scourges of corruption, nepotism, and penury?

Kilonzo impressed Ward on first sight with his smooth veneer, certainly one of his strong points. It was impossible not to be struck by the martial punctilio of the commissioner's garb. Kilonzo often appeared in public in a smart military-style uniform, complete with garlanded epaulets.

The commissioner at first seemed to view the visit as little more than a courtesy call. He greeted Ward and Ferguson with a sincere expression of condolences, offering them coffee as he motioned them into chairs. But Ward was inclined to waste no time in showing the commissioner that he was present on business. Abruptly, he cut short Kilonzo's speech with the question: 'Given the postmortem report, are the police now finally treating this as a murder?'

Kilonzo's composure evaporated as if from an affront. He said he could not yet characterize the inquiry as a 'murder investigation.'

'At this time my investigations are still continuing,' he said stiffly. He might have been reacting to Ward's determined tone of voice rather than to the question itself. 'In fact, I have not yet seen the report of my investigating officer.'

Ward could not understand how Kilonzo could delay an investigation any longer. 'Commissioner, how can there be any doubt that this is a murder? We have the evidence of your own police pathologist. You've seen the doctor's report, I take it?'

'Yes, I am familiar with the report,' Kilonzo said without hesitation. He adopted the air of a superior trying to restrain a headstrong subordinate. 'But there is still my investigating officer's report to come. And until I see that, I am not prepared to come to any conclusion about this matter.' He paused as if searching for something with which to appease the father. 'Three CID officers have already been reassigned from Nairobi to the Narok team,' he said, referring to the Criminal Investigation Division. 'I can assure you that full and proper investigations are in progress at this very moment. All I am prepared to say right now is that suicide has been ruled out.'

Well, that was something. For the moment Ward seemed to be mollified.

'I'm glad to hear there's some investigation in progress,' he said, 'because that's very different from the impression I got initially.'

Kilonzo spread his hands apologetically. 'You can understand why I prefer not to announce a murder investigation publicly at this time. One does not want to send a warning to the perpetrator, after all. You've seen the reporters waiting outside in the waiting room – I've told them already that the police have not ruled out murder.'

'Will there be an inquest?' Ward asked. 'And what form would it take?'

'I am not sure one will necessarily be held,' Kilonzo said equably. 'A death certificate in a case like this can be issued by any of the proper authorities. They can authorize the disposal of the remains without the need for an inquest, if that is what you wish.'

'Would it be helpful if I offer a reward for information relating to the murder?'

Kilonzo dismissed the suggestion with a wave. 'I have

ample funds available for such a purpose,' he said. 'If I think it is necessary.' He stressed the '*if*'.

As the visitors prepared to leave Kilonzo's office the commissioner shook his head bemusedly.

'It's strange, you know – this area, the Masai Mara, is normally trouble free. Poachers usually just shoot their victims and leave them. They don't do things like this.' It was Kilonzo's only mention of poachers as potential perpetrators. In fact, the Mara was less bedeviled by poachers than some other Kenyan parks, possibly because it was relatively compact and situated far from the region where armed bandits were known to range. Still, violent raids on the Mara's tented tourist camps were not unknown, although they tended to be efficiently hushed up.

In any event, the commissioner quickly brightened, like a doctor assuring a nervous patient of a positive prognosis. 'Well, don't worry. The Kenya Police have a strong track record in solving crimes of this nature,' he said confidently.

Kilonzo might have honestly underestimated the complexity of the task confronting his investigators. But it was public knowledge that a crime like Julie's murder was precisely the type that was squarely beyond the force's capabilities.

In acceding to British High Commission pressure to grant Ward an audience, Kilonzo may have staved off, however briefly, the father's grasp of how inadequate the Kenya Police was as an investigatory force. Had Ward started in at the base of the pyramid, he could not help to have been appalled.

Most people in need of police assistance in Kenya absorbed the situation in a hurry. A visitor needed to make only one visit to the central police station on Harry Thuku Road, down the street from the Norfolk Hotel, to be struck by its atmosphere of indolence. Officers and clerks lolled indifferently behind a long wooden counter, greeting all inquiries with the same bored expression. Anyone tenacious enough to pursue a complaint – more often than not a tourist needing to report a stolen passport or money, for citizens and residents knew how fruitless a police report would be – was eventually ushered into a damp conference room to stand in line awaiting an officer's attention. Finally, the officer might agree to take a statement, grasping for whatever stray paper he might have handy. Often as not it was a days-old newspaper. He would scribble the details in the margins, pointlessly take down the complainant's address (for it was rare indeed that a follow-up would be pursued), and indicate his work was done.

At the time of Julie's death the police force was well along its slide in the Kenyan public's esteem. Once when the police issued a suicide ruling in a case that reeked of political murder not long after Julie's death – the victim was Kenya's foreign minister – angry riots exploded in Nairobi and two other cities amid cries of 'cover-up'. Already the signs of a widespread loss of confidence were evident.

To begin with, the street force was permeated with an ethos of petty corruption. If graft infected most other Kenyan institutions, why should the police be exempt? No motorist stopped on a city street for a traffic infraction needed instruction in the body language of the officer who hopped into the passenger seat to discuss the consequences. The offender could drive up to traffic headquarters, at the far end of a suburban avenue impossibly congested at midday, the officer would explain, or he could pay a fine on the spot . . . 'but unfortunately I cannot give you a receipt.' Those unfamiliar with the protocol of offering a bribe were hastily educated. One expatriate who casually waved a couple of hundred shillings at a pair of traffic officers remembered being met with horrified glares. 'No, you do it like this,' one instructed him, folding the money neatly within the cardboard fold of the motorist's driving license. 'You hand me the whole thing together.'

Then there was the increasing politicization of the police, which was becoming a public scandal. Inept as the force was in apprehending burglars or killers, it was quite active in supervising political orthodoxy in President Moi's increasingly stringent state. One technique the force employed in this job was torture. 'Being in custody is becoming more dangerous than walking through a slum at night,' remarked one Kenyan around this time. 'In the latter place, if you are attacked your cries might attract help; in the former you are doomed.'

The drive to root out dissidents in Kenya was becoming more and more arbitrary, it seemed. 'You'd not even need to be guilty to be in a police cell,' wrote the same critic: 'you only need to be suspected. That means that those of us who think the problem does not concern them may well find themselves there. Then who will hear your wails?'

Dozens of people could tell stories of being bundled into the trunks of unmarked cars and transported to the headquarters of the police Special Branch, in a hideous orange skyscraper in downtown Nairobi. There they were kept in tiny cells half-filled with fetid water, so that they could not sit or lie down, and interrogated naked through the night.

Common criminals had fared scarcely better before Kilonzo's anti-torture policy took force. For years tourists strolling between the Norfolk Hotel and the curio shops of downtown heard the thud of truncheons and the wail of suspects as they passed the police station: This was the sound of 'investigations' taking place.

This tradition of brutality was one of the bequests, as it happened, of Kenya's colonial history. As recently as the early nineteen-eighties the physical embodiment of law enforcement in independent Kenya had been a white man.

Patrick Shaw had been one of the last of the British police officers to bind over into the postcolonial police. While he was alive, holding an ambiguous top-level portfolio as head of the Kenya Reserve, there was scarcely a criminal in Nairobi or its environs who could be sure of escaping a well placed pistol shot.

'He was a killer,' observed one of the retired white Kenya Police officers still living around Nairobi at the time. It was not an admiring remark, for Shaw was not technically a policeman, and many legitimate officers regarded his identification with their force as a nasty affront, as if the professionalism with which they had tried to approach their job in post-independence Kenya evaporated in his burly wake.

Until his death in 1987 the impossibly fat Shaw was ubiquitous. People knocked down and mugged on a teeming Nairobi street would look up in their daze from the muddy sidewalk to see Shaw holding a booklet of mug shots in hand, asking the victim to identify the assailant. Leaving a movie or night club at a late hour, one might find the insomniac Shaw parked in his little Volvo, which fitted him like a tight corset, on the lookout for suspicious characters.

Still, in many ways Shaw was an aberration. Some of the old Metropolitan Police officers who had come down in the nineteen-fifties and stayed on after independence had striven to instill a genuine esprit of professionalism in the rapidly Africanizing police. Many Kenyans could still remember the old days when 'you would file a complaint and it would be thoroughly investigated', as one recalled. But in time the British officers retired. Their trained African successors were brushed aside and passed over for promotion in favor of people with superior political or tribal associations. In that era 'all that the police used to go for were confessions,' said a lawyer familiar with police activities both as detainee and counsel. If they could not beat a confession out of somebody, the prosecution would not go forward. Formal police skills languished and atrophied, like a broken limb in a plaster cast. When Kilonzo banned torture, the rate of prosecutions dropped sharply, because few police officers had experience in any alternative investigatory technique.

Ward could not have comprehended this background as he walked dismayed out of Kilonzo's office. But the political environment swirling around the Kenya Police would have a lot to do with the course of the investigation of his daughter's death. Meanwhile the police commissioner's words of reassurance ringing in his ears did not entirely free Ward of his misgivings. After all, Kilonzo still had not committed himself to a genuine murder inquiry. Ward could only ask himself, why not?

The long day was to end with yet another drive across town to the promised second meeting with Dr Youssef. At this point in late September the so-called 'short rains' of Kenya's autumn were just beginning to announce their advent. The rains would not reach their peak for more than a month, at which time they would come virtually every day in late afternoon or evening, sometimes on a brief but punishing scale that would turn the hillside streets of the suburbs into white-watered rivers swirling around stalled vehicles. For now the approach of the wet season was heralded by a sudden graying of the sky in midafternoon, a substitution of the piquant touch of the sun shining out of a blue sky by a chilly, misty foreboding of rain.

CHAPTER SEVENTEEN

The second meeting with Youssef would not take place in
the depressing chill of the city mortuary, but at Youssef's
private office at the Nairobi Coptic Centre. About a mile
past the mortuary roundabout Ward and Ferguson turned
off the Ngong Road on to a dirt path. They slowed
sharply, for someone had indulged Nairobi's taste for
speed bumps all along the way; the obstructions were
unmarked and almost invisible in the dirt and the car kept
jouncing and scraping bottom. They turned a corner and
came to a stop in front of an overgrown compound with a
gate and a sign for a Coptic church.

As they entered Youssef's office they found a man
plainly in the grip of some unpleasant emotion. Sweat
beaded on his forehead and flattened the thin hairs of his
scalp. He chattered nonsensically about the weather and
offered his visitors Cokes, all in an attempt, it seemed, to
avoid the subject at hand: the promised postmortem
report.

The visitors managed to steer the conversation back to
the main issue. The reason for Youssef's fretfulness
suddenly became clear. The pathologist explained that he
had been visited by the police that very morning – in fact,
just after the British visitors had taken their leave.
Ferguson suddenly remembered the Kenyan who had
brushed past him on his way up the mortuary drive as he
and Ward were leaving that morning.

A plainclothesman had demanded a copy of the postmortem report, Youssef related, and insisted on waiting as
the pathologist typed out the document himself. Before
leaving the policeman had gathered up all of Youssef's
copies.

Neither Ferguson nor Ward fully believed this. 'Certainly you must have kept one for your own files,' said Ferguson. 'Or notes.'

'No, the police took the notes as well,' the pathologist replied. Then he made an odd admission. 'It is no matter. It is all' – he tapped his temple with a forefinger – 'up here. You don't have to worry. I did the typing myself so no substitution could be made. And I signed it myself, in Arabic,' he said proudly.

Then he added, 'You know, I am a religious man. I will always tell the truth.'

Youssef could offer the exasperated father one item of physical evidence. He could not provide, as he had promised, a plaster cast of Julie's jawbone. But reaching into a cupboard he pulled out a cardboard box, and from this extracted the jawbone itself. Proudly, he showed Ward and Ferguson his handiwork. He had glued the two pieces together.

'You see how they fit,' he said, holding the completed piece in his moist fingers. The line of glue holding the two halves together was as straight and precise as a carpenter's join.

'This could not have been caused by animals,' he said. 'And someone put the leg on the fire after it was severed. That is the proof of murder. There is no other explanation.'

The visitors left the Coptic grounds deeply troubled. On the one hand Youssef four times now had confirmed his finding of murder. But that had to be weighed against Kilonzo's evasiveness. Didn't one hand know what the other was doing in this country?

The father was struck by the stark difference between Britain and Kenya. That very morning he had flown in expecting to clear up the misunderstandings about Julie's death. Instead, he was sinking into a morass. In England, he reflected, there would be an all-out, tireless, day-and-night effort to solve this mystery. But this wasn't home, notwithstanding the British-style institutions and the lilting English spoken by its bureaucrats.

133

That night he brought his concerns to dinner with Doug Morey at the aptly-named Carnivore, the restaurant where Stephen Watson had waited one last time for a date with Julie so many long days ago. In its open-air dining area the tables were arranged around lush flower gardens, creating a sort of oasis from the lion-hued scrub and grass of the district.

Ward and Morey sat among the other diners with sizzling metal platters in front of them. An army of white-aproned waiters went from table to table with carving knives and skewered haunches of beef, pork, and game. There were piquantly seasoned breasts of chicken, and stringy, gamy chunks of crocodile. A steamy hiss rose from each table as carved slices were forked on to the hot platters.

At Ward's table the procession of skewer bearers was suddenly interupted by a British correspondent from the *Daily Mail*. Ward sighed. There was no escaping the press. This reporter brought news that the *Daily Telegraph* that morning had once again questioned the cause of Julie's death. 'FRESH DOUBT ON BUSH GIRL'S "MURDER"', the headline said, emphasizing its skepticism with the quote marks around the word *murder*.

The article quoted 'a reliable source close to the police pathologist' stating that Julie could indeed have been killed by animals 'despite her father's assertions,' suggesting bizarrely that it was Ward himself who had first raised the murder issue. It said that the pathologist who conducted the postmortem 'reached no clear conclusion as to how cuts on her remains were made.'

This was blatantly untrue, Ward knew. Scarcely a few hours earlier Youssef had reiterated his conclusion. Now the father had to wonder if someone had got to Youssef and made him change his mind. It was another unpleasant blow.

Ward figured the time was ripe to get all the evidence out in the open. The press pack were calling at all hours, waylaying him on the street, interrupting his meals. He could barely get in a good night's sleep for the ringing of the telephone in the small hours.

With the extended comedy of the elusive postmortem report consuming his time and attention, Ward had diminishing patience for the pack of howling reporters, whom he viewed as a sheer nuisance. Reasoning that he might be able to kill two birds with one stone, satisfying all the reporters at once and clearing up the matter of the postmortem findings, he scheduled a press conference at the Inter-Continental for 22 September, a Thursday. Perhaps with everyone in the room together he could set the record straight: Julie had been murdered by person or persons unknown, not by animals, he wanted to say, and it was up to the police to find the killers.

As a diplomatic gesture Ward alerted Kilonzo to the conference and invited him to send an observer. For all Kilonzo's evasions he had confirmed that investigators were working on the case, and it might not pay to seem uncooperative. Kilonzo agreed to Ward's offer, but a bare fifteen minutes before the press conference began he sent a message: Would Ward please avoid making any suggestion that Julie's death was the result of foul play?

The request fitted with Kilonzo's expressed concern about alerting a murderer, and Ward wearily resolved to try. Accompanied by two officials from the British High Commission he entered a small meeting room tucked behind the Hotel Inter-Continental's hall of curio shops and newsstands. Ward felt tired as he scanned the room. It was filled with British journalists, along with a handful of Nairobi's resident foreign correspondents stirred to idle curiosity by the discovery of Julie's pathetic remains in the Mara.

Many in the room were instantly alert to the evident toll on the father. The runaround with Youssef and Kilonzo had left its mark. Ward looked exhausted and emotionally overwrought, and some of the reporters thought they detected a catch in his voice, as if he were holding back tears. His barrel chest sagged. As if trying to put off a few minutes more the chore of publicly confronting his daughter's violent death, he began by seeking out a particular reporter for a waspish scolding.

'Who have we got from the *Sunday Mirror*?' he asked, scanning the room. A South African named David Barritt spoke up. 'Ah. Thank you very much for calling me from the airport at midnight last night shortly before I got to sleep. Very considerate.'

There was an uneasy pause. Then Ward collected himself. He started by trying firmly to bury any suggestion that his daughter's death was caused by an animal attack. He related briefly the essentials of his meeting with Dr Youssef, saying the pathologist's report 'indicates that the pieces that he examined did in fact suffer cuts with a sharp instrument prior to an attempt being made to burn those pieces.'

Ward predicted that the police would 'probably issue a statement within a couple of days,' and added that he was confident they were carrying out a 'very thorough investigation.' But he then trampled all over Kilonzo's plea for circumspection. 'I am convinced,' he said, 'that she suffered a violent death and was not just a girl who wandered off track and was eaten by animals.' He paused before pointedly adding, 'Which has been the story so far.'

When one of the reporters asked him to comment on the suicide theory – Tham had repeated it in an interview with the *Telegraph* – he dismissed it out of hand. 'If your leg has been cut off with a sharp instrument and subsequently burned, it doesn't really point toward suicide.'

He seemed to be trying to persuade himself, as well as the reporters, that the police were handling the job properly. 'I think the police authorities have this now well in hand, and whereas they may not be quite ready today to say, "Yes, we are conducting a full-scale murder inquiry," I think that is what they are doing,' he replied to another question.

Much of what Ward said would have brought a rueful smile to his face a few eventful months later. He allowed as how he was 'impressed' with Kilonzo 'when I had the pleasure of meeting him.' He pooh-poohed the suggestion that the police were resisting his inquiries. And he was still disposed to be generous about the country his daughter had enjoyed so much. Graciously, he said he might allow her ashes to be buried in the last place she had lived.

'She was very happy here for the last six months of her life,' he said. 'She had lots of friends here. And we will probably bury her here.'

But he let no chance go by to defend her reputation as a responsible, bright woman not prone to harebrained adventure, even if some of the circumstances left questions about her behavior. Some of the reporters had already spent some time snooping around the Mara, and they were familiar with the gully. One asked Ward why he thought Julie had not walked up the hill or followed the river back to Sand River gate.

Ward as yet had no explanation for Julie's failure to seek help so near at hand. The point obviously bothered him, and he admitted so. 'Bearing in mind that I know her to be an intelligent girl, a practical girl, it is unexplained,' he said.

More than six months would pass before John Ward's apotheosis in the press as a solitary man fighting an official cover-up. This was his first public appearance since the 'Lion Girl's' remains had been found strewn over a forlorn clearing in the Masai Mara, and few of the correspondents knew what to make of him. Some of the stories to emerge from the press conference retained their tone of skepticism. One pointed out that despite Ward's insistence that the pathologist's report was 'unequivocal' in establishing that Julie's remains had been cut by a sharp instrument, 'the "unequivocal" report has not been released and Ward does not have a copy. The pathologist has told two British journalists that the wounds on the body could have come from the claws or teeth of wild animals.'

Meanwhile, John Ward took an important step to preserve the key evidence. Calling John Lee, the Nairobi mortician who had taken custody of his daughter's remains, he canceled plans for her cremation.

CHAPTER EIGHTEEN

That night Ward was haunted by misgivings, visions of the tangled claims and counterclaims of the Kenyan authorities. He had planned to spend the next day on a visit to the Masai Mara, but in the morning he canceled the trip.

To Ferguson he confided that his unhappiness about Kilonzo's refusal to announce a murder inquiry, and his unease about the still unproduced postmortem report, mandated his staying in the capital at least a little while longer.

That morning, as if to answer Ward's fears, the police called Ferguson to notify him the report would be ready in the afternoon. Immediately after lunch Ferguson went to pick it up.

Shortly after two o'clock the embassy diplomat convened a large gathering at the British High Commission office for the unveiling of the report. Ward arrived with a business associate named Frank Ribeiro in tow, to find Ferguson, Jenny Jenkins, and John Lee of the funeral home waiting for him. Ferguson was in a state of high excitement, as if the long-awaited document opened up some new and unexpected chapter in the saga. Ward rapidly read it over, and instantly understood that it did.

To someone unfamiliar with the events of the past few days the report would have seemed unremarkable. But nobody in the room misunderstood its coded subtext. The report said that the deceased's leg had been torn off and the jawbone cracked in two. The instrument of death was described as something blunt, and the cause of death was listed as 'blunt injuries, subsequent burning.'

The language was as transparent as a pane of glass. The

leg 'torn off'? The jaw cracked in two? The carefully chosen words describing the injuries as blunt? The picture made a strong case for death not by murder, but by accident. The document plainly supported the police version of Julie's death and consigned to oblivion, as if by simple erasure, Youssef's insistence on foul play.

That was very close to the truth indeed. Ward did not have to read twice to discern that Youssef's version of events had been physically erased from the pages in his hand. The new report was interposed with shocking clumsiness directly over the original.

Next to where the word *torn* described the injury to Julie's leg, someone had originally typed 'cut'. That word was obliterated by three overtyped x's. The same thing had occurred where the report now stated that the jawbone had been 'cracked' in two rather than 'cut'. In the space where the weapon was described as 'blunt', someone had originally written 'sharp'.

No-one in the room could remember having seen the likes of it before. In Ward's furious grip was not one but two postmortems, the first one obscured, like an artist's canvas lightly repainted, by a maladroit hand.

Whoever altered the report had not even seemed to worry about exposure. Not only were the original words still visible, but the overtyping was off line from the rest of the typescript, as if the report had been rolled clumsily back into the typewriter to make the changes.

Most telling, whoever did this had overlooked what still remained as the key evidence of murder: that the limb had been severed and 'subsequently burned'. This finding, the key to Youssef's verdict, was unaltered. No animal known to inhabit the Mara cut up its food and then put it on a fire. None, that is, but man.

Ward sat in the silent room, angry and apprehensive. There was no alternative now but to confront Youssef directly. Outside, Ward, Ribeiro, and Ferguson jumped into John Lee's car and headed for the city mortuary. The flaming blooms of the Uhuru Highway roundabouts rushed invisibly past.

The men found the Egyptian cowering in his dim office. Youssef had clearly expected Ward to return, and he seemed to have exactly anticipated his state of mind. When Ward charged through his door, the question 'Who changed this report?' on his lips, Youssef scarcely hesitated for a second before miserably blurting out: 'It wasn't me. You must see my boss. He did it.'

The pathologist got up from his desk to follow them to the door. As Ward turned to leave, Youssef added, 'But it still shows evidence of foul play. It still says the leg was cut with subsquent burning. You see?'

Ward brought Youssef along to confront the man's superior. His introduction to Dr Jason Kaviti thus took place under less than optimum circumstances. Kaviti was a fixture of the Kenyan justice system. The secret of his survival, if it is possible to read between the lines, was a certain talent for obscurantism. He was cosseted by the judiciary, his findings generally accepted by unquestioning judges. Kaviti was destined to become one of the most controversial figures in this case, but for now he was a formidable obstacle to anyone seeking to prove a forensic point with which he had reason to differ.

The Britons bearded Kaviti in his office at Jomo Kenyatta Hospital, the filthy, overcrowded public institution located across Ngong Road from the private Nairobi Hospital, where rich Kenyans and European expatriates went to be treated with crisp efficiency.

The found a short, gray-haired man resistant to giving answers. The electricity of this moment would stay with Kaviti for a long time. Months afterward he could still describe Ward's livid expression. 'He was fuming,' Kaviti would describe the occasion simply.

Ward had dropped all pretence at politeness. Kaviti had precipitated a crisis, and as his junior pathologist stood nearby shivering in a state of nervous collapse, the father confronted him.

'Why did you alter this report?' Ward asked.

Like most Kenyans, Kaviti viewed raised voices and aggressive approaches as insulting. He reacted in the usual way, smiling wanly without answering.

Ward repeated the question in an angry tone.

After a long silence Kaviti answered. In a low voice he took the first step toward an entanglement that would ultimately expose him to public ridicule. As Ward and Ferguson recalled later his version was this: The day before – that is, 22 September – he had come into Youssef's office in the city mortuary and happened upon the postmortem report in the typewriter. Reading through it, he concluded that Youssef had simply by mistake written 'cut' instead of 'cracked and torn'. For the same reason he had changed 'sharp' to 'blunt'.

'His English is not very good,' Kaviti said equably of Youssef. 'He meant to say these other things. Therefore I took it upon myself to change the report.'

'Do you make a practice of altering other pathologists' reports?' Ward asked.

'I am the chief police pathologist. I am entitled to alter my subordinate's reports if I wish,' Kaviti replied with indignation.

'How many of Dr Youssef's other reports have you changed like this? How many has Dr Youssef done himself?'

Kaviti stayed silent, so Ward directed the same questions at Youssef.

'How many?'

'I've carried out one hundred postmortems,' Youssef said, 'and this is the first one that has been altered by Dr Kaviti.'

Ward turned back to Kaviti. 'I don't understand how it is possible for you to have come to such a conclusion, that the leg was torn from the body. The report still says it was subjected to subsequent burning!'

Kaviti was tiring of the confrontation. He recounted later that at this point he was on the verge of throwing the rude Englishmen 'all out of my office'. Now he chose to maintain his silence in the face of the father's presumptuous interrogation. As Ward continued shooting increasingly infuriated questions at him, Ferguson interposed his smooth diplomatic tones to make – as it turned out – an indispensable suggestion.

'Dr Kaviti,' he said, 'since you have now admitted making these alterations, don't you think it is necessary and proper that you initial the changes and date them with the day they were made?'

Kaviti mulled over the request under Ward's glare. Evidently finding it innocuous, he agreed. Ward was quietly amazed that Kaviti would confirm his alteration in writing, but as he looked on the pathologist placed his initials and the date '22.9.88' – the previous day – next to his three alterations on the report. As the Britons prepared to leave the office, Ward turned back to Kaviti one more.

'I'll be taking this matter further,' he said. 'If I have to, I'll have a proper examination done!'

'Well, you are at liberty to do so,' Kaviti said formally to Ward's back.

Ward's uncertainty about relying on the Kenyan government to solve his daughter's murder had now hardened decisively. If Kilonzo's temporizing had left him slightly uneasy, combined with Kaviti's alteration it began to look more like there was a conspiracy to keep the real nature of Julie's death from reaching daylight. Laid out before him was the spectacle of a government tying itself in knots to avoid accepting clear evidence of murder.

Ward would later say that it was at this point that the prospect of a high-level cover-up occurred to him. Who could order officials of the Kenyan government to falsify an official document? And for what reason? It now occurred to him that if anyone was going to investigate his daughter's murder, he would have to do it himself.

The first step was obvious: to get the remains professionally examined. The only place he was sure of getting a dependable postmortem was the UK, and he began arrangements to repatriate Julie's remains, preserved in formaldehyde, back home.

Meanwhile, he and his friend Frank Ribeiro returned to the Mara, this time driven by the urgency of collecting

142

evidence for a British examination. It was Ward's first visit to the park since the day he had found Julie's jeep and remains, and now he thought it crucial to assemble with his own hands whatever was still lying around the two sites. The thought of burying his daughter in this land she seemed to love had by now been extinguished. Her ashes were still lying around out there, he reflected. That simply was not right. Anything he could still exhume from beneath the sausage tree, he decided, would get a proper burial in England.

The two men flew to the Keekorok airstrip on Saturday, 24 September. There to greet them on alighting were two police officers. One was George Othiambo, the skinny officer who had taken custody of Julie's remains the week before. The second was a tall Kikuyu superintendent with nineteen years on the force. Ward learned from the man that he had personally been assigned by Kilonzo to be the chief investigator in Julie's death.

Ward eyed Superintendent Muchiri Wanjau with interest as the officer drove him and Ribeiro in his Land Rover back to the sausage tree. This was the man on whom all of Kilonzo's assurances rested, whose report the commissioner was awaiting with such tangible anticipation. Wanjau was smartly, if monochromatically, turned out in a dark brown jacket and an Oxford shirt in checked earth-tones. A busily patterned tie, also in dark colors, completed the ensemble, a dull stab at some weird stylishness. Wanjau wore his hair cropped very short over a trim moustache and his long sideburns flared out under the ears. They gave him a strangely fifties appearance, like someone trying to catch up with Western style thirty years too late.

Wanjau was not exactly a garrulous sort, especially with whites. He spoke in clipped sentences, sullenly; it would be a rare moment over the next few months when Ward would see him with anything but an unhappy look, brooding over some unarticulated dissatisfaction. Wanjau peppered his conversation with an overdramatic flourish of diction. The police 'moved in', they 'swung into action', that sort of thing. So far, Ward was beginning to get the impression that all the action was in the talk, and the rest was largely inertia. In any event, he could not hope to get much insight into Kenyan police thinking from the unhappy, taciturn Kikuyu policeman who sat next to him in the car.

For his part Wanjau did little to hide his discontent at his new assignment. White people could not hope to understand the importance of tribe and ethnicity among Kenya's Africans, but Wanjau felt it deeply. He felt he had been transported to some unfamiliar world, where the people did not speak his language and he received more suspicion and hostility than cooperation from the park rangers who were supposed to be helping him out. The Masai of this part of Kenya were like an alien race to Wanjau, and he would never get over his discomfort at having to depend on these strangers for translations, directions, and driving.

Also Wanjau hated flying, especially in helicopters, and it seemed that scarcely a moment had passed since he drew this distasteful case that he was not required to go up in the air to get somewhere, see something, or photograph something else. Ward would frequently find him pacing irritably along the gravel airstrip at Keekorok, torn between his eagerness to get out of the Mara and anxiety at the aircraft that was coming to take him away.

Of all the people Ward met in Kenya, the police superintendent might have been the most sensitive to the father's increasingly strident tone of voice over the next few months. Given the frustrations he faced, Ward had a certain right to consider himself the soul of patience. He could not have comprehended how his bluntness grated on the deliberate, easygoing Africans. But Kenyans prized politeness and courteous patience over all other qualities in personal intercourse: It was a poor tourist guidebook that failed to stress the need to approach Kenyans politely and to expect even the most rudimentary transactions to take longer than expected. Of course, the definition of courtesy differed from culture to culture. Busy European expatriates found it rude and irritating when Kenyans began their telephone conversations with 'How are you?' and waited silently for an answer before identifying themselves or stating their business; to Kenyans the whites' way of plunging into the gist before passing the civilities was grating and impertinent. They were insulted if personal greetings were not exchanged at length before even the most urgent transaction.

The government at large reflected this insistence on its own definition of civility and graciousness. To the outside world it might have seemed that no people on Earth had such highly developed antennae for international slights and affronts. Kenyan leaders always seemed to be complaining about the impudence of some other government, often one like Canada, Germany, or the United States whose foreign aid kept it afloat. Foreign visitors protested aloud at their peril about poor service or bureaucratic bungles; not long before John Ward's first visit to Nairobi the authorities had jailed a German businessman for two weeks because he complained in an imprudently direct manner about African inefficiency.

Acculturated to the dynamic world of Western business, Ward found it hard to imagine that his insistent badgering of the police could have any effect other than snapping them into action. In fact, it would have the opposite effect.

Wanjau, the butt of most of Ward's scoldings, gave up accommodating the pushy *mzungu*, this white man, very early in the investigation, much earlier than Ward knew. He never confronted the father directly. He just withdrew gradually, nodding silently at Ward's investigative discoveries and quietly discarding them. It was his way of expressing a desire for this whole business to simply go away. That wish only grew stronger as the Julie Ward killing continued to make his life difficult. Wanjau had no more clue than the girl's father about what could possibly have happened to the tourist, and in this strange place of wild animals and indifferent Masai he had scarcely an idea about how to begin. Getting constantly upbraided by

John Ward did not make him any more enthusiastic about his task.

Wanjau and Ward never clicked from the first. By the end of the investigation they would detest each other.

On the day he first met Ward, Wanjau had been involved in the case for scarcely more than forty-eight hours. It had been barely enough time to get a sketchy briefing from the local policemen and to make a preliminary reconnaisance of the two key sites. Othiambo had escorted Wanjau to Sebastian Tham's compound to examine the Suzuki, only to discover that Tham's workmen, lulled by the police force's evident noninterest in the vehicle for the ten days that had passed since the discovery of the remains, had hosed down its dusty outside and swept out its interior. Not even a trace of the muddy 'SOS' remained.

Wanjau later said he checked the jeep for fingerprints, but it had been a cursory check indeed. He had simply looked over the washed vehicle and concluded there was no point in even trying.

When Ward and Wanjau reached the fire site it looked even more desolate than it had on Ward's first visit. He took a brief general look around the area. There was not much to see among the unremarkable brush. For this visit Ward had come equipped with a handful of polyethylene bags, and at length he began filling the bags with ashes and debris.

Ward would always find it hard to express how he felt as he dug his hands into the thick pile of gray ash, the crudely cremated remains of pieces of his only daughter. At the time he simply closed off his emotions. He worked methodically, professionally, as though he simply had a job to do. Then he took a series of photographs of the thicket, including the sausage tree, its lower limbs still burned and blackened from the fire.

On the way back to Keekorok, Ward asked Wanjau to drive the group over to the Suzuki site for a last look around. All that could be seen were the tire treads marking the spot where the jeep had been mired before Tham's workmen hauled it away. Ward quickly surveyed it for what he thought would be the last time, and the group returned to Keekorok.

That night Wanjau knocked on Ward's door at the Keekorok Lodge. It was his responsibility to take an official statement from the father, he explained, and Ward steeled himself mentally to retrace the painful ground of the last two weeks. But it soon became evident that Wanjau was pursuing some wayward thread of his own. He pressed Ward for information about his daughter's character, and then mentioned that he had heard that shortly before she disappeared, she had had a quarrel with her traveling companion, Glen Burns.

'I don't know anything about that,' Ward said.

Wanjau was easily discouraged and, on the face of things, just as easily misled. Investigators who followed his tracks much later would be appalled to find that he was one of the least methodical police officers they had ever met. He failed to take written notes of his interviews of many key figures, much less suspects, and did not even record their dates. Whatever characteristic is the opposite of initiative, Wanjau had it. It would be reasonable then and later to ask what the superintendent, seconded down to Narok by Kilonzo himself to take over from the undermanned local constabulary, was planning to do with his time. For the next eleven months he seemed to do almost nothing in investigating Julie Ward's death without first being prodded by her father, and so when he acted, it was not with enthusiasm or determination, but resentment. It is not the quality most useful in solving a crime.

CHAPTER NINETEEN

The next morning Ribeiro and Ward met Simon Makallah, the chief warden. Makallah was still wearing his smug half-smile and he was full of enthusiasm as he agreed to guide Ward and Ribeiro to Sand River Camp, the campsite where Julie and Burns had pitched their tents.

'I can show you the exact site where she camped,' Makallah said.

They piled into a borrowed white Suzuki jeep with the stylized panda logo of the World Wildlife Fund stenciled on its side. Makallah took the wheel.

At Sand River Camp, Makallah stalked across the uneven ground. 'This is the place,' he said, as if proud of his own discovery. 'But of course it has been used since she was here.' Still, Ward got out his camera again. As it happened, Makallah was indicating the wrong place, several hundred meters away from the actual tent site. No-one would later be able to figure out where Makallah got his information, assuming he did not simply make it up. But his small misplacement of the tents would create greater confusion later on.

On the way back to Keekorok, Makallah suddenly stopped the jeep about five kilometers north of the campground. The warden pointed out his window toward a trackless expanse of browning bush.

'I believe this is where she turned off the road to drive across the bush,' he said.

To Ward, Makallah might well have selected a spot at random. Here and there the dual tracks of vehicles or the faint traces of old trails left the road, but they vanished into the thick grass before reaching fifty yards. In that direction lay nothing but uninviting ridges and rocky outcroppings, and some low humpbacked hills beyond. Perplexed, Ward compared the inconspicuous tracks indicated by Makallah with the graded and groomed road on which they were standing. If Julie had gone just another fraction of a kilometer she would have come into view of Keekorok's cluster of buildings and black roofs visible through a distinctive stand of trees. Often after this day he would ask himself why Julie would turn off a perfectly good and straight road on to a scarcely visible trail leading off into absolute nowhere. Only an idiot would do a thing like that for no reason. Could somebody have led her down that way? Or forced her?

But Makallah seemed to suggest that she had gone off the road on a frolic. Ward was irked at the Kenyans' apparent impression that Julie was an impulsive scatter-brain. First she would heedlessly turn off a paved road into bush where it was evident she could get irretrievably lost in minutes. Then she would wander off from her car as if on a weekend stroll down the High Street. Add to that the misgivings the father had about Wanjau's pursuit of irrelevancies, and it looked like the Kenyans were scattering off in every direction but the right one.

He wondered again about Makallah's headlong dash across this unforgiving country to find Julie's body. The warden's explanation about following footsteps out of the gully and seeing vultures in the distance seemed ever more implausible as Ward saw more of the trackless waste around here. Makallah had not needed much more than an hour to find the body after leaving the jeep; he could not have homed in on the spot faster if he had been shot from a cannon. Maybe these blokes were great trackers, but it must have been a real stroke of luck to find it so fast.

Or something else. As the two Englishmen were lifting off from Keekorok on the 11 a.m. flight back to Wilson Airport, Frank Ribeiro prodded Ward. 'I wouldn't trust that guy,' he said. Ward had to agree. From that point on Makallah was fixed in John Ward's mind as a potential participant in his daughter's killing. Almost everything he did after that day was aimed, directly or indirectly, at finding the evidence to prove Makallah's guilt.

Nairobi harbored one last mysterious encounter before the father's flight home. As they exited a downtown bank, Ward came upon Youssef standing at a newsstand in the busy sidewalk traffic. Like most downtown newsstands this one was a display of mostly secondhand British periodicals laid out on the ground, their covers faded from the sun. Ward stopped the pathologist to thank him for signing the papers for the swift repatriation of Julie's remains to the UK.

Youssef seemed grateful for the approach, then became furtive. He confided that he had examined the remains again. 'Everything is in order,' he said. 'When you get them to England you will see.'

'What are you saying?' Ward asked. 'Do you mean your original findings were correct?'

'Yes, yes. You will see when you get them home.' As he went shambling off into the crowd he turned and said, 'You will understand why I could not speak.'

That night John Ward caught the midnight British Airways flight to London. In the cargo hold under his seat, pickled in formaldehyde and packaged in a pair of small metal caskets, were his daughter's remains.

Two days later Ward met the pathologist who would perform the second postmortem on his daughter's corpse. He felt he could not be any farther from the squalid surroundings of the Nairobi city mortuary than at Cambridge's Addenbrookes Hospital, which rises in a jumble of brick and glass towers on the south side of the university town. On the fifth floor, high above the bustle of starched whites that gives Addenbrookes its air of clinical professionalism, sat Geoffrey Austin Gresham, professor of morbid anatomy.

Gresham had thirty-five years behind him of postmortems and autopsies, the search for criminal clues in the microscopic features of human tissue. Small and erect in bearing, tidy and precise, Gresham was the very model of a British university don. The frame of white-gray hair around the balding top of his head, his neat salt-and-pepper mustache, and his gold-rimmed glasses gave him an air of informal eminence that would have fitted perfectly into a novel by P. D. James, where the police pathologist is not only above suspicion but indispensable to the tidy plot. He puffed ruminatively on a metal-shanked pipe as John Ward described the circumstances of his daughter's death and the suspect postmortem performed in Nairobi.

Gresham had a pained reaction to the slovenliness of his professional confrères. This business of retyping the postmortem report was scandalous, he thought. Simply unacceptable practice in England.

Where Youssef and Kaviti were vague, even mysterious, about their procedures, Gresham took genuine relish in describing his. With professional pride he walked Ward figuratively through the process of conducting a postmortem. There would be X-ray examinations of bone, which would be able to establish the age and even the gender of the deceased. These would also help to show what sort of instrument was responsible for the severing of the pieces, Gresham assured Ward. He explained in painstaking detail how a thin bone responded to blows differently from a thick bone. Mildly he told Ward he was confident he could tell the difference between an animal assault and a human attack with a sharp instrument.

There would be a comparison of Julie's dental records with the teeth left in the jawbone. If necessary, there would be consultations with colleagues in the department. Gresham would describe his findings directly into a microphone as he examined the remains, thus preserving the record against manipulation.

Dealing with Gresham was liberating after the appalling display at the Nairobi city mortuary, where not even professional scientific judgments could be uttered without consideration of political implications and not even an official forgery could be accomplished competently. Ward was relieved to hear Gresham talk fluently of X-ray examinations and chemical tests and consultations with a

151

faculty of respected experts. Gresham talked about professional standards with an air of pride that meant they would not be lightly breached.

'Well,' the pathologist said finally. 'Let's have a look, shall we?' He meant Ward to take this as a signal to leave him to his work, but the father stopped him.

'I want to watch,' he said.

Behind his gold-rimmed glasses Gresham's blue eyes blinked. *This is unusual*, he thought. In his experience there had been some people who wanted to be in the room during an autopsy – West Indians, mostly – but even they shrank from actually watching the cold procedure. Still, if Ward wanted to stand at his shoulder and look, that was all right with him.

Gresham's mortuary attendant had a bit of trouble prying open the sealed metal boxes, cutting his hand on one sharp edge. Gresham reached in for the leg, took one look, and said, 'It's been cut.'

Ward had felt a little addled after all the time he spent in Kenya hearing talk of wild animals and suicide. More than once he felt a twinge of doubt. *Maybe I'm crazy*, he thought. But from here on in he knew he could always come to Gresham to hear him say, sure as could be, 'John, she was murdered.'

CHAPTER TWENTY

In the Masai Mara, Wanjau continued to flounder
aimlessly. At the outset he ruled out the possibility that
any of the park rangers might know more about the
tourist's death than they were volunteering, much less that
they might even be suspects, but that left him without any
leads. Moreover, he felt isolated among the nearly entirely
Masai ranger force of the Mara. To him their language,
known as Maa, was a totally unintelligible jumble of words
and inflections compared to the simple melded Arab and
Bantu phonetics of Swahili.

The superintendent made several more visits to the fire.
Leaving Othiambo there one day, Wanjau walked toward
a Masai manyatta that had been spotted not far from the
site, roughly between the fire and the distant Makari
ranger post; he measured the distance as 1.7 kilometers.
Constructed of dung, the manyatta sheltered two middle-
aged Masai who ducked inside one of the huts as they
saw Wanjau approach. After a time a third man, much
older, came by.

Wanjau found the herdsmen even harder to communicate with than the rangers. He tried for a while to indicate
he was looking for a lost camera. Finally he gave up and
dispatched some men to comb the compound and the
surrounding area, without result.

A few days later he returned with a Masai who could
communicate in Swahili: Simon ole Makallah. Wanjau
would be mercilessly second-guessed for selecting as an
interpreter someone he should have considered a suspect,
especially when he had to admit that the resulting
interview was a bust. The people who were there when the
remains were found had already headed south across the

Tanzania border, he was informed. No, Makallah said, they couldn't be traced.

Two weeks later, in England, Ward had a second meeting with Gresham. Reassuringly pedantic as ever, Gresham escorted him back to his examination room, where he had displayed a number of X-ray pictures of Julie's leg and jawbone.

With colleagues the pathologist had also pored over the extracta from the fire beneath the sausage tree. Some of the larger items were also human bones, he concluded, probably from the fingers.

The leg had been severed from Julie's body by a single blow, Gresham confirmed. The diminutive professor used a forceful bit of stage business in delivering this judgment, swiping his arm like the swing of a scythe to show how the weapon had struck the inside of the leg. The blade had traveled slightly upwards to clip the kneecap from behind, slicing it cleanly in two.

It was the same with the jawbone, which Gresham believed had been bisected by a single swipe with a sharp blade, so swift that it had sliced a lower tooth in half, leaving the root canal embedded in the bone.

In addition to his sessions with 'the prof', as he called Gresham, Ward was trying to pick up the loose ends strewn untidily about the case by Wanjau's less than fastidious approach. On his next trip to Nairobi – he was going every few weeks now – he talked with Julie's last known traveling companion, the Australian zoologist, Glen Burns. Burns by now had returned to Nairobi after a trip through Rwanda and Tanzania. He had been appalled to learn of Julie's death from Paul Weld Dixon, and one day he arranged to meet her father at Weld Dixon's house.

John Ward questioned Burns closely about his and Julie's last trip together. 'Did you and my daughter have a quarrel on September fourth?' he asked, remembering Wanjau's curious question. Burns assured him there had been no quarrel.

Burns appears to have left Ward cool. He assured Ward

that he was only a casual acquaintance of his daughter, made a reasonable account of his actions in leaving her and the Suzuki in extremis in the Mara, and left the father reassured that he had nothing to do with her death. But something about Burns made it hard for Ward to take a shine to him. Much later Ward would find it difficult to describe why. He could not shake the opinion that Burn's offhand attitude about his decision to fly off, leaving Julie alone and stranded in the Masai Mara, was just wrong. In the diary he had kept since deciding to pursue the investigation on his own, the father made an entry about Burns. He called him 'weak-willed', a 'wet' who took no responsibility for Julie's safety.

Others who came to know Glen Burns would regard that assessment as unfair. Glen Burns never forgave himself for leaving Julie alone in the Masai Mara. He had an acute sense that had they remained together she would still be alive. With his Australian air of self-confidence and unconcern he might not show it to a stranger right off, but from time to time the devastation with which news of Julie's death struck him emerged: in a very real way, he felt, he was responsible.

Meanwhile Ward was busy on other fronts. He had posters printed up offering a reward – *zawad*, in Swahili – for information leading to the recovery of Julie's missing camera. After they were distributed around the Mara, Ward got many calls offering information. But the camera was never found.

Ward had made this trip to Nairobi specifically to discuss Gresham's written autopsy report with the police. It was days before Kilonzo finally agreed to a meeting. The 18 October session was their third. This time Wanjau was a sullen presence in the room.

Ward quietly laid his yellow-covered copy of the Gresham report in front of Kilonzo. 'Have you read it?' he asked.

'I have read it,' Kilonzo said, 'and I accept its contents. In fact, you will be interested to know that I have started a new line of inquiry' – he nodded vaguely in Wanjau's direction – 'but still, we will need more time.'

Ward began to protest, but Kilonzo stopped him short.

'I want to assure you that we are treating this matter very seriously,' he said. 'If there is a murderer in the Masai Mara National Game Reserve, we want him caught before he can do this again.'

'If?' Ward tried to keep his temper. 'If? The time for "if" is past, Commissioner. How can you doubt any longer that there is a murderer? You now have a pathologist's report stating clearly that my daughter's leg was severed by a sharp instrument! Cut, and subsequently burned! What more proof could you possibly need?'

'Mr Ward, I certainly don't rule out murder. But I still wish to wait for the report of my investigating officer.' He tilted his head in Wanjau's direction. 'We have channels here. Ways of doing things. Perhaps they are just different from yours.'

'But what else could it possibly be but foul play?' Ward insisted. He turned to the page in Gresham's report that revealed that a lock of hair recovered from the fire had been cut at both ends, as if once by a hairdresser and once by a panga. 'Now how else could that be explained?'

'I prefer to wait for my officer's report.'

Kilonzo's impassive resistance made Ward, for the first time in the commissioner's presence, lose his patience.

'Commissioner, I am increasingly concerned at the reluctance of the police authorities here to accept the obvious evidence I have presented. Between all this, and the fact that the postmortem report was altered—' He trailed off.

Kilonzo's serene expression had turned to puzzlement.

'Did you not know that Dr Youssef's report was altered?' Ward reached into a briefcase and brought forth a copy of Youssef's report. 'This report was written by Dr Kaviti.'

'How do you know this?'

'He admitted it to me himself. The significance of this is that the report is not by Dr Youssef, as it indicates.'

Kilonzo called out loud for his secretary. 'Bring me the

postmortem report on the late Julie Ward,' he said. As she turned through the door, he called: 'I want the original, the one that was handwritten.'

From the office they could hear the secretary rummaging among files. Ward showed Kilonzo the copy Kaviti had initialed and dated. The secretary came back into the office and muttered something to the commissioner in Swahili.

'She says she cannot find the original report. Well. I can not understand what is happening here.'

'What are you going to do about it?'

'Superintendent Wanjau will bring Dr Kaviti and Dr Youssef here tomorrow so I can get to the bottom of this,' Kilonzo said. 'I will find out what is going on.'

The meeting closed with a ritual exchange.

'I'm asking you once more to open a full murder inqury,' said Ward.

'Again, I prefer to wait for my superintendent's report.'

That day Ward unburdened himself to Ferguson. It seemed clearer with every meeting that Kilonzo was purposely stalling. It was October already, a month since Julie's death. What did it take for them to admit it was murder?

Perhaps they were hoping Ward would just go away. But he would not go away. John Ward was now more resolved than ever to keep the investigation alive, if he had to do it himself.

Ward brought along a copy of Gresham's report for the junior pathologist. He stood by as Youssef leafed through the report with mounting glee.

'He agrees with me!' Youssef said, finally. 'A Cambridge professor!' Youssef could barely contain himself. He was like a schoolboy awarded a gold star. He kept repeating, 'A Cambridge professor!' Ward decided to press his advantage.

'Now can you tell me now how your report got altered?'

In the flush of victory Youssef agreed. 'Dr Kaviti came into my office at the mortuary that day and asked specifically for the Julie Ward file.' The senior pathologist had looked cursorily at the leg, but not the X-rays Youssef had taken. Then he had rolled the report back into Youssef's typewriter, the junior pathologist admitted, and made the changes.

Late the next day Ward received a visit from Wanjau accompanied by another policeman. Wanjau had three more questions to ask him: where had Julie gone to school, what had become of the maps found in the jeep, and what was her blood type?

'What's the significance of these questions? Does this mean you have found some blood?' Ward asked.

'We may have done so.'

Ward had reason to be skeptical. There had been no sign of blood around the fire in the Mara – some damp spots indicating bodily fluids, perhaps, but certainly no evident bloodstains. In fact, Ward's working hypothesis was that Julie must have been killed somewhere else, and her remains transported somehow to the fire. But he agreed to send the maps back from Britain and to get Julie's blood type. (As it turned out, this was a problem: No-one seemed to have a record of it.) As for the third question, Ward responded sharply. 'I think that's totally irrelevant. What significance could her schooling have on this case?' he said. Wanjau had no answer. Ward filled the silence by grilling him about his progress.

'What about this ranger Peter Kippeen? Is he a suspect?'

Kippeen's name had appeared weeks earlier in an article by a *Sunday Times* reporter who had hired a four-wheel-drive shortly after Julie's jeep had been found. He and others set out to retrace her route. Bouncing along the rutted landscape, the troupe of newsmen missed the gully, but managed to get themselves stuck very close by. Kippeen had appeared over a nearby ridge, evidently after hearing them revving their engine to extricate the vehicle.

'Perhaps if he heard their vehicle, he could have heard Julie's,' Ward suggested.

Wanjau shrugged, trying to dash cold water on the

theory. 'Kippeen was not assigned to that area,' he said. 'He was only there temporarily to assist in keeping an eye on a Swiss television crew working near there. He has been reassigned.' To Ward it seemed another lead had been disregarded by the police.

Wanjau would later complain to acquaintances about *wazungu* telling him how to do his job. He gave the Swahili term its full derogatory weight – rich, overfed, arrogant whites. On this occasion Wanjau smoldered as Ward warmed to his subject. He crisply upbraided Wanjau, losing the temper he had tried to keep in Kilonzo's office.

'There's been a total lack of progress here,' he said, 'despite the evidence which I have provided.'

'I am still investigating,' Wanjau mumbled, annoyed at the father's badgering tone.

'Well you haven't given any indication to me that you've made any progress. The only things you have are what I've given you.'

After that meeting Ward called Kilonzo, curious about what his session with Kaviti and Youssef had turned up. As usual, the commissioner was noncommittal, prompting Ward to remark, 'You now have two postmortem reports, Commissioner. Do you think it's necessary for me to get you a third one?'

Kilonzo tried to placate him.

'I do not think it is necessary, as I consider both reports now to be generally in agreement,' Kilonzo replied.

Youssef later told Ward what had really happened at the meeting. 'The commissioner accepted my findings and those of Professor Gresham,' he said. And Kaviti? Youssef was buoyant over having scored one on his boss. 'Dr Kaviti maintained his position . . . but he wasn't happy.'

The next day Ward and Ribeiro returned to the Mara with a new member of Ward's investigative team. Bob Whitford was a florid survivor of colonial days, an aging Welshman with terrier eyebrows and a brogue you could slice with a knife.

Whitford was one of those people who as a youth

acquire a dream of being a policeman and never relinquish it. After joining the Metropolitan Police in London following wartime service with the Royal Navy, he served as a constable for two years and spent another four and a half as a detective assigned to Scotland Yard. By then Kenya was beckoning as an opportunity to escape the grinding competitiveness of the home force; it was long before Hola, long before the trial of Jomo Kenyatta. In the early 1950s one could still look out over the rolling green of the highlands without detecting the imminent end of empire, although the change would not be long in coming. In 1955, at the age of thirty-eight, Whitford signed on and mustered out to Nairobi to join the colonial police at the height of the Mau Mau emergency.

Most of the Kenya Police force was white and it had a distinctly martial character. A good number of the men were ex-soldiers who had experienced imperial service in India; it was as if the British continued to view their oldest and richest colony as a source of reliable manpower for Africa. As a member of the first class of genuine policemen recruited for the force, Whitford was among those who began slowly to change it from a paramilitary outfit into a legitimate investigatory and law-enforcement institution.

In those days cattle rustling and the pacification of disorderly visitors from up-country consumed much of the force's time, but serious crime like murder was far from unknown. The tribal and clan animosities aggravated by the Mau Mau insurgency, which was largely a Kikuyu phenomenon, filled the force's files with stranglings, drownings in pit latrines, and tribal lynchings.

Murders of Europeans were relatively rare, if not murders *by* Europeans. Whitford himself was assigned to perhaps the most infamous white crime of the era. As much as Hola, the case of Peter Poole may have marked an important milestone in colonial psychology.

Poole was a former Kenya Police Reserve officer who was found guilty in 1959 of the shooting death of an African houseboy he had caught throwing rocks at his dog. In 1960, when Colonial Secretary Iain Macleod refused to intervene in the case and rejected a request for a royal pardon, there was fear that bands of armed white settlers would attack the prison to free the condemned man. But the violence never materialized and in August 1960 Poole came to a bad end as the first white in Kenya history to be hanged for murdering an African. 'Later there was despondent drinking, and a renewed realization that Kenya was no longer "white man's country",' wrote the historian Robert B. Edgerton. Whitford took a less grand view of the case: 'I felt sorry for him,' he said of the man he had helped bring to this sordid end. 'He was a bit crazy, I think. He wasn't normal.'

By then the colonial government was operating a reasonably integrated force, and there were Africans even among the senior officer corps. 'They were quite efficient, some of them,' Whitford allowed.

After independence the white police officers were permitted to stay on, partially in recognition that their experiences and training made them indispensable. The tribal tensions engendered by the struggle for independence were gradually giving way to a different environment for crime: The steady economic decline that afflicted Kenya, like most African countries, in the 1970's and 80's bred violent robberies and burglaries. Newspapers fattened up on stories of husbands and fathers who articulated their feelings of defeat amid the country's chronic underemployment with panga attacks on their wives and children. Soon the Europeans, long accustomed to feeling themselves exempt from the conditions of the country, took to locking their doors even in Nairobi's most salubrious suburbs. Most whites felt secure on the streets in daylight, but it was a rare executive house that was unequipped with strong bars on the windows and a so-called 'rape gate' in the hallway. This was a padlocked steel door to seal off the sleeping quarters from marauders who might be raiding the rest of the house.

Most such homes were protected by night guards hired from the numerous private firms springing up to provide the kind of security well beyond the competence of the increasingly ill-equipped police force. In truth these guards were weak reeds to lean on in the event of a concerted attack. Most of the firms trained them in only two subjects. One was how to summon help, and the other was what the companies called 'customer relations' and amounted to instructions not to get into arguments with the homeowners. But inside and outside the houses radio buttons, often labeled *Hatari!* ('Danger!'), were installed to summon the patrol vans that the security firms hired to cruise the neighborhoods, loaded with hulking Africans armed with baseball-bat-sized clubs known as *rungus*.

Meanwhile the police force was gradually becoming 'Africanized', as the white officers put it, and of course the pace picked up as the Metropolitan Police recruits began to retire. Whitford saw his chance shortly before he would have reached mandatory retirement at fifty-five, signing on as general manager of the Kenya branch of a big private security company called Securicor. A few years later he formed his own security and investigative firm, which he named Vigilante Services.

Ward had realized soon after the affair of the post-mortem report that if he were to pursue his daughter's killers himself he would quickly exhaust the capacity of the British High Commission, diplomatic and otherwise, to help him. From the High Commission itself he took a list of suggested private investigators, and presently he put Whitford on his payroll.

Whitford had an incisive grasp of the steps that should have been taken by the police in the days immediately following the discovery of Julie's remains. He was appalled, if not particularly surprised, at the spectacle of their wandering about aimlessly.

'It was no investigation at all,' he remarked later. Whitford was not convinced that a reasonable investigation of Julie's death was technically beyond the police force's capacity. He preferred to see the problem as a lack of initiative, an absence of enthusiasm. He thought the Kenyans expected Ward to react like most other people would have to the implacable inactivity and indifference of the police – that the expense and effort would be finally too discouraging. They hadn't counted on his determination, or his money. Without Ward's constant goading, Whitford figured, there would scarcely have even been the overt appearance of an effort to solve Julie's killing.

The old colonial cop did not agree with his client's growing feeling that the lackluster investigation was the product of some grand conspiracy to keep Julie's murder a secret. Ward was beginning to turn his attention to why the government was going to such lengths to cover up a murder. But Whitford privately doubted there was any grand conspiracy. The Kenyans had a way of trying to ignore things they could not handle. If there was a meningitis outbreak in a remote province with not enough vaccine, the government would simply deny an outbreak existed. Whitford saw a similar thing happening here. If they could have solved the case, they would have had no problem calling it a murder. But since they couldn't, they would call it something else – wild animals, suicide, the will of God. It did not require a conspiracy for everyone to fall into line in a case like this, his experience told him; by instinct everyone involved knew exactly what was expected of him.

The day Whitford accompanied Ward to the Mara they discovered something odd: Simon Makallah had been placed on indefinite leave. Ward was disappointed and curious. He wanted to talk to the warden again. Even more, he wanted to know what the suspension was about. But no-one at Keekorok could tell him.

The visitors borrowed a car and driver from Tham and drove out of Keekorok followed by a carload of rangers. Julie's trail was steadily being worn away by nature while the police sat on their hands. The campfire looked like it had given up all of its secrets, but Ward wanted to take further samples of the soil and to familiarize Whitford with the scene.

As the father dug out the earth from under the fire the air filled again with what Whitford recognized as the sickening stench of burned flesh, a fetid reminder of the events of two months earlier. The investigator wrinkled his nose and turned away. Ward took more pictures, and then he led the convoy back toward the Suzuki site. At the gully there was no sign that a car had ever been there. Even the Suzuki's tire treads had been eroded and washed away.

Ward had been intrigued by *The Sunday Time*'s yarn about its marooned journalists and piqued by Wanjau's easy dismissal of the lead, as usual. At midday they drew up at Makari for Ward's second visit to the pathetic ring of tin-roofed huts not far from the gully. Like most of the ranger stations in the park the Makari post was a combined office and bivouac for the small team of rangers given responsibility for as much of the reserve they could patrol on foot and survey from the nearest rise. Four rangers were lolling around the circular enclosure when Ward and Whitford arrived.

Whitford began to question the men in Swahili. 'I'm looking for Peter Kippeen,' he said. There was a rustle, and one of them stepped forward to identify himself as Kippeen. Whitford showed him a photograph of Julie.

'Have you seen this woman?' he asked. He showed it around to the other young men.

The rangers grinned absently without answering. Ward looked over at the clump of policemen and wardens standing nearby. None of them stepped forward to help. He pulled out a copy of *The Sunday Times* piece, with Kippeen's name underscored and a photograph of the grinning ranger. 'Is this you? Do you remember this car?' Whitford asked. Again there was no answer. Without success Whitford continued with a number of routine questions, such as how many rangers were assigned to the post.

Meanwhile, Frank Ribeiro was doing a spot of reconnaissance of his own. Rooting around behind the ranger huts, he found a dusty, compact object that unrolled into a tube of Macleans toothpaste. It was a British brand, Ribeiro knew. He picked at it to see if there was any identifying mark. On the bottom crimp a serial number could be seen stamped on the soft metal. Ribeiro pocketed the tube.

When he walked back around to the clearing Ward had pulled aside James Sindiyo, the deputy warden, who had followed them in a park vehicle, to question him about the rangers' routine.

'What do they look for?'

'Poachers,' Sindiyo said. He directed Ward up a hill. 'From there they can see for miles around. They can also keep track of animal movements.' Ward saw enough to be sure he could spot Julie's gully from its crest. Not for the last time it occurred to him that if somebody wanted to hold a person prisoner for days in the Masai Mara, they could hardly find a better place than this one.

CHAPTER TWENTY-ONE

Ward long believed it was his furious upbraiding of
Wanjau that sent the police superintendent back into the
field in late October. One of the points he made in his
lecture, he remembered later, was that if a case like this
had arisen in the UK the police would have cordoned off
the area for a kilometer around and combed it painstakingly for evidence. As it happened, Wanjau returned
to Keekorok on 20 October with a team of ten constables
and a Masai officer. The next morning he loaded them all
into two Land Rovers and had them all driven out to the
fire site, which he called the 'main scene'.

Standing parade style shoulder to shoulder, they were
sent off to comb the ground for a radius of two kilometers.
After a fruitless day they trudged back to the Land Rovers
and drove back to base empty handed.

It was the same for most of the next morning. But at
around noon, Wanjau later recalled, almost a kilometer
due south of the fire, one of his men trod on a skull that
was missing a lower jaw.

Wanjau got up to the place instantly and examined the
find. There were sixteen teeth in the upper mandible,
some of them with fillings. The superintendent ordered an
intensified search of the area. They found even more
bones, including some that looked like parts of a spine and
five ribs. Wanjau had them all packed up and delivered to
the Mara Bridge station, with instructions to photograph
them and send them on to Dr Kaviti in Nairobi.

Ward heard of the discoveries on his next trip to Nairobi.
Kilonzo projected a more cooperative mood than Ward
had seen lately, even if it did not last. Laboratory tests

Ward commissioned in London had shown that gasoline had been used to fuel the fire under the sausage tree, and Kilonzo confided that the Kenya Police laboratory had come to the same determination. The commissioner said that accordingly a 'full effort' was under way to arrest the guilty parties.

For a moment Ward was encouraged. 'What progress have you made, then?'

Kilonzo became shifty again. 'Our investigations are continuing. We have no results to report . . . as yet.' It sounded like the old story.

'Does this mean an inquest will definitely be held here in Kenya?' Ward asked.

'It's possible,' the commissioner agreed. 'If the investigation ends without a result, the file will be forwarded to a magistrate.'

Kilonzo spread his hands. 'I wish to assure you, Mr Ward, that I am determined to get to the bottom of this affair. No stone will remain unturned. There will be no cover-up.'

Ward was unsatisfied. 'What about Dr Kaviti, then?'

'What about him?'

'Has he been charged?'

Kilonzo looked surprised. 'Charged with what?'

'What about attempting to pervert the course of justice? You can see as well as I that Dr Kaviti is a most unreliable pathologist. I am concerned to have my daughter's skull resting under his control.'

Kilonzo stirred uneasily. 'Whatever you think, Mr Ward, Dr Kaviti is the chief police pathologist.'

Ward had a collection of new evidence to give Wanjau, and he brought the items out one by one. One was the Macleans toothpaste tube. He handed it to the superintendent, explaining that he had already had the serial number investigated and determined it belonged to a consignment sent to Kenya for sale six years earlier. That meant it could not necessarily be traced to Julie, but Ward was under the impression that Africans in the bush brushed their teeth with sticks rather than toothbrushes and paste. For their

167

part, the Kenyans considered this suggestion insulting. ('The fact that rangers live and work in the bush hardly makes them wild game!' said an official report on the case later.) In any event Wanjau did not find much significance in the find. As soon as he had a chance he threw the object away.

Next was a stack of aerial photographs Ward had taken of the two sites on his way out of the Mara days earlier.

'You may be interested to know,' he paused, 'on the very first day I was at the Makari post, I noticed something that didn't mean much to me at the time. There was on the ground a little button battery – like the kind that goes in a camera. Since Julie's camera is missing, perhaps it's significant.' Wanjau and the other officers listened with polite expressions on their faces, silently. Ward let it pass.

'We welcome any help,' said one of Kilonzo's assistants.

One evening two police officers arrived at Ward's hotel room, one carrying an envelope and another a bulky plastic bag. The envelope contained a death certificate for his daughter; the other object was Julie's skull.

Ward called John Lee to pick up the skull and arrange its transport back to England, where Gresham would give it a going-over. Meanwhile, he scanned the certificate. Under 'Cause of death' it read: 'Blunt injuries, subsequent burning.'

That night he would recall as one filled with macabre reflections. The plastic bag with its horrible contents sat in the room like a grim shade. Not many fathers, he reflected, have to spend the night in a room with their daughter's skull in a dark corner.

The next day he went to Keekorok with Whitford and John Ferguson. As Ferguson had never been to the scene of the crime, Ward decided to trace Julie's route for a fourth time, now following as closely as possible the exact path he understood her to have taken: first to Sand River Camp, then backtracking up the road to the detour suggested by Makallah, and finally as far as the gully. It turned out to be a lucky decision.

Wanjau was at Keekorok with a police vehicle and James Sindiyo, and the two cars set off. For the first time in weeks Wanjau appeared to have developed some information of his own. It related to Julie's short stay at Sand River. The campsite policeman had seen his daughter arrive from Keekorok on 6 September, Wanjau told Ward, and had even helped her strike the two tents she and Burns had left there several days earlier. His name was Gerald Karuri.

Ward had not been back to Sand River since the day Makallah showed him Julie's campsite. As they pulled up to the gate Wanjau was explaining that the small building on the side of the gatehouse was where Karuri kept his office and home. The gatehouse was a stucco affair that spanned the road with an arch. Julie had passed through the arch, crossed over the bridge, and turned up a track to the campsite.

After she had taken down the tents, Wanjau said, she was stopped at the gate by the rangers.

'Why was that?'

'The tent had been in the camp for two extra days for which she had not paid. She was instructed to pay an additional two hundred shillings.'

Wanjau escorted the party into the gatehouse. It was a bare room with a couple of counters and shelves fashioned out of lumber. In a corner was a small two-way radio. On one shelf was a stack of logbooks and receipt pads.

Wanjau flipped open a register book. Along the top of each page were columns marked for the date, visitors' names, the registration numbers of their vehicles, the number of adults and children in each car. At the end of each line was a space to show how much the visitor paid, and a blank for his or her signature.

'The rangers fill in the amount paid,' Wanjau said. 'All the rest the visitors sign.'

In the dusty shadows of the room Ward turned the book to the entries for September and ran his finger down the page until he came to his daughter's name. He could not be sure in the unlit interior, but he had a feeling that the scribbled *Julie Ward* was not his daughter's handwriting.

Ward carried the volume outside, his eyes squinting against the sudden glare of sunlight.

'Who signed this book here?' Ward asked. Wanjau passed the question to the gate clerk, who answered nervously in Swahili.

'The lady signed it,' Wanjau said.

Ward was skeptical. He propped the book up against the wall, open to the page with her name on it, and snapped a picture. He could compare it to her signature on something at home.

From there they retraced the road part of the way back to Keekorok, turning off at Makallah's suggested point. It was a jarring ride across the rocky, rutted bush as the party tried generally to follow the lazy, muddy Sand River east. After a few miles they had wandered off course, doubled back, tried again, and after much trying finally found the gully.

On a tiny ridge they could still see vestiges of the fire someone had set by the jeep. As Ward took some soil samples from the darkened spot, Wanjau spoke up.

'We have found some cigarette papers nearby, which we think she might have used as toilet paper.'

For his pains he got an exasperated look from Ward. 'I hardly think so. After all, I found a roll of toilet paper in the jeep that day. You'll find it listed on the police inventory.'

'Perhaps you're right,' Wanjau said uncaringly. Evidently the *mzungu* did not want to hear his evidence. 'Maybe we found it elsewhere.'

The group left for another jolting ride across bush to the scene of the remains. There was not much to show Ferguson. Then they backtracked to the Makari post.

'We made a thorough search of the place,' Wanjau volunteered. 'There was nothing.' Two rangers watched the party move around the clearing, peering briefly into each hut with its rickety camp bed. One had a kerosene lamp, and Ward asked permission to take a fuel sample, hoping to compare it to the petrol that had fueled the fire under the sausage tree.

Ward thought again of the little button battery perched on a coin in this compound on the day they had found Julie. Someone had told him that was a way to recharge a dead battery, laying it on a coin in the sun. 'Do any of the rangers wear a watch?' he asked Sindiyo. 'Digital watch, perhaps?'

'No, they don't have a watch?'

'How do they tell the time, then?'

Sindiyo gestured at a transister radio on the ground. 'They listen to the radio.'

'There were four rangers the last time I was here. Where are the other two?'

Kippeen was on leave, Sindiyo said. He did not say what had happened to the other one.

Back at Keekorok Ward took gasoline samples from the fuel pumps at the lodge. Julie's Suzuki was still parked behind the lodge at Tham's house, and he drew a fuel sample from its gas tank.

Ward got back to London the next day, but it was his shortest stay: on unpacking his baggage he found that his camera and film were missing. Gone were the latest photographs he had taken of the Mara sites, and even more important, the pictures he had shot of the suspect Sand River logbook.

Pausing only long enough to deliver the latest soil and fuel samples to his London laboratory, he boarded a plane to Nairobi barely forty-eight hours later to take another set of photos.

The irksome theft of the camera only seemed to under-score the discouraging results of his efforts so far. Whitford had spent a lot of time in the Masai Mara trying to get the names of campers who had stayed at Sand River around the time Julie had pitched her tent. He had been in touch with tour operators he knew had driven clients through the same area. Some were able to give him just the first names of tourists they had signed up for day drives, but Whitford had taken the names back to Nairobi and begun comparing them with the full names of tourists who had checked into the leading Nairobi hotels in the same period. He had already tracked down a few tourists, although none who could shed light on Julie's last movements.

Whitford was also pursuing the possibility of finding an informant among the Masai who frequented the park. He asked an assistant named Gertrude Kibete to research Masai customs to determine how best to approach a reward and how the Masai might react to a murder in their midst.

Her first suggestion was to offer a reward not of cash, but of fifty head of cattle. 'They would think more of that than of money,' Kibete explained. The argument was not without a certain familiarity to an old Kenya policeman; a lot of the cattle rustling that annoyed white ranchers in the old days was laid to Masai herdsmen acting in accordance with the ancient tradition that the Masai owned all the world's cattle as a gift from God. But Ward preferred to deal in cash.

Kibete's other finding brought little comfort to her client: The Masai would be so spooked by a murder in their area that they would move quickly away, to some other land being tended by members of their clan. Whitford and Kibete thought it likely that any Masai who might have witnessed Julie's death or heard a violent commotion would have relocated to Tanzania, just a few kilometers away. No-one would ever learn any more about where the inhabitants of the manyatta had gone.

Wanjau was having no greater success at things. One day the police officer unburdened himself to the father with a rare confession of frustration. He had no leads, he said. He seemed to have reached a dead end.

Ward was still skeptical about Wanjau's resoluteness. 'What about this policeman at Sand River Camp who helped take down her tents?' he asked. 'It sounds like he might have been the last person to see Julie alive.'

'No, he has been transferred, and I cannot find where.' This inability of the police to delve through even their own departmental records was striking. How did investigations ever take place in this country? Ward sighed as Wanjau tried to give the impression he was carrying on. 'This file will never be closed,' Wanjau said.

The remark probably owed more to Wanjau's over-developed sense of drama than to any feeling of duty or resolve. Wanjau had all but withdrawn from the case. He would take a few more statements from time to time, but from this point on the police investigation effectively rumbled to a halt. More determined investigators than Wanjau would long ago have abandoned any quest to make the Mara give up its recondite secrets, and without will or a commitment to detail Wanjau faced an impossible task.

On his side, Ward's lack of confidence in Wanjau was being confirmed almost daily as he made his rounds of Nairobi, collecting statements. Almost no-one he talked to had been interviewed by Wanjau or any other policemen. One example was Perez Olindo, the wildlife chief, who described to Ward his day's aerial search of the Mara with Paul Weld Dixon – the very first search for Julie. Olindo might not have much to contribute, but he was an obvious starting point, and he had never been asked for a statement.

Olindo admitted this one day when Ward visited him to say he was preparing to post notices in the Mara offering a reward of 300,000 shillings – $15,000 – for information leading to the arrest and conviction of Julie's killer. The news disturbed the director. 'I hope you will be in touch with Commissioner Kilonzo before taking any action,' he said. Ward went ahead without the commissioner's approval.

CHAPTER TWENTY-TWO

In the first week of October the telephone rang in the Wiltshire office of Guerba Expeditions, the tour company employing Steve Watson, with a call from Harare, the capital of Zimbabwe. Martin Crabb, one of Guerba's principals, took the call to hear the voice of a journalist on the line.

David Barritt had been the man from the *Sunday Mirror* owned by Robert Maxwell who two weeks earlier had drawn Ward's complaint at his Nairobi press conference for waking him up at midnight. This time he told Crabb that he was working for *The Sunday Times* of South Africa. (The tabloid *Sunday Mirror*, he said later, had temporarily lost interest in Julie Ward.)

Over the telephone, Crabb remembered later, Barritt seemed a serious sort. He said he was doing a thorough study of the Julie Ward killing, aimed at actually solving the murder. And he was very interested in talking to Steve Watson.

Barritt had worked hard in Nairobi to unearth Watson's name. He had begun with a casual remark Ward dropped at the press conference that Julie had had a boyfriend in Kenya named Steve. From people at Paul Weld Dixon's compound, he recalled, he had determined that 'Steve' was an overland tour driver. Eventually he found that the only firm with a driver named Steve in Nairobi was Guerba, and that led to his call to Crabb.

For his part Crabb was struck by how much Barritt already seemed to know about Watson's tour schedule and whereabouts. For one thing, he knew that the young guide was at that moment conducting a group through Rwanda and Zaire to see the mountain gorilla parks.

Crabb thought fast. The last thing he wanted was to have this journalist interrupt Watson in the middle of a tour. This tour in particular: There was a BBC television crew along, and Crabb did not want the company's name associated with whatever Barritt was up to. Moreover, he knew Watson would be busy. As soon as he sent his current clients home another group would be flying in. In any event, as long as the British press was making a big thing about the Julie Ward case, Crabb thought he ought to warn Watson in advance. He asked Barritt to put his questions in writing and send them to England by telex.

Barritt agreed and rang off with an ominous word of advice. Crabb should be careful about letting Watson return to Kenya, he said. The police were interested in him. They might even consider him a suspect.

'I considered the whole idea of Steve Watson being a murder suspect quite ridiculous,' Crabb said later. He had heard enough of the story to know that Watson had a full tour of twenty clients with him in Kenya during the time of the girl's death. Julie had waved them all off from the Serena the day before she disappeared.

But before contacting Watson he called the British High Commission in Nairobi for advice on bringing the young tour guide back to Nairobi. The embassy was firm: Watson should certainly return to Kenya as planned – anything else would look suspicious.

On 12 October Crabb telexed Watson at the Meridien Hotel in Kigali, the capital of Rwanda, to fill him in on what was happening. *Ref. Julie Ward*, the message began, *This has been big news here. Newspapers still fishing*.

It was the first Watson knew that Julie's death had become a media event. In Kigali he read on. The telex described Barritt as a reporter for *The Sunday Times* of South Africa and mentioned his remark about the Kenyans' suspicions of Watson. But it advised him to return to Nairobi as scheduled.

Crabb later said that if he had known what Barritt was really up to he would never have let things get even this far. For soon after the call Barritt got the *Sunday Mirror* interested again in the story. The *Sunday Mirror* was one of Britain's less salubrious weeklies. Part of its stock in trade was sleaze and sex, written in the overheated, pun-riddled and clichéd style memorialized as 'tabloidese'.

At home in Johannesburg, Barritt was the editor of something called *People* magazine, a weekly that owed much more to the *National Enquirer* and other American supermarket tabloids than to the glossy US weekly of the same name. Salacious gossip about celebrities, UFO sightings – that was the weekly fare of *People*.

For his part Watson found the whole affair mystifying and the idea that he stay out of Kenya laughable. Like Crabb he figured his alibi for Julie's last days was ironclad. But he felt he did not have time to spare for Barritt. Watson had a busy week to spend in Nairobi. October was the height of the tour season, and he had to prepare for the next group coming in. Guerba sent a message to Barritt telling him Watson was unavailable, but it missed him in Johannesburg. He was already in Nairobi.

Almost immediately Barritt managed to track Watson down in a large downtown wasteland behind Nairobi's post office, where the lumbering overland tour trucks were permitted to park. The tour guide tried to shrug him off. But Barritt continued wheedling until Watson finally agreed to meet him at his hotel, the high-rise Nairobi Safari Club, the next morning.

In the rich atmosphere of the hotel Barritt exuded friendly solicitude. 'There'll be a lot of journalists coming here to Nairobi over this,' he warned Watson. 'They'll make a mess of it, for sure.'

Watson did not fully understand what Barritt was getting at. 'What kind of article are you writing, exactly?' he asked the reporter.

Barritt replied airily. 'It's an in-depth piece,' he said. 'Looking into every aspect. Your story is a very small part of the whole thing, of course.'

'Have you talked to John Ward?'

'Oh, we've already talked to him.' Then Barritt asked, 'Are you aware that the police have been looking for you?'

176

Barritt would say later that Watson showed 'no hesitation' about talking. 'He was quite anxious to talk to me,' he said. 'He was concerned people would think he was involved in the murder.'

In fact Watson knew he could prove his innocence, but he felt that Barritt's information might have had a nugget of logic. Some friends of Julie's knew him, and knew he had spent time with her. He was deeply conscious that he might have been the last European to have seen her alive. It did not seem to him completely ridiculous that the police might consider him a suspect.

But the only evidence he had of that came from the telex from Crabb – and that was based on what Barritt had said. Nevertheless, he replied, 'I know. But I have nothing to hide.'

By then it was late Saturday, too late to move a story for the next day's *Sunday Mirror*. But the newspaper was now fully on board. The editors smelled an exclusive brewing, and they instructed Barritt to keep Watson isolated from other reporters, if possible. For the next week Barritt hung on to Watson as if he were a rare gem.

The following Sunday Barritt's article dominated the front page of the *Mirror* under a screaming headline. The furor it caused would never disappear.

There was the story Watson had told, in his view inflated and twisted beyond recognition into a schoolboy's sexual fantasy. Both he and John Ward objected strongly to what they saw as a lurid story insulting the memory of Julie Ward. Stephen Watson began proceedings against Barritt in South Africa; Barritt stood by his story.

Friends of Julie felt that the *Sunday Mirror* article could not be right. Watson's description of her, with its graphic details, seemed so inappropriate when applied to Julie that it appeared to be about a completely different person. Equally, people who knew Watson would not expect the soft-spoken young man to talk this way about a woman. When Crabb saw the article clipped and lying on his desk, his first reaction was that someone had made a bad joke. 'Steve Watson was not what I would call a bragger,' he said later. 'He was not the type to stand up in a pub and talk about his exploits with women.' But that was how Barritt's piece appeared to him.

Still, it did catch the imagination of some people. From that time on the Kenya Police seemed to assume the victim in the Mara was a woman of loose morals. They questioned Watson and cleared him, and Glen Burns too. But months later, Inspector Wanjau harbored an impression of Julie Ward he seemed to have gleaned almost entirely from the *Sunday Mirror*. 'She was a woman,' he said, 'who would go with any man.'

In truth, John Ward had assumed that his daughter and Watson had had an affair in the Mara. That did not disturb him. But the *Sunday Mirror* article did, and Ward furiously resolved to have Watson explain himself. On his next visit to Kenya, he made a side trip to Tanzania and tracked down Watson's touring party.

Watson was appalled to read what Barritt had made of their interview. He could remember making some of the quotes on the page, but even those seemed turned on end. There were places where he felt that Barritt had confused the answer to one question with some entirely different question. The salacious remarks about Julie and sex – Watson flatly denied he had said anything of the kind. Of the twenty-nine quotes attributed to him in the article, Watson stated that he could only remember making nine.

'I'm going to take action against this man,' Ward told him.

Ward would later bring a complaint against the *Sunday Mirror* before Britain's Press Council, a body that rules on infractions of truth and decency. He later dropped the complaint because he would have had to abjure any further legal action. Instead, he planned to finance a libel suit by Watson against the newspaper.

From that time on Barritt said he was 'astonished when I heard Steve was saying he hadn't said those things.' He would add, 'I stand by every word of that story.'

And from that time on John Ward would speak to no

reporter without first asking whether they were from what he chose to term the 'Maxwell press'. The controversy produced strong and irreconcilable feelings that affected the early part of the investigation.

In Wiltshire, Crabb wrote Barritt a telex of his own. 'If I had known you wrote for the *Sunday Mirror* I would never have entered into discussions with you,' he wrote. 'Perhaps one day you should consider the effect of what you are writing.'

Christmas at the Ward house that year promised to be a dismal occasion. Every previous yuletide had been Julie's affair. She was the one who decorated the house and arranged the tree, always managing to come up with the most delightful presents for everyone. The thought of the house without her spirit about was too awful to contemplate. Ward decided to take the whole family off on vacation to the Caribbean. It would be the first break any of them had had from the misery of the last few months. Ward figured it would be good medicine. He had immersed himself in the investigation, perhaps as a way to distance himself from the very great loss of his only daughter. But the rest of the famiy had no such outlet. Janet still felt the tragedy deeply, as if she had lost her oldest and dearest friend, which exactly described Julie. John Ward kept the press away from his wife and sons until the very end, when Janet felt strong enough to visit Kenya herself and see the place where her daughter had enjoyed her last months. Not long before that she also issued a statement to the press, the only public remark she ever made about Julie. 'Most of her leisure time was spent with me, her mum,' she said. 'She was my best friend and companion, and I miss her dreadfully.'

As the new year opened Wanjau stirred himself to take a handful of statements in the case. One was from Watson, who on Martin Crabb's suggestion presented himself at CID headquarters in Nairobi.

For Watson the episode was an introduction to an odd

aspect of Kenyan police procedure: the taking of statements. In dealing with Europeans, if not Africans, the police observed all the courtesies, but what remained was a bizarre mixture of interrogation and suggestion that often exposed the questioner's thought processes more than it shed light on a crime. Investigators who would read Wanjau's sheaf of collected statements later would throw up their hands in frustration at the way opinion and impertinence permeated the documents in a disorderly mix. Non sequiturs shouldered promising clues right off the page. Irrelevancies were explored in painstaking detail and significant leads ignored.

Wanjau also showed some trouble with the English language. Watson recalled later that he had to keep correcting elementary mistakes as Wanjau questioned him.

Watson opened his statement by identifying himself as a British subject working for Guerba Expeditions. 'Our expeditions cover the whole of the African continent,' he began.

'Do you go to South Africa?' Wanjau interjected pointlessly.

'No, we don't go there . . . or where there are wars.'

Watson continued on, describing the route his tour group had taken to reach the Masai Mara on 3 September. He told Wanjau about finding the stranded jeep and towing it to the Serena. He acknowledged he had shared Julie's room but not her bed, and recalled what she had said about meeting him in Naivasha. Finally he described his role in the search.

At the end Wanjau asked him about the *Sunday Mirror* article.

'I was very surprised and annoyed by what they put down in their paper,' Watson said. 'Most of what they put down wasn't said by me.'

Wanjau nodded and appended the remark to the end of Watson's statement. But he did not believe him.

Late in January another meeting convened in Kilonzo's

office. In front of Ward, Ferguson, and Ribeiro, Kilonzo asked Wanjau to bring everybody up to date. There was not much to report. Wanjau seemed to have made no inroads in the case since his informal meeting with Ward the previous November, when he had confessed his frustration and indicated he was pursuing a new lead.

'The superintendent is one of my most experienced officers,' Kilonzo volunteered.

Ward broke in. 'One thing I'm very interested in is what happened around the time my daughter is supposed to have left the Sand River Camp,' he said. Then he explained that handwriting experts he had hired in the UK had concluded that Julie's signature in the camp registry book was a forgery. Ward was becoming convinced that Julie had not left Sand River under her own steam at all – that she might have been abducted from that very spot.

Ward turned to Wanjau. 'You have samples of her handwriting,' he said. 'Haven't you taken the elementary step of checking them against the writing in the book?'

Wanjau replied that he had never seen samples of Julie's handwriting.

'All right.' Ward laid out on the table copies of Julie's letters he had brought with him. Next to them he placed a photograph of the Sand River log.

The policemen all nodded in agreement. The logbook looked to be a forgery.

'Can you get us more samples of the handwriting?' Kilonzo asked. 'This certainly looks like a breakthrough.' The other policemen nodded eagerly in assent. 'A breakthrough.'

For a time Wanjau made as much as he could out of the suspicious forgery. He returned to the Mara to confront the revenue clerk, David Nchoko. One day he informed Nchoko that he was a suspect in a murder inquiry and threatened to haul him off to jail. At that the clerk came clean. The girl had forgotten to sign the book herself, he said. After she left he wrote her name in himself, to make sure the auditors did not find any blanks. But it was an innocent act.

Ward was convinced that the suspicious doings at Sand River Gate disguised a genuine clue to his daughter's disappearance, especially given that she was never seen alive after that point. When Wanjau recounted the clerk's revised story, Ward's eyes narrowed.

'Do you believe him?' he asked Wanjau.

The officer gave an unconcerned shrug. 'That's what he says,' he replied.

CHAPTER TWENTY-THREE

By the beginning of 1989 John Ward had spent close to one hundred thousand pounds sterling on trips to Kenya and all over Europe, and all he had managed to prove was that the police themselves had done a hell of a bad job. Ward's investigation still left gaping holes in the fabric of Julie's last mysterious weeks. All that his interviews and forensic tests established – to his own satisfaction, if not the police's – was that a murder had been committed, but not how, why, or by whom.

He had to admit, moreover, that much of his activity came under the category of spinning wheels. It was a boring slog, this effort to track witnesses without a bit of help from the authorities. Tracing the other Sand River campers was a case in point. Ward had photographed the pages of the visitors book covering the days of Julie's stay. There were about one hundred other names to pursue, only a handful of which had addresses in Kenya or elsewhere.

The problem was that most of the more than one hundred campers had been members of four tour groups going in and out of Sand River Camp around that time. Often the tourists were all simply logged in under the group leader's name.

One person he managed to contact was a camper who had not seen Julie, but remembered a tour vehicle marked with the name Best Camping Safaris. Bob Whitford tracked down the firm and cadged from their agents a list of the first names of their clients on that Mara tour. Reasoning correctly that most foreign tourists in Kenya spent at least one or two nights in Nairobi before heading to the game parks, he stopped at all the tourist hotels in Nairobi and tried to match the first names with their guests from the same period. Surprisingly, Whitford was able to complete a short list of British tourists this way, which he sent up to Ward in Bury St Edmunds.

Everything Whitford came up with sparked a frisson of excitement. Ward and his two sons set about calling all the names on the list. But no-one they found had seen her leave Sand River. There seemed no way to establish that she had left the camp at 2.37 p.m., as Nchoko's logbook indicated, and no way to establish that she had not.

That was the unchanging pattern of their inquiries. One French doctor Ward reached thought he had a photograph showing Julie's tent in the background. Ward flew to France to take a look. But it was not her tent.

It was ninety-nine per cent frustration, but he was intent on checking every detail. Who knew where the key clue might be found?

Ward had made nearly a dozen trips to the Mara, but for every tiny clue unearthed there were a dozen red herrings like the toothpaste tube, or a score of silent rangers. One day Ward and Whitford brought down to the gully a twenty-five-pound magnet suspended on a string. For hours they dredged it through the stagnant ponds around the site, fishing for Julie's keys or any metal object that might have given them a nugget of information. Nothing.

Continually frustrated, Ward was beginning to test whether direct political influence might cause the Kenya government to budge. He was meeting with officials of the British foreign office to solicit their help, and one day in January he tried someone with even better connections in Nairobi: He called Roland 'Tiny' Rowland, the chairman of a huge company called Lonrho.

Tiny Rowland was a man who could understand the impelling force of a personal campaign, for over the previous few years he had been engaged in one himself. His vendetta dated from a failed attempt to take over Harrods department store, perhaps the premier retailing name in the world. In 1985 the prize was snatched from his grasp by a mysteriously financed family of Egyptian brothers, the Al-Fayeds.

Dr. Adel Youssef Shaker, whose initial autopsy report on
Julie Ward was clumsily rewritten. Was he a 'man without a
backbone,' as Byron Georgiadis remarked at the inquest? His elation
at discovering the key evidence of murder evaporated once it became
clear that he would have to publicly contradict his own boss.
AP/WIDE WORLD PHOTOS

Chief pathologist of the Kenya Police, Dr. Jason Kaviti found himself in a tense confrontation with John Ward after his role in changing the autopsy record was exposed. But the Ward case was not the first time his findings had muddied the waters of an important police case.
AP/WIDE WORLD PHOTOS

Simon ole Makallah, chief warden of the Masai Mara Game Reserve, gave evidence at the inquest. His performance on the stand was roundly attacked by Mr Ward's lawyer, Byron Georgiadis.

Kenyan Police Commissioner Philip Kilonzo may have been ill-served by the inept subordinates he assigned to investigate Julie's death. He resisted John Ward's increasingly desperate badgering by consistently refusing to acknowledge that the incident should be treated as a murder case. AP/WIDE WORLD PHOTOS

John Ward (*left*) and Byron Georgiadis (*right*) with Paul Weld Dixon (*center*) became a familiar pair around the Law Courts building in Nairobi. The veteran Kenyan barrister used his long experience to reinforce his client's conviction that the government was engaged in an active cover-up of Julie's death. AP/WIDE WORLD PHOTOS

Ward and Georgiadis conferred daily during the inquest, to which Ward himself was not admitted until after he gave his own testimony late in the proceedings. AP/WIDE WORLD PHOTOS

Eccentric and blunt but devoted to Julie, Paul Weld Dixon (*right,* with John Ward) first raised the alarm about his former tenant's disappearance in the Masai Mara. Later he was present the first time the word *'murder'* was mentioned in connection with her death.
AP/WIDE WORLD PHOTOS

Ward spent hours with witnesses like Weld Dixon, who, like many others involved in the case, became a close friend and the father's source of insights into the Kenyan character.
AP/WIDE WORLD PHOTOS

Magistrate Joseph Mango, promoted soon after the inquest to a judgeship on the Kenya supreme court. He treated many of the government's witnesses with skepticism. In issuing a verdict of murder he praised the police for their investigation but rejected all of their conclusions. AP/WIDE WORLD PHOTOS

A happy Julie Ward with her camera, in a photograph taken during the overland tour with Ho-Bo. Leaving the stifling atmosphere of a full-time job in England, she dreamed of settling in Kenya and photographing wildlife. Was it overconfidence or sheer misfortune that led to her death? AP/WIDE WORLD PHOTOS

Since then Rowland had pursued the Al-Fayeds like a lion deprived of a kill, trying to prove that they had lied to the British government about the source of their financing. Rowland was convinced their money came from secretive millionaires like the Sultan of Brunei and arms dealer Adnan Khashoggi. Lonrho published exposés about the Fayeds, including one about the eldest brother called 'The Hero from Zero'. At one point Rowland got a leaked copy of a British government report largely corroborating his suspicions. He published it in the esteemed Sunday paper owned by Lonrho, the *Observer* – in a special Thursday edition. It was all in vain; eventually the Thatcher government decided to let the Al-Fayeds keep Harrods, even though it conceded the family had lied about their background.

Lonrho was enormously influential in Africa in general and Kenya in particular. The company's Kenyan holdings included industrial works, hotels, distribution companies, and the *Standard* newspaper, one of the three English-language dailies in the country. Lonrho maintained its influence and enviable ease of maneuver in Kenya through what appeared to be a cunning, if obvious, device. It appointed Mark Too, a leading official of KANU, the ruling party, as its local chairman. Too was a man whose striking physical resemblance to President Moi himself was said to derive from very close ties of blood. This was an old stunt, in fact; during the presidency of Jomo Kenyatta the same position in Lonrho had been held by Kenyatta's son-in-law.

Rowland returned Ward's call on 30 January. The desperate father outlined the story of Julie's death and the runaround he had subsequently received at the hands of Kenya's bureaucrats. He knew Tiny Rowland slightly as a fellow hotelier, and even remarked to the industrialist that Julie had been a Lonrho shareholder; that dated from many years earlier, when Ward had given each of his children five thousand pounds to invest and she had put some of her stake into Lonrho shares.

Rowland sounded reassuring on the phone. Why, he

was about to have a meeting with President Moi himself, he told Ward. 'Leave it to me,' Ward remembered him saying. He seemed full of confidence he could help Ward break the case.

John Ward never heard back from Tiny Rowland. He called Lonrho several times, finally getting the impression the chairman did not want to talk about it. Much later Ward managed to corner Rowland at a hotel-industry function in England. Better to let it all drop, Rowland seemed to be suggesting.

That was obviously what the Kenya government hoped would happen. But Ward pressed on through another month of dead ends. Then one day he remembered the Swiss photographers.

It was amazing how some things entirely slipped one's mind. The Swiss camp had been mentioned several times by people on the periphery of the case. Wanjau had even remarked that Peter Kippeen, the mysterious ranger who helped the *Sunday Times* people, had been posted to Makari just to keep an eye on the Swiss. Now Ward remembered how he had noticed the Swiss team's Land-Rovers at Keekorok Lodge on 14 September, the night he spent grieving after his terrible discovery in the bush. He got in touch with some friends in Switzerland and asked them to help trace a group of documentary photographers who might have been at Keekorok in the middle of September, 1988. Eventually they got back to him. They had tracked down a documentary filmmaker who lived near Geneva, in Montreux, by the name of Henri Berney.

CHAPTER TWENTY-FOUR

Henri Berney had to be one of the best equipped campers ever to come through the gates of the Masai Mara. He and his team of twelve photographers arrived for a four-week stay at the very end of August 1988, as laden with goods and equipment as a Sahara caravan. In addition to such customary camping gear as tents, stoves, and provisions, they had enough machinery to erect and service a veritable lodge in the bush. There were seven tents and four four-wheel-drive vehicles. There was radio and stereo equipment and a refrigerator stocked with provisions. A 3,000-watt dynamo powered all these things as well as the floodlights to be installed around the bivouac's perimeter.

Berney had also brought along one device that had probably never been seen before inside the park's boundaries. Known by the trade name of Navstar, it was a navigating receiver that could pinpoint the camp's location to within one hundred meters by picking up signals from satellites orbiting the Earth 23,000 feet above the savannah.

Berney and his team fell into the category of visitors with special needs, and so they found themselves dealing directly with Simon Makallah, the chief warden. They were in the country to prepare a series of wildlife documentaries for Swiss television, a task that called for a campsite remote from the most-traveled routes inside the reserve. Makallah was an exceptionally agreeable man. He nodded knowingly: it was a demand he had heard before – a fair source of a little extra money in under-the-table fees from time to time. Cadging extra money from tourists was against the Masai Mara rules, but Makallah was the chief, after all.

The Swiss photographer found much to praise about the guide who promised to find him a suitable spot in the rugged southern quadrant of the park. He liked his polite demeanor and his manifest familiarity with even the remotest corner of the vast savannah.

The Swiss spent only a night at Keekorok Lodge before Makallah led them to the campsite he had selected for their month-long stay. It was ideal, a heavily treed spread near the V formed by a creek and its tributary in the rocky undulating country east of the Keekorok–Sand River road. Nearby was a gentle rise. The hillock was a good feature. It gave Berney's crew a vantage point from which to scan the ground for a couple of miles around. Not long after their arrival the team discovered a den of hyena near the hill, and one member of the crew or another would climb to its summit every morning to watch them.

Over the next month the activity of the sprawling camp made it a beacon in the south-east quadrant of the Masai Mara. The Swiss photographers worked hard, maintaining a constant shuffle, day and night, of the four vehicles into and out of the camp. Music played and the radio telephones with which each car kept in touch with the camp crackled constantly. At night the lamps were lit and a fire blazed until dawn.

Yet the Berney team was not so isolated that its members failed to hear about the disappearance of an English tourist somewhere in the park; Berney thought later that one of his crew must have picked up the story while passing through Keekorok Lodge. The photographer's first reaction was to help. He had four sturdy vehicles at his disposal, after all, and he approached the rangers at the Keekorok station to place the cars at the authorities' disposal.

That was when he got his first hint that something about the affair was odd. Berney and his wife, Monique, later searched for a way to describe the sinister atmosphere they detected among the rangers at Keekorok, and it was Monique who found the apposite phrase.

'It was like a Mafia code of silence,' she recalled. No-one wanted to talk, and no-one seemed to welcome Berney's natural curiosity either. 'They told us to mind our own business,' he would later tell John Ward.

The mystery only deepened when Monique ran into Simon Makallah just before the Swiss were due to leave the reserve. A dark shadow seemed to have fallen over the polite, accommodating Makallah of a month earlier, she thought. The warden confided something to the Swiss woman: After the remains were discovered, he had received a summons to Nairobi. Monique thought she understood him to say he had been called up to see the President himself. She felt Makallah was deeply fearful of something having to do with this extraordinary summons. It was as if he were not sure he would ever come back.

In April 1989 Ward finally reached Berney by telephone at his office in Montreux. Berney sympathized, but he was too busy to give Ward much of his time. Eventually, however, he sandwiched the hotelier in between trips out of the country, and on 19 April Ward was on an airliner coming in low over the manicured farms of Switzerland and stepping on to the tarmac into the bracing air of a Geneva spring, with an interpreter at his side.

In his studio Berney took the measure of the stocky, weary-looking hotel-owner from England as Ward recapitulated the story of his discouraging quest to force the police to investigate Julie's death. Berney could not suppress a rush of admiration for this man: perhaps something about his intent, methodical campaign appealed to the Swiss psyche. Much later Berney would stress in his recollection of the meeting the cool – nay, 'cold' – approach Ward had taken to pursuing justice for his daughter.

Ward had nearly eight months behind him of nearly constant prosecution of this end, and like anyone confined in the same environment for so long it had lost its capacity to shock, or even to elicit any emotion. Like a surgeon inured to gore, he had locked away the horror of what must have happened to Julie in her last days into some dark room that he never opened in public, only perhaps in his most secret, private moments.

Ward's sheer determination was a quality the Swiss also recollected vividly. 'Anyone else would have just forgotten it,' he said later. 'But not Mr Ward.'

The father had brought to Switzerland a sheaf of maps and a pile of aerial photographs of the site where Julie's Suzuki had been found. 'I've come to ask whether you might know of anything that might help,' he said. Berney hauled out his own maps to compare with the father's.

Ward's finger traced Julie's path, starting at Sand River Camp, up the meandering thread of blue that marked the Sand River. When it paused at a marked X, seemingly far from any established trail, Berney's attention was seized.

'I know that river,' he said. 'That is the same one we were on.'

'This is the place where we found her jeep on September thirteenth,' Ward said. 'We figure it must have got there on the sixth of September.'

Berney interrupted him with an outburst: 'That is totally impossible!'

Ward stopped as Berney showed him his Navstar location.

'Here,' the photographer indicated, 'latitude one degree thirty-seven minutes, seventy-three seconds south . . .' He traced a horizontal line on the map. 'Longitude thirty-five degrees, fifteen minutes, twenty-five seconds.' The vertical line met the other at a spot that looked to be little more than a third of a kilometer from Julie's jeep – three or four hundred yards. Berney's camp must have been just on the far side of a hillock from this X on the map. Here was the rise, Berney said, that his team strode up every morning to scan for game. If Ward was right about the location of Julie's jeep, it could not possibly have been overlooked by his crew for six days; it would have been sitting in a trench almost at their toenails. And with SOS scrawled on its roof in mud?

'Impossible!' Berney repeated. 'Living in this area without anybody around, we would certainly have seen this jeep. We were looking for animals. We spent every minute meticulously combing the area. Every tree, every bush – anything to find an animal, a reptile, a bird.'

He looked at the map again. 'This hill,' he said. 'From this observation point we looked over the whole area with powerful binoculars. So how could it be that we would not see this jeep? Do you think we would take it for a rock? Mr Ward, we are expert observers. I do not think that jeep could have been there for more than one night. Impossible!'

In eight months, Ward probably had never heard anyone utter a word with such finality. The Swiss photographer's reaction was like a searchlight in the darkness.

In the months to come there would be testimony that Berney's camp was three, even four kilometers from the jeep, or that his spotters missed seeing it in their single-minded search for wildlife, but Berney was resolute. His camp was 400 meters from the gully at most, he insisted. A spotter overlook a vehicle? Absurd. They were trained to look for vehicles, he said: Where the cars stopped, there was likely to be game showing itself to the tourists.

And suppose, implausibly, they had missed the jeep. So what? With the dynamo roaring all day and night, music playing, the radio crackling, twelve friends and workmates joking, singing, laughing, shouting – how could Julie have missed *them*?

There was only one hitch. Berney was reluctant to commit himself to deliver his testimony in person in Nairobi, given the press of business and the unpredictability of an African timetable. But the photographer did agree to provide Ward with a full written statement of his position. If that were not enough and only if it were absolutely necessary, he finally conceded, he would try to make time to testify in person.

With Berney's resolute 'Impossible!' ringing in his ears, Ward found that a number of jigsaw pieces instantly fell into place. If Julie's jeep had not been in the gully for the whole period of her disappearance, then the police needed a new theory. The idea of her setting off stupidly across unmapped countryside could not stick. Nor could the slander that she would have been heedless enough to leave the jeep alone, or that she had headed off in manifestly the wrong direction, or had ignored the vantage point offered by the hill. Given Berney's evidence, only one theory was possible: She had not been in the jeep when it got stuck in the mud.

Ward had reason to be elated and disquieted at the same time. The attempt to denigrate his daughter's intelligence had to fail. That was a victory. But if Julie had disappeared on 6 September and been killed on the 12th or 13th, where had she been in the meantime?

However ghastly the implications, from that point on Ward never relinquished the new theory. It would be the touchstone and pivot of his case against the government at the inquest.

Berney's evidence solved many unanswered questions. What was her jeep doing out there? Why did she leave instead of waiting? Why was there no note? Why didn't she just follow her tracks back to the main road?

It was not like just getting one piece of the jigsaw puzzle, Ward reflected. It was getting half a dozen pieces all at one go.

The case coalesced around this one critical nugget like a pearl around a grain of sand: Julie must have been abducted sometime around the 6th, days before her kidnappers drove the Suzuki into the gully, perhaps even as the search planes and helicopters were buzzing overhead. Berney's evidence created many other mysteries, such as why someone wishing to cache a stolen jeep that was evidence of murder would draw attention to it with a scrawled SOS, but they did not seem so important in the excitement of solving the principal mystery.

What was even more important, Berney's evidence had appeared at an ideal moment. Pressured by John Ward,

192

the international press, and the British High Commission, the Kenya government was just about to announce that it would hold an inquest into the death in the Masai Mara of Julie Ward.

Part Two

'Is She Haunting You?'

CHAPTER TWENTY-FIVE

There would be talk later that John Ward had approached several barristers in Nairobi about representing him at the inquest before he finally found one courageous enough to agree to challenge the government. The lawyer he finally chose hinted himself that the case had scared off some of his colleagues at the bar: 'I had no hesitation,' he once said, 'although I was aware that some other people were looking over their shoulders.'

It may have been so, but to most well-informed people in the European community of Nairobi, Byron Nicholas Georgiadis was the indispensable man. There was little question that Georgiadis was the region's best barrister by such a wide margin that there was scarcely anyone in second place.

He was sixty-two when the inquest began, a silvery-haired icon of the Nairobi bar. There were many other lawyers known for their aggressiveness on behalf of a client, their courtroom skill, and their long history in the country, but there was none who had Georgiadis's combination of polished Oxford tones and his fearless approach to Kenyan judges and witnesses, and especially his record in extricating people from hopeless legal entanglements.

Georgiadis had been born in what was then Tanganyika to a family of Cypriot tobacco growers in the time between the wars, long after Germany had been forced to relinquish its lone African colony to Britain. Characteristically, the English had wanted the vast territory not out of any lust for its natural riches but out of suspicion over Germany's designs on Uganda. This concern was not entirely ill-placed, for the Germans had, after all, tried to run a railway from the Tanganyikan coast to Lake Victoria at exactly the time that parliament was debating the Lunatic Express. Still, Bismarckian Germany would just as likely have ignored Africa except for a German adventurer named Carl Peters, who spent years trying to present Berlin with the fait accompli of a territorial claim in Africa. In the end Germany's brief empire on the East Coast was the product of an even deeper absentmindedness than Britain's, and in any event it was relinquished for good when the final pages of the First World War were written at Versailles in 1919, ceding the land to the English.

In his youth Byron Georgiadis had been packed off to Oxford to read law, following the tradition among wealthy European settlers of educating their sons overseas. Before his studies were finished, the family had decided to sell their holdings to British American Tobacco Co.; they were the first family to do so, and with his father's health failing Byron was summoned back to Tanganyika to represent the family in the transfer of the farm to its new owners.

That task accomplished, Georgiadis had supervised his way out of a job. A legal career was the obvious next step, and the young Oxford transplant pursued it with a great deal of energy.

By the time of his introductory meeting with John Ward, Georgiadis was white haired and stocky and locally famous. He had defended many of the first Europeans to be charged with crimes in the courts of the fledgling black governments of Africa after independence, but he was not exclusively a lawyer for whites. Not a few prominent Africans relied on his skills as well. In Kenya, where a politician's disgrace often hinged on the outcome of a trumped-up trial, Georgiadis was available for the defense; to a certain extent he regarded that as his political insurance. 'I often think that's why they keep me around,' he said.

In court his demeanor was proper, but he could explode in rage to terrify a recalcitrant witness. Short of fireworks he needed only to fix an overmatched African with his skeptical cold blue eyes and the witness would collapse; he could puncture holes in a prosecution case simply with the practiced body language of contempt. Bob Whitford, reflecting on the Peter Poole case on which he had cut his own teeth in Africa, thought the condemned man had made the wrong choice of counsel. 'If he had Georgiadis, he probably would have got off for insanity,' he said.

It was not an arbitrary judgment; something of the sort had happened not long before when Georgiadis defended one of the better known single women in Nairobi. She had fired a gun point blank at a shameless and promiscuous lover from the front stoop of her home, but Georgiadis got her off. Her plea was that the man had demonstrated his sleazy and contemptible nature by launching an incestuous affair with his own daughter. So he deserved it.

Charmingly accessible as he talked about his client's daughter, this victimized 'gel', Georgiadis was the darling of the reporters flooding Kenya to cover the inquest. His Oxford-educated voice had the rounded tones of an Alec Guinness. The British press liked to compare him to Rumpole of the Bailey, John Mortimer's fictional barrister, with whom Georgiadis obligingly expressed an affinity.

But there was nothing of the disheveled and uxorious Rumpole in Georgiadis's immaculate clothes and precision of speech. Discovered at home amid his fishing trophies and dogs, he would equally haul out his scrapbooks of clippings, reliving his prosecution of Mau Mau insurgents and his defense of Sullivan, the thick-witted scapegoat of Hola. He might put the dogs through their paces in the hooped and gated obstacle course he had built for them in the yard of his Langata home. Or he might invite an interviewer along for a round of golf, graciously abjuring the motorized cart he kept because of his arthritis, instead struggling over the links on foot with his guest.

WILY LAWYER PROUD TO BE A THORN IN SIDE OF AUTHORITY, the *Daily Telegraph* headlined one feature about the distinguished barrister. His increasing disgust with the manipulation of law and precedent in Kenyan courtrooms rose unmistakably from quotes like this: 'I have always been a thorn in the side of whoever is running this country and I am proud of it. You have to pursue the line of legal right and let the chips fall where they may.'

None of the stories revealed the thing that would enliven Georgiadis's uncompromising behavior during the Julie Ward inquest. Almost immediately after the proceeding was finished, he would announce his retirement to Cyprus, giving a farewell speech to his partners so pointed and detailed in its disdain for what Kenyan justice had become that an immediate legend sprang up in Nairobi to the effect that one lawyer in the audience decided on the spot to leave the country as well. Like an old thoroughbred winning one final race just before going out to pasture, Byron Georgiadis was going to make the Ward inquest his last hurrah.

Armed with Berney's evidence Georgiadis could not only place before a court a complete and consistent scenario for Julie's demise, but punch gaping holes in the government story. He had polished it to a sharp edge.

'The rangers' official version,' he would tell listeners, 'is that she arrived at Sand River at 2 p.m., packed her tents, and left through the gate at 2.37.

'They say she left the Keekorok road for some reason and went off across country, downhill, in trackless waste, and got stuck in the mud.

'But – she's rushing to Nairobi. Why, in a problem car, take off across country?

'Then they say that, like a congenital idiot, she leaves a locked car with provisions, and in flip-flops meanders across the country to ten kilometers away, where she's eaten by carnivores. In the car are a good pair of sneakers, two maps of the Mara. Twenty litres of petrol she had just bought was missing, as was her camera.

'So would she carry petrol away from the car? And go in the wrong direction? Why not backtrack? Her alleged track' – he stressed *alleged* – 'crosses a major road. Why not stop on the road and flag down a car?'

He would wave his arm in contemptuous dismissal. 'Her

father immediately perceived that this was a cock-and-bull yarn.'

The family had a better theory.

'We think she came back to Sand River from the Serena to stay the night and to go to Nairobi in the morning. Someone in authority saw or spoke to her. She says, "I've come to stay overnight," and so on.

'We think he said, "Go up river and see some game, I'll show you a good drive. Follow my vehicle."

'We think she was prevailed upon to go toward the Makari post, and her guide imposed his unwanted attentions. And she spent the next four or five days a prisoner, if you like, in that area.

'When the perpetrator heard about the search and fuss, he panicked and killed her, dismembered her, then, using his own vehicle, distributed the remains near where tourists don't go, where animals might carry the body away. He cut off the toes and fingers and dismembered the lower jaw. He might not have known about dental charts being used for identification.

'Then he drove her car into the mud. He may have got stuck himself.

'But he wouldn't have done all this at night himself, hoofing it across the Mara. So he was followed by an accomplice.'

Who did it? 'You have to look at the facts and work backwards,' Georgiadis would say. The murderer had to be someone who knew the park, he would say, someone who could find his way to and around its most remote corners. Someone with free movement around the park, so he could be confident he would not be stopped by the authorities. And someone who had authority over underlings, so he could order clerks to forge logbooks and drivers to ignore the vehicle logs.

In all the 750 square miles of the Masai Mara, Georgiadis figured, there could be only one person who fitted this description: Simon Makallah.

CHAPTER TWENTY-SIX

More than just opportunity and means made Simon Makallah an inviting suspect. His elevated position in the Masai Mara also seemed to justify what Ward and Georgiadis viewed as the government's conspiratorial cover-up.

Ward had been increasingly mystified by the extent to which Kenyan officials seemed to have gone to obscure the circumstances of Julie's death. Georgiadis reinforced his suspicions, particularly as the scale of Wanjau's noninvestigation became clear.

'This deliberate refusal to investigate,' he scoffed, reviewing the case later. 'It's risking more than his career is worth unless there is some official sanction.' Wanjau was Kilonzo's hand-picked man, the barrister pointed out: 'The investigation could not be that bad without some official acquiescence behind it.'

Then who or what was the government protecting? Speculating about the hidden beneficiary of the cover-up became something of a parlor game in Nairobi as the inquest began. One school of thought was that not even Makallah was prominent enough for the whole machinery of Kenyan bureaucracy to be mobilized on his behalf: A Masai game warden could easily have been sacrificed to assuage the foreign press, if it came to that. Rumors circulated about highly-placed officials having a hand in the rape and murder of a tourist in the Mara. One rumored suspect was a politician's son who had a supposed yen for white woman and – propinquity being an important element in the story – a farm outside the boundary of the Mara. A government cover-up to protect a political family – there was a story that made sense. (Nothing ever came of this theory.)

Georgiadis resisted the impulse to look for a highly placed beneficiary of a cover-up. He thought the whole affair could be explained by the government's need to protect not a single person, but an all-important export: tourism.

In truth, Kenya had been identified with tourism for most of its existence as a separate entity. And as inviting as its Indian Ocean beaches were for wintertime vacationers from Italy and Germany, there was no doubting that its wildlife and game parks were its premier attractions.

Tourism had its origins in the hunting safaris of old, when European royalty and the American industrial élite were the clientele of a small but growing cadre of professional guides. Theodore Roosevelt had burnished his reputation as a man of action with a published report of his hunting safari in 1909. The Prince of Wales was said to have learned of his troublesome succession to the throne as Edward VIII while on a hunting trip to Kenya in 1936; in 1952 his granddaughter Princess Elizabeth was game viewing at Treetops Lodge in the Aberdares with her husband, Prince Philip, when they learned of the death of her father, King George VI. Industrialists and socialites alike had made the bagging of the Big Five – lion, rhinoceros, buffalo, leopard, and elephant – part of the mystique of the grand life. ('Ah yes, Aly Khan,' remembered Bunny Allen, a hunter who had run a safari for the playboy husband of Rita Hayworth. 'He failed to get a leopard.')

Hunting was inescapably part of Kenya's mystique as well, enhanced by Hollywood. William Holden came out to shoot a film called *The Lion* and stayed to buy into a small lodge on the slopes of Mt Kenya which he developed into the Mt Kenya Safari Club, still a byword today among luxury safari-goers. The most famous and successful Great White Hunters – among them the partners Bror Blixen and Denys Finch-Hatton, respectively husband and lover of Karen Blixen (Isak Dinesen) – had kept it a secret among themselves that the root of success was less marksmanship and courage than the ability to run an efficient catering service in the bush. The latter skill was much in demand when filmmakers discovered Kenya. The hunters traded stories about the care and feeding of the likes of John Wayne and Ava Gardner and yarns about directors who ordered up at whim an invasion of elephants to trample a prop hunting camp. 'The first thing you would do was try to talk them out of it,' remembered Terry Mathews, a veteran who turned from hunting to wildlife sculpting after a client took out his eye with an errant gunshot in 1968. Hollywood continued to be Kenya's best advertising agency even as recently as the 1980s when the film version of *Out of Africa*, shot in Kenya, unleashed a new flood of American tourists upon the land.

By then hunting was out, banned in 1977. The decision had been forced on the government by the disturbing decline of game populations, particularly elephant and rhino, shot to pieces by poachers. Kenya no longer supported herds at their prewar size, when game hunting was not a conservation issue because there were so many animals that blasting away at them provoked no more second thoughts than sweeping ants off a table at teatime. By 1973 the elephant herds in Kenya numbered 165,000 head. Four years later they were down to 50,000.

No-one thought the organized hunters were guilty of heavy illicit killing, and many agreed that the presence of trained huntsmen in the bush probably deterred some native poaching. But with some of the animals being pursued to the point of extinction, hunting was unseemly at best. Already an ethos of conservation had overtaken the tourist trade, and even such old-line hunting firms as Ker & Downey Safaris had shifted to conducting more photo safaris and game-viewing tours. Some of this change was mandated by alterations in the clientele. With bigger aircraft and cheaper fares hundreds of thousands of people could afford vacations in Kenya every year, not just royalty and industrial nobility. They would have mixed poorly with a handful of rich target-shooters. When the Masai Mara was established as a game sanctuary in 1961 it excluded hunters. Over time more of the country's game ranges were set aside to protect the fauna rather than expose it to gunfire.

With seven hundred thousand foreigners coming to Kenya each year to see game, tourism was the country's only growth industry, bringing in more than $350 million a year. Threats to the business were often seen as challenges to national security, as when a surge in poaching raids by Somali bandits provoked the government to round up its entire ethnic Somali population for a 'screening' to determine which were legitimate Kenyan citizens and which illegal aliens.

But in 1988 the threat to tourism was even more direct: Several visiting foreigners had been attacked in the game parks. The first case came in September 1988, around the time Julie disappeared, when a Dutch tourist was shot in the chest in the remote Meru National Park. The crime was blamed on *shiftas*, Somali bandits. Then Julie disappeared, bringing a horde of British correspondents and inspiring a disturbing outbreak of stories about the sinister atmosphere of the tourist parks. The following April, three German tourists stumbling on a group of poachers in the isolated landscape between Tsavo and Amboseli parks were shot and seriously wounded. Two French tourists were killed in Meru that July.

The government took Western press coverage of these episodes personally. 'They are the kinds of events which the Western press simply dotes on,' editorialized the *Kenya Times*, the quasi-official organ of the ruling party, KANU. 'The correspondents love to blow them out of all proportion, using them as scarecrows to deter Western tourists from visiting our country. By making a mountain out of a molehill after the killing in our national parks of a single Briton or other Westerner, they can poison the minds of all would-be tourists, thus robbing our exchequer of an important source of foreign cash, to our detriment.' The *Times* responded with stories about the dangerous streets of New York and London, wondering aloud why tourists did not avoid those places if a couple of killings in the bush frightened them.

So in a way the impulse to minimize the menace in the Masai Mara was understandable, if misplaced. Still, in June and early July, when the government and Ward and Georgiadis were preparing to undertake the inquest into Julie's death, no-one could foresee how bad for tourism the coming summer would be.

CHAPTER TWENTY-SEVEN

At her desk in a building on London's Fleet Street, Caroline Davies contemplatively absorbed Kenya's announcement of an inquest into Julie Ward's death.

Davies was a petite woman with dark hair who had been raised on an island off the remote Scottish coast. In British popular mythology the people of these tight little islands are repositories of an arsenal of quirks and impossible eccentricities born of their remarkable solitude, but Davies had the air of self-confidence and gregarious habits characteristic of people who make their way from places of isolation to succeed amid the frenetic pace of a big city.

The newspaper she wrote for, the *Evening Standard*, occupied a comfortable niche in England's press spectrum. At one end were the national 'qualities', exemplified by the *Telegraph, Guardian*, and, holding tenuously on to distinction despite its ownership by the unspeakable Rupert Murdoch, *The Times*. At the low end were the tabloids, Maxwell's *Daily Mirror* and Murdoch's *Sun*, which guaranteed bare breasts on page three and blaring headlines sliding disreputably all over the page like slithering streams of oil. The *Standard* was in the middle of this pack. Along with its corporate siblings, the *Daily* and *Sunday Express*, the newspaper had once earned a reputation for high standards and slick literacy under the ownership of Lord Beaverbrook. Its latest proprietors were about to be the last to move their newspapers out of union-bound Fleet Street and into glittering new quarters – then under construction off Kensington High Street – and they were preparing an advertising campaign based not on journalistic distinction but on a printing process that kept ink from rubbing on to readers' hands. But the *Evening Standard* was the last afternoon newspaper remaining in the London market, and that often gave it a leg up on scoops against even the big national dailies, which all appeared in the morning.

Davies had carved out a comfortable niche herself on the paper's staff, covering the stories of British subjects who had mysteriously come to grief overseas. There had been a young girl, much like Julie Ward, murdered in Greece – and like John Ward her father was pursuing an investigation on his own – and a young nurse pitched off a balcony to her death during an illicit drinking party in Saudi Arabia. Julie Ward's death was from the same mold. Like a stockbroker cold-calling a prospect, Davies dialed Ward's number in Bury St Edmunds.

Soon after Ward's Nairobi press conference the previous September the press had begun to lose interest in the case. The one squalid exception had been the *Sunday Mirror*'s 'Lion Girl' article, but if anything that had reinforced Ward's own inclination to avoid the whole howling mob.

The Julie Ward story had more or less dropped from sight, as sensations eventually do. From Davies's standpoint she was operating in a clear field. In truth, many of Davies's colleagues in the London press believed John Ward to be not much more than an ill-tempered character, 'a mean old man', as she put it later. The discovery of Julie's remains in the Masai Mara was nearly a year old. There were other stories, other excitements, and there seemed little point in pursuing a year-old case with an uncooperative father.

Ward would later describe how he came to believe that the British press could lend a hand in pressing for justice in Kenya, but in truth the perception was forced upon him by Davies's call. Now, with months behind him of frustrating contacts with Kenyan officialdom, he responded instantly to the opportunity. Instead of meeting the mean old man of Fleet Street gossip, Davies found Ward an affable man. He invited her to come talk to him about the case, and for the first, but scarcely the last time, he displayed to a reporter his documentary evidence that the Kenyan government was engaged in the cover-up of a murder in the Masai Mara.

Davies's story appeared inside the *Evening Standard* on 1 August, wrapped around a furniture ad and beneath a headline quoting John Ward: MY DAUGHTER WAS MURDERED . . . AND I HAVE THE PROOF.

Under her blond bangs Julie smiled out at the reader, cuddling a chimpanzee in a picture taken during the Cameroon stop on the Ho-Bo tour. From a thumbnail-sized photograph in the center of the page Ward's face gazed toward his daughter, his eyes narrowed in determination.

The story covered all the important points of Ward's and Georgiadis's case. Not sparing the characteristic frisson that makes the British press so distinctive, it began:

> Businessman John Ward – who flies to Kenya this week for the inquest of his daughter Julie, found dead in the African bush last September – claims he has proof that she died at the hands of a vicious killer.
>
> He opened his files to the *Evening Standard* and revealed how he found his twenty-eight-year-old daughter's remains . . . and discovered a cover-up spiked with incompetence, forgery, and deceit.

Davies recapitulated Ward's investigation, touching on the altered postmortem, the confrontation with Kaviti, and Kilonzo's refusal to convene an official murder inquiry. Ward was quoted criticizing Wanjau for refusing to accept evidence of Julie's murder, and he cast a sidelong shot, the first in public, at Simon Makallah, who the article noted 'has since been suspended'. (This left the impression that Makallah's suspension stemmed from his possible involvement in Julie's death, but in fact it came out of the malfeasance charges drummed up by the Ntimama clique on the Narok council.) The article ascribed the initial theory that 'she had been eaten by wild animals or had somehow set herself alight' to Makallah himself.

Davies spent many more hours with Ward in Bury St Edmunds. For the paper she described how he had perfected something of a music-hall routine acting out the indolent mannerisms of the Kenyan constables and clerks at whose hands he had suffered so much trouble. Ward's exposure to the low-grade investigations of the Kenya Police had given him a very constrained impression of the better qualities of African character, the way a slum patrolman sees nothing in human nature except drug-induced stupor and aimless violence. John Ward had been scantily exposed to the charm and dignity of the average Kenyan, especially one unsullied by too long an association with metropolitan Nairobi. Beneath his amusing gesticulations and his denigrations of Kenyan intellect, there lay the desperate frustration of a father trying to whip a Third World police force into undertaking a modern and responsible murder investigation.

Davies knew her story was likely to set off another press frenzy; even the national papers were sure to pick up her lead, now that the inquest was definitely scheduled and available as a hard-news peg. But she had been first out of the box, and a week later she was in Nairobi with Ward when, days before the inquest was to begin, he stopped by Sebastian Tham's office at Wilson Airport for another look at Julie's Suzuki jeep.

The vehicle stood forlorn and abandoned, like a forgotten old dog, rusting at the side of the safari company's shed. Tham had made little use of his doleful gift from Ward; the window he had smashed to gain entry was still broken, and the vehicle could not have been used much since it had been driven north from the Mara nearly ten months before. The police had forgotten about it once Wanjau made his indifferent search of its vacant interior and snapped some useless photographs at the Mara Serena Lodge.

Ward opened the door in scant expectation that the Suzuki had any more secrets to give up. As if to punish the inert object he ripped away its cheap door panels and pulled some worn lining off the metal floor.

There, soaked in grease in the well under the front passenger seat, he found a white receipt for a tankful of gasoline.

The receipt, dated 2 September at a service station in Narok, showed that Julie and Burns had filled the Suzuki at one of the last service stations before entering the Mara. It was now eleven months after his daughter had died and ten since the Kenya Police had supposedly given the car a good going-over. Ward mumbled angrily about how such important evidence of the route and timing of Julie's final journey could be so sloppily overlooked.

At his next meeting with Wanjau he presented the inspector with the receipt, along with a crisp rebuke for having missed it.

For all the frustrations and disenchantments of the previous year, Ward still saw the inquest as an intermediate step in the investigation of Julie's death, and he harbored the impression that the police, embodied by Wanjau, were still on the case. What he did not know was that Wanjau had long since made his final report to his superiors on the death of Julie Ward. It was dated 6 April, some four months earlier. Ward would not learn of its conclusions for another month to come. Byron Georgiadis would learn of them first, and he was prepared to spring the report on his client at a moment of maximum possible impact, when the astonishment and fury it provoked would be displayed on Ward's face for everyone to see.

Wanjau did not volunteer that he had washed his hands of the investigation. He pocketed the stained receipt without comment, and very shortly threw it away. He thought it unlikely, he said later, that Ward could possibly have found it in the place he claimed. After all, the police had already examined the jeep.

CHAPTER TWENTY-EIGHT

On the morning of 27 July a group of American tourists visiting Kenya under the sponsorship of the Audubon Society piled into three Toyota vans in front of their lodge at Amboseli National Park.

The convoy had been scheduled to leave at 9.30 for Tsavo National Park, the home of Kenya's largest elephant herds (and not coincidentally, its greatest incidence of armed poaching), but the party had been informed as they dressed for breakfast that the departure time had been moved ahead to nine. The group, all hailing from in and around Hartford, Connecticut, were just scrambling to get themselves and their luggage into the vans when they were informed of a second change: An armed ranger was going to ride with them. The man was standing in front of the first bus, dressed in greens and toting an Uzi submachine gun.

Allen Sullivan hesitated. If he had been told the night before that this trip would require an armed escort, the retired schoolteacher reflected, he would have taken care to oversleep. But he steeled himself and got into the front seat of the first van in line. Sitting behind him was a woman named Marie Ferraro, a fifty-year-old mother of two grown children. Marie was traveling alone; she had left her husband home because his doctor had warned him that the bumpy rides around the African bush would be bad for his back. The ranger climbed in the bus with them. To American tourists used to policemen armed with nothing more obvious than holstered pistols, the sight of Kenyan police with their big automatic rifles always inspired a combination of anxiety and confidence; the same feelings surged through the van as the guard stepped

212

up with a sinister-looking carbine in his hands.

As the three vans moved out of Amboseli the terrain grew steadily worse. They stopped twice, once at a trading post midway between Amboseli and Tsavo, and again a short while later to take in a picturesque Masai village. When they moved out again it was high noon. The ranger had moved from bus to bus at each stop, and now he was in the last van. The convoy was stretched in a line along a heavily rutted dirt trail, the vehicles scarcely visible to each other in the dusty distance.

Suddenly, as Sullivan stared out the front window of the lead van, a figure stepped out into the road from behind a bush. He aimed what appeared to be a rifle directly at the van's windshield and squeezed off two shots. Sullivan felt a burning streak along his right cheek. He felt his face and turned round to Marie Ferraro. There was a red streak around her ear and she was slumped over, killed instantly.

There was more firing and the van listed sharply as the attacker shot out its tires. On the side of the vehicle Sullivan could make out a second man, holding an ax. Now the attackers were banging on the side of the van, shouting what the driver described later as Somali-accented Swahili.

'Throw everything out! They want you to throw everything out!' screamed the terrified driver. 'They want American dollars!' A hail of pocketbooks and wallets fell to the ground. The luggage was pulled out of the hold into the dirt.

By then the second van had pulled up and been motioned to a halt by the rifleman. Pocketbooks and wallets and luggage piled up beside it too. There was no sign of the third vehicle. It had turned back to Amboseli with mechanical trouble after departing the Masai village, the group's armed guard among its passengers.

Sullivan and his companions were herded into the second van and sent on, leaving behind by the side of the road their suitcases, money, passports, and Mrs Ferraro's corpse. Later a Kenya army detachment would be sent off to retrieve the body and the baggage. The rest of the

213

travelers were airlifted back to Nairobi from Tsavo early the next morning, along with their horrific story.

The killing of an American housewife in Kenya added a new dimension to stories about tourist security in the country. Here was a group of innocent tourists assaulted with automatic rifles by bandits who disappeared into the woods (and would never be found). With the Ward inquest about to begin, the newspapers in America and Great Britain had two grisly yarns to tie together.

It was a commonplace in newsrooms around the English-speaking world that it takes three anecdotes to make a trend. Very shortly, within a month, there would be a third. And the third story would bring the issue of tourist security in Kenya to the attention of the entire world.

CHAPTER TWENTY-NINE

With the words 'The deceased is called Julie Ward,' Deputy Public Prosecutor Alex G. A. Etyang began on 9 August the inquest the girl's father had sought for eleven months.

The colonial-era Law Courts building stands aloof at the northern edge of downtown Nairobi, diagonally across a beflowered traffic roundabout from the sprawling gray pile that is Nairobi City Hall. From a distance the court-house building is an imposing structure of mustard-yellow stone with all the elegance and solidity of Edwardian architecture. Up close some of the elegance melts away. Gracing one entrance is a tarnished bronze fountain that functions irregularly; the front steps are often strewn with debris from a nearby garbage-collection point. Over the arched entranceway the crossed spears and Kikuyu shield of the seal of independent Kenya watch proudly, patched over the remains of the old British colonial crest that crowned the arch before.

Inside, the courtroom doors open off hallways connecting small courtyards framed by arched columns or rails. Even on the ground floor one has the sense of walking along a verandah, except in the dark crowded sections of corridor where two courtrooms face each other.

Courtroom Four, where Chief Magistrate Joseph Mango would preside over the Julie Ward inquest, was located near the end of the long main corridor, on the right as one headed down the straight hall toward the rear of the building.

Almost directly across the hall was the venue of perhaps the most celebrated trial of a white man in Kenyan history, the tribunal charging Sir John Henry Delves Broughton with the murder of Lord Erroll, the Kenyan playboy who was the hereditary chief of the Scottish nobility. This was the case reintroduced to public notice after fifty years by the book and movie *White Mischief*. That three-week proceeding, according to the author James Fox, generated a six-hundred page transcript. Nothing so revealing would come out of Courtroom Four in August and September 1988, when the transcript would be taken by two stenographers imported from England by John Ward, straining against a booming din to hear the testimony. Every morning of the inquest Georgiadis would step up to the bench to hand Mango a copy of their transcript. A police functionary at Etyang's table also took longhand notes, but he was often interrupted and sent scurrying out the door in search of files and evidence.

The courtroom was entered from two heavy wooden doors opening on either side of the judge's podium, which allowed spectators and officers of the court to stop and make ceremonial bows to the bench before proceeding to sit in a paneled gallery thrust forward from the rear of the room. Two lines of half-moon windows stretching down the long walls on either side, a good fifteen feet over the spectator's heads, opened on to the upstairs hallways at foot level, so that the proceedings inside were continually overwhelmed by the echoing tramp of the foot traffic on the floor above. The room itself might have been designed as some perverse sort of echo chamber, so resounding was the roar of intruding noise and so faint the sound from the witness box.

From the very beginning the inquest attracted a full gallery. If it did not represent the colorful range of British colonial classes that filled the seats for Broughton's ordeal, the crowd laying claim to the scant spectator space in Courtroom Four did represent a wide variety of interests.

First among them was the press, which seemed to have segregated itself into Kenyan and foreign with the same instinct that preserved the racial and class divisions of the society at large. The Kenyan reporters generally crowded into the jury box situated along the right wall as one came into the room, about even with the witness box in front of the judge's dais. They sometimes squeezed in so tightly they jokingly referred to it as the *matatu* bench, after the brutally crowded vans and buses that ferried Kenyans between the capital and the provincial towns.

The British reporters, including a large group sent directly from London for the sensational case, headed for the three rows of padded leather stalls directly behind the lawyers' tables. At first they were so frustrated at the dim sound of testimony from that vantage point that some tried a morning or afternoon's sojourn with the Kenyans in the jury box. But a few hours of sitting on a bench with all the comfort of a seat in the stocks sent them back to the cushioned seats of the gallery, to which they would come early in the morning to place a notebook as a claims marker before regaining the corridor for a last puff on a cigarette before the judge's appearance.

A smattering of white spectators, often old British ladies, would sometimes try to seize a front seat, but they would be shooed off by Byron Georgiadis so the journalists could have the best view. The last couple of rows of seats were generally taken up by Kenyan law students. They all seemed to be skinny men in nondescript suit jackets and women in glimmering polyester skirts, and sustained an amused whispered commentary throughout the inquest full of admiration for Georgiadis's withering cross-examinations and contemptuous ridicule for Etyang's stammered flounderings.

As in public courtrooms anywhere the period before the convening of court was a time for interested contemplation of the character of the courthouse population. Here there was a conventional collection of moping defendants and appellants and prideful attorneys. From time to time one's attention would be arrested by something different. One morning the Ward spectators gathered in the corridor outside the courtroom to watch a detachment of police guards form itself around the back entrance. Presently a file of prisoners, manacled to each other and dressed in the most pitifully ragged motley, was marched in to disappear down a dark staircase. On another morning midway through the inquest, the bustling but flowing crowd outside the building was transformed into an impassible mob of milling people awaiting, as it turned out, a judge's ruling on one of the interminable electoral disputes that vivified Kenyan politics. The hallways inside were made nearly impassable by the press of political cliques. While a witness was testifying stupefyingly about some irrelevancy in the Ward case, suddenly the torpor was broken by unrestrained shouting and cheering outside the room. Spectators emerged from Courtroom Four into a gleeful crowd carrying the victorious party member out of the courtroom opposite on their shoulders and out the front door and into the street, where their exuberance jammed traffic for an hour.

Magistrate Mango cut an impressive figure sitting at the raised bench of Courtroom Four. He was a small, stocky man, but an air of great dignity was lent him by a square black beard, pharaonic in appearance. Mango was one of a cadre of increasingly beleaguered judges in the Kenyan system. After the 1982 coup attempt President Moi had taken steps to accumulate more power in his own hands. One key step was a constitutional amendment, railroaded through parliament after a debate taking a matter of minutes, making the tenure of all judges subject to his own pleasure. The amendment remained by far the most troublesome and controversial move Moi had ever made. It was true that even in the days of constitutional tenure for the judiciary Attorney General Njonjo had stacked the courts with short-term 'contract' judges forever worried that their jobs would not be renewed if they angered the leadership, but the new amendment destroyed all the Kenya judiciary's residual independence with the stroke of a pen.

Magistrates had a poor reputation even within this system. As the chief jurists of the lower courts, they were conveniently situated at just the location where a little illicit money would go a long way. It was common speculation that among the magistracy and in the public prosecutor's office legal results could be had at specific price tags, like objects in a boutique. It cost so much to keep the prosecutors from opposing bail, so much to have a case transferred to a compliant judge, and so on. Some people claimed that certain magistrates had even resisted promotion to high-court judgeships because their incomes would drop sharply once they were removed from this thriving marketplace. Mango was politically ambitious, however. Not long after the Ward inquest he accepted just such an appointment, to a judgeship on the high court. His ultimate ambition was thought to be the Chief Judgeship of Kenya.

Alex Etyang, the man who opened the inquest by presenting the State's case, had a deceptively distracted look to him. He was an orphan of the system, in some ways like Kilonzo: a man of much more ability than the political environment permitted him to display. Etyang, who as a Pokot was a member of one of the smallest and most isolated tribes of Kenya, had once won high marks as head of the prosecutor's bureau in Nakuru, in the heart of Kikuyu country. 'There he was running his own office,' an acquaintance said later. 'He could make decisions and act on them.'

In Nairobi, however, he had more or less been promoted into a subservient position, subject to the rulings and orders of the public prosecutor and of Attorney General Matthew Muli. Like most civil servants he seemed to have adopted the practice of keeping his head down and staying in line. The foreign press would amuse itself at Etyang's expense by cracking wise about his befuddled manner and his way of searching the air for a new question to ask a witness. In fact, he was more likely looking for a line of inquiry in this delicate, troublesome, and politically explosive case that would just keep him out of trouble.

Like almost every element of Kenyan jurisprudence, from its vocabulary and the judges' garb of robes and wigs to the very rules of evidence, the inquest in a Kenyan court was based on the British model. That meant that it was designed not as an adversarial joust like a trial, but as a fact-finding affair aimed at assisting a magistrate to determine whether a subject's death merited some further legal inquiry.

'It shouldn't be an adversarial proceeding,' Georgiadis told the reporters who trooped to his downtown office as the event commenced, 'but in this case it is.'

Georgiadis blamed that on the government and the magistrate, who he complained had ruled early on that the rules of criminal procedure, rather than looser civil rules, must be applied because the inquest could lead to a criminal prosecution. Hearsay, for instance, was barred. Still, as much as he cursed the ruling as having turned the inquest into something resembling a trial, he lost few opportunities to portray it as a battle between two radically different theories of Julie's death.

'Etyang and I have the same interests at heart inside that room,' he would begin, generously. 'But in practice they've spent a year conducting a disinformation campaign in order to postulate that animals have consumed her.'

The word *disinformation* rang out with contempt. Georgiadis's lustrous voice left no doubt in the minds of his listeners that he was going to place that theory on trial. He let his passions blaze away like the fire under the sausage tree, as if he had taken on the job not only of putting his client's case before a magistrate but of unleashing the fury John Ward had so far kept publicly in check.

One did not have to listen to Georgiadis for very long to perceive that his view of the inquest went beyond how it was seen by his client, who was simply trying to goad the sluggish police bureaucracy into finding his daughter's killer. He was going to elevate this case beyond a question of murder to put the system of Kenyan justice itself on trial.

In truth, Georgiadis did not have to contrive much of his passionate contempt. Among his familiars Georgiadis's disenchantment with the deteriorating rule of law in

Kenya was a byword. It had become as much a part of his character and image, even of his legend, as his passion for deep-sea fishing and golf or the canine obstacle course laid out behind his house.

It was not only the judicial-tenure amendment. The same year lawyers were required to obtain trade licenses from a government agency empowered to deny them for any number of reasons. There were more cases of detention without trial and more of prisoners dying under torture at Special Branch headquarters. The last few outspoken dissidents in parliament had been raucously hounded out of KANU and their legislative seats.

Now, with the Julie Ward inquest poised to begin, Byron Georgiadis suddenly found himself with unexampled access to an international stage. His audience was greater than any he had had since his defense of Sullivan, the thick-witted Hola Camp commandant. Given thirty years' advance in telecommunications, it was even better. And it came to him at an exceedingly propitious moment.

The inquest would be Georgiadis's last hurrah in Nairobi, and he was resolved to make it memorable. Just when he had reached his point of deepest despair about the decline of law, the multiplication of rank inefficiencies and political hypocrisy in the land he had served for three decades as an officer of the court, just as he had reached his decision to retire and put this country and all the humiliations of corrupt jurisprudence behind him, the world's press was in town to hang on his every word.

Long experience in the corridors and chambers of the Law Courts had given Georgiadis a matchless feel for how the government could manipulate proceedings to its own advantage. He had seen too many verdicts that swore at common sense. He used one particular case to illustrate the myriad pitfalls confronting his client in seeking justice through the Kenyan courts. It was an inquest in which he had not been personally invoved, but several other actors in the inquest over Julie's death had: Mango had been the magistrate and Alex Etyang the prosecutor. And the police pathologist who had examined the deceased, and whose evidence bulked large in the confusion in which the proceedings ended, was Dr Jason Kaviti.

The 1987 inquest into the death of Peter Njenga Karanja touched on all of the darker shadows falling over the Kenyan police establishment, including the politicization that was draining the force of its public reputation. Karanja's family had faced some of the same obstacles as Ward in trying to find what had befallen their breadwinner. At the center of the case was the Kenya government's all-purpose bogeyman of sedition, a shadowy organization of unknown aims or size known as Mwakenya.

Mwakenya was a dissident group, but most of what was known about it ended right there. That to the average Kenyan it was by far the best-known such group probably had more to do with the government's incessant drumbeat of anti-Mwakenya propaganda than with anything it plotted or accomplished. In fact, more than a few people around Nairobi suspected it was largely a figment of the government's imagination. Occasionally the authorities would haul in for questioning or arrest a hapless schoolteacher or truckdriver. He would be charged with possession of 'seditious' literature, but no-one could ever quite describe what about these mysterious flyers made them seditious. The scant Mwakenya literature reaching the light of day was so politically naive as to be ludicrous as a blueprint for revolution.

Mostly the government used Mwakenya to smear its opponents, including political exiles critical of the administration. There would be vague charges of complicity with foreign enemies, assertions of financial irregularities, and so on, all linked somehow to Mwakenya.

Anyone labeled Mwakenya could expect to be in for a bad time. When Peter Karanja was arrested in 1987 some seventy-five Kenyans had already pleaded guilty to Mwakenya-type charges and twelve others were being held without charge.

So it went with Karanja, a forty-three-year-old coffeeshop owner in Nakuru, the prosperous onetime provincial center of the White Highlands, when he was picked up by police for questioning. Twenty-two days later he was pronounced dead of mysterious causes at Jomo Kenyatta Hospital. He had been interrogated as a suspected threat to national security for sixteen straight days, four to six hours a day, while being fed a diet – which police claimed he requested – of milk, tea, and bread.

At the inquest Senior Superintendent James Opiyo, a police officer who was in charge of interrogating Mwakenya suspects and determining 'the truth', hinted at his standard technique.

'Some people are good talkers, some are not. You keep talking with him, questioning him, until some day you make some headway. The headway always happens.' When Karanja was brought in, he said, 'he pretended not to know why he was arrested. Initially he was not cooperative. But later he became cooperative.'

Soon after he 'became cooperative', Karanja was taken to Kenyatta Hospital. On arrival he was loaded into a wheelchair and wheeled before Dr Peter Carberry. Carberry saw a man who was weak, incontinent, febrile, and showing sores on the bottoms of both feet and up and down his legs, including a suppurating crater of a wound on his kneecap affording a view down to the bone itself. He was malnourished and dehydrated, and showed a touch of jaundice.

Carberry asked him if he had suffered any trauma to account for the wound. As the magistrate observed dryly at the conclusion of the inquest, 'This would have been his last chance to tell anyone in the outside world what could have happened to him.' With four policemen standing around the examining table, he passed up the opportunity. Thirty-six hours later he was dead.

Then came the episode that could not help but have arrested Ward's attention: Twelve days later a postmortem was conducted by Dr Jason Kaviti. He determined that the body, of a male African adult in good nutrition, had been dead for about twelve days. He found blood in the abdominal cavity and gangrene in parts of the small and large intestines. Kaviti acknowledged the presence of bruises and wounds all over the legs, on the right shoulder, and the right elbow. Then he expressed no doubt as to the cause of death: pneumonia.

The family contended otherwise. These injuries, Karanja's relatives argued, were characteristic of torture.

At the inquest Kaviti firmly ruled out blunt force as a cause of the abdominal injuries, on grounds that there had been no bruising of the abdominal wall. At that point the family's lawyer, a well-known liberal attorney named Ben Oki Ooko-Ombaka, produced a standard forensic pathology textbook which noted that fatal internal injuries can occur with no external evidence of trauma. Kaviti reluctantly assented.

Still, Kaviti's testimony served its purpose. Mango was clearly troubled by what at the very least appeared to be police negligence over the health of a suspect they had held for twenty-two days. 'The deceased was not treated well, and one is left surprised that a human being could treat another like that,' he remarked. He considered that the evidence did tend to show 'that the wounds that covered the body of the deceased when he was taken to Kenyatta Hospital to die could have been caused by the application of force.'

Mango continued, 'I only fall short of so holding because of the disagreement by the two vital witnesses in the proceedings. The two experts: Professor Alfred Kungu of the University of Nairobi forensic pathology department (the family's witness), and Dr Kaviti.

'The basic difference between these two medical giants,' Mango remarked, 'is that one says the wounds were definitely caused by some force and the other is doubtful as to whether there was any force.'

Mango's even-handed treatment of two sharply contradictory findings was typical. He had nothing if not a talent for the inconclusive conclusion, cut to measure to serve all conceivable masters. In this case he declared torture a possibility in Karanja's death, which pleased the family. But he stopped short of making specific accusations against police officers, the force, or the government, which pleased all those important parties. Then he shoved the whole thing into the lap of Attorney General Matthew Muli, and the issue died.

Given his own experience with Kaviti and knowing the standing of the gray-headed pathologist within the police department, Ward had reason to be disturbed when Georgiadis showed him Mango's ruling, with its apparent willingness to let Kaviti obscure the issues. As new reporters came flocking around in the early days of his daughter's inquest, Ward added a copy of Mango's ruling to the papers he obligingly showed them. He would display Shaker's altered postmortem report, with its misaligned corrections in type. Then he would show the Karanja decision, copied out of the pages of the *Nairobi Law Monthly*, featuring a photograph of the magistrate with his pharaonic beard.

'See what I'm up against?' Ward invariably commented.

Still, Mango had shown a little spine. He had specifically objected to the policemen's standing over Karanja during his examination by Dr Carberry. 'The deceased was with three people. If he survived, he would go back with them. If they had beaten or otherwise molested him would any reasonable human being expect that he would accuse them in their presence? The deceased was like a caged animal.'

There was one final element to the Karanja inquest that Ward did not mention to the press; had he known about it, his confidence in the power of international attention might have been undermined. The Karanja inquest was to be witnessed by two very prominent human-rights advocates. Doctor Robert Kirschner was a Chicago medical examiner and a representative of a world-famous group named the Physicians for Human Rights. Marvin Frankel was a former New York federal judge who had been asked to witness the inquest by the Lawyers' Committee for Human Rights. They had both received visas to Kenya after openly stating their business. By law, court proceedings in Kenya are open to the public. Nevertheless, after sitting in the courtroom for less than an hour, they were arrested.

Kirschner related later how they were motioned outside and bundled into unmarked police cars. For eight hours they were held incommunicado at a Nairobi police station after being informed, incorrectly, that it was illegal for anyone but accredited journalists to take notes in court. Kirschner was interrogated on the twenty-fourth floor of Nyayo House, the Special Branch headquarters, and accused of being an agent of Amnesty International, a human rights group against which the government harbored a particularly acute resentment. Frankel had been discovered carrying a letter from a Kenyan exile in New York to a friend and dissident lawyer in Nairobi, and was questioned harshly about the message. Both men were refused permission to contact the US Embassy until that night, when they were released, taken out a side door to evade an American consul badgering the police over their arrests, and returned to their rooms at the Nairobi Hilton. Frankel left Kenya that night. Kirschner stayed another day, securely protected by embassy personnel.

Georgiadis seemed constantly to expect some similarly abrupt reaction by the authorities to the international interest shown in his final case. He kept predicting that a suspension of the proceedings was imminent. If such a thing happened Georgiadis knew he would be powerless. So he appeared to hedge his bets by making sure that a suspension or any other transparent government stratagem would look like a confirmation of Ward's charge of a cover-up.

In all he had no choice but to play to the outside world because he was convinced that inside the courtroom, come what may, he was going to lose.

'It's a conspiracy of a very puerile, infantile order,' he would say. 'Bloody system.'

John Ward had a very different approach from his passionate barrister. He received reporters in his room in the Nairobi Safari Club, sitting with his back to a big bay window looking out on the city skyline. Visitors could not help but be impressed by the geniality with which he welcomed them (as long as they were not from the 'Maxwell press') and the composure with which he discussed the murder of his only daughter.

Ward had a way of dropping his eyes and staring at his fingernails as he talked, giving him an air of studied nonchalance. 'There's only ever been one target,' he would say. 'I want to get the man who killed her. Because he must have put that little girl through a lot of pain and terror before she died. I want him caught because if he's not then he goes free, and that's unacceptable. And it's unacceptable that the government should help him get away with it.'

Only very occasionally would he let a bit of hard temper stray into his words. 'I can't force these idiots to start a murder investigation until they agree that there's been a murder,' he would say.

Time was a healer, and only in the last six months had he found it much easier to contemplate what had happened – certainly easier to talk about it. But sometimes he would still turn introspective, and his face would go a little slack, its creases deepening with his reflection on the pain and grief he had confronted.

'There had never been so much as a broken leg in our family, let alone a murder,' he would say quietly. 'But now – now I've seen that leg so many times – you just get hardened to it, even though it's your own daughter.'

At times like this he would touch very carefully on the unfillable vacuum Julie's death had left in his family, particularly on his wife, Janet. 'She still cries,' he would say. 'Cries too much, I think.' There would be the barest hint of a deeper force impelling him to pursue his implacable campaign for justice. Julie had been closest to her mother, but it had fallen to the father to put aside the business he had built to instead devote to his daughter's memory the kind of single-minded attention that usually only a mother has for her children as a father builds a career.

Occasionally someone would wonder if he were not

somehow compensating now for some unconscious neglect of his daughter during her life, even if it were only the inevitable distracting influence of an entrepreneurial business on family life, common enough. But Ward could explain his motivation in other ways. His definition of a man's responsibilities included protecting his family, he said. If he could not have protected Julie from rape and murder, he was going to safeguard her memory and her reputation. 'I want to get the man who killed her,' he repeated, and that was all he needed to do to inspire a listener's respect for his unceasing determination over the space of nearly a full year.

In the court of international public opinion Ward and Georgiadis began the inquest firmly in the lead. Etyang was not receiving reporters, and even if he had, the soft-spoken prosecutor could not have hoped to put his case across with the distinguished white barrister's verve. Georgiadis had succeeded in creating, at least among the European press, considerable suspicion about the government's position. Etyang could not have dispelled it even with a good case. Given the case he had to put forward, he was a helpless man indeed.

But there was another element that affected how the proceedings would be viewed inside Kenya, this one unspoken. To anyone who had lived through the ordeal, as Ward had, the suggestion that his investigation into Julie's death was racially tainted was preposterous. But once the inquest got under way in Room Four a pattern emerged in the lineup of the two sides. Simply put, everyone on Ward's side was white, and everyone he was accusing of incompetence, mendacity, and murder was black. Even the press seemed to be segregated by race: white reporters on the padded seats in the back, Africans on the hard wood of the jury box in front. As it did in so much else about life in Kenya, the racial aspects of the inquiry into Julie Ward's death emerged only subtly. Even then they had real meaning only to those who considered themselves once again the victims of racial injustice, like the Kenyans themselves.

228

CHAPTER THIRTY

Etyang and Georgiadis spent much of the morning of 9 August sparring over the procedural rules of the inquest. Finally they each rose to make brief opening statements – Etyang contending the case would show itself to be one of death by misadventure, and Georgiadis that he would demonstrate that a murder had been committed. Then the first witness was called through the wooden door of Courtroom Four, bowed stiffly in Mango's direction, and stepped up to give his testimony.

The authority of Paul Weld Dixon's upright, martial bearing in the witness box was slightly undermined by his trouser legs, which were so short that a wedge of pale white skin showed between them and his socks. But in demeanor one could not have asked for a more agreeable witness. Under Etyang's questioning he related that he had lived in Kenya for almost twenty-five years as a documentary filmmaker. He first met Julie in early June 1988.

'She was a tourist who had fallen in love with Kenya,' he said. After the rest of the Ho-Bo contingent had scattered, 'I told her she could camp in my garden. This she did.'

Ward Dixon's portrait of a quiet, introverted Julie would not be seriously challenged during the inquest. 'What really caused a small friendship between us was two husky dogs which she owned,' he said, explaining that his own property was populated by dogs of every description. 'That is all I learned about her.'

Etyang raised the issue of Julie's social life, a line of investigation pioneered by the *Sunday Mirror*. Weld Dixon answered sternly that his young tenant had kept to herself. 'I had no intention of prying into her affairs,' he said.

Still, Julie was hardly a stranger. Weld Dixon described how easily she had fallen into the casual scheme of Langata hospitality. She would drop in on the couple without invitation, stay long, occasionally cook a meal for them. 'She visited me in typical Kenyan style,' he said. 'She arrived at ten or eleven in the morning and asked for coffee. She asked me and my wife to go to her guesthouse. We liked her.'

Eventually, Weld Dixon testified, he and his wife offered to drive her to the airport for her departing flight in mid-September.

The retired filmmaker related his rising anxiety as 9 and 10 September passed with no sign of her. He relived his calls to the Flying Doctors and the police on the night of the ninth and five Nairobi hospitals and the mortuary the following morning. 'All were negative.'

Then he related how he and John Ward visited the Sand River Camp during the father's first day in Kenya, and that a 'scout' at the gate had said in Swahili that he well remembered Julie. She had left Sand River about 3 p.m., he remembered, but that it had been about a week earlier.

Of a reward for information about Julie's disappearance that Weld Dixon posted, he said, 'It produced one red herring. Two Masai said they had seen Julie in a small jeep with an African sitting beside her.'

'Did you refer this to the police?' Etyang asked.

'No,' the witness answered. 'I just felt it was wrong.'

In the afternoon Georgiadis took over the questioning, walking Weld Dixon through Adel Youssef Shaker's post-mortem examination. Weld Dixon confirmed Youssef's assertion of murder.

'Do you recall Dr Youssef saying, "The forepart of the leg is in a straight line – the position when running"?'

'Yes.' Weld Dixon's answer stirred interest among the British reporters. The next day's newspapers reported that Julie might have been running away from her captors when she was cut down from behind. But it was just a red herring. Weeks later there would be testimony that the leg could stiffen in that position from rigor mortis, or from having been wedged tight against something for some period. Georgiadis himself instantly dropped the point, never bothering to suggest further that Julie might have been struck while running.

'Did this leg show any signs of a strip of flesh having been removed from it,' Georgiadis asked, 'as if the vultures had had their go?' He meant to undermine from the very first Makallah's explanation of how he had found the body.

'Certainly not.'

Ten days after the postmortem, the witness went on, he was called to see Commissioner Kilonzo. 'I saw him for ninety minutes on Friday, September the twenty-third.' That was the same day Ward discovered the alteration of the postmortem report.

'Did you bring your notes of the postmortem?' Georgiadis asked.

'I had my notes with me, but I didn't open the book except to show the commissioner one sketch of the leg. He didn't take any notes.'

Georgiadis asked how the conversation proceeded.

'We talked in very general terms,' Weld Dixon allowed. 'The police commissioner was unhurried, interested, and charming. He gave me the impression of wanting to help. He told his staff, "I want no telephone interruptions." I left the office very satisfied.'

David Weston made a very different impression in the stand from the proper Weld Dixon. His face bisected by a jet-black moustache and topped by a shock of razor-cut black hair streaked with gray, the balloon pilot from Florida peppered his testimony with surfer slang that had the Kenyan note-takers – as well as the British – poising their pens over paper in bewilderment.

Weston recalled how he had first met Julie on the fifth of September in front of the reception desk at the Mara Serena. He repeated their conversation, said he tried to help the mechanics fit the fuel pump, and recalled only one 'strange thing.'

'This one guy – Burns – had left her behind. I thought that made him a jerk.'

Weston invited Julie to his room 'to hear some tunes and drink a couple of brews,' he recalled. 'Everything was copacetic.' Etyang stumbled over this untranslatable Americanism.

'Pardon me?'

'Everything was fine.' They had dinner, then he escorted her to her room in the Serena. He did not go in, he testified.

Etyang pressed for some indication that she might have parted less than amicably from Burns. Weston shrugged. 'After she went missing there were rumors around she had argued with her boyfriend. But she told me that he wasn't her boyfriend.'

The next day Weston had taken Julie on her balloon trip, leaving in the early morning and getting back to the lodge about 9.30. The pilot recalled how he had tried strenuously to dissuade her from leaving for Sand River and driving to Nairobi alone on the same day. She would be fine, Julie insisted. She assured him she had 'been around' and could take care of herself.

'It was just another adventure for her,' Weston said.

'How was she dressed?' Etyang asked.

'Jeans, flip-flops, a shirt . . .'

Etyang asked if she seemed upset or depressed.

'No, she didn't. She wasn't depressed.'

In his turn Georgiadis had some very brief questions.

'Was she aware that meandering around the Mara on foot was not allowed, and not advisable?' he asked Watson.

The balloon pilot replied, 'I thought she knew that you don't go out for a stroll.'

CHAPTER THIRTY-ONE

The next two days of testimony were to give Georgiadis a
new crack at something that still bothered him and Ward:
the suspicious logbook entry at Sand River Camp.
Georgiadis was irate at Etyang's plan to put the revenue
clerk, David Nchoko, on the stand to testify about Julie's
movements at the campsite without mentioning at all
that he had forged her name in the visitors' book and lied
about it.

'What I question is this,' he said before the testimony
began. 'The police are well aware this guy originally
forged her signature. Having committed forgery and given
false information to the police, how can an assistant
deputy public prosecutor call him to the stand to give
evidence of the final result – his recollection of having
filled in the book himself – and produce no evidence of his
original assertion that she had done it?

'Are they so uninterested about a lying revenue clerk,
who is so crucial to the point whether she left on the sixth
as alleged or went out through that gate?'

Nchoko's story and the acquiescence of Constable
Gerald Karuri, a young policeman assigned to Sand River
Gate who claimed to have watched Julie leave the area,
could only mean they knew more about Julie's disappearance than they had told, he thought. Georgiadis grimaced
as if having tasted something foul. 'If you're going to solve
a murder . . . The police in the States and the UK can
open a chink in the door with one lie.'

David Nchoko certainly looked like a person with
something to hide. He stepped up to the witness box with
a haunted look, visibly trembling. Mango's clerk, holding
a Bible in one hand and a Koran in the other, asked him in

Swahili if he was Christian or Muslim, and at his answer handed over the Bible to swear him in.

Georgiadis started to throw Nchoko off balance even before Etyang began, insisting from his seat that the witness testify in English, not Swahili. Nchoko nervously resisted, claiming his English was poor. Finally, with Mango's clerk acting as an English interpreter, Etyang was allowed to proceed.

Nchoko first saw Julie and Burns arrive on 2 September, he said, at about 6 p.m. 'The lady asked about a camping site, and I showed them . . . They pitched two tents about 200 meters from the gate.'

'Is this the lady you saw?' Etyang handed him a photograph of Julie.

'*Ndiyo.*'

'Yes,' the interpreter said.

Nchoko next saw Julie on 6 September, when she entered from the Keekorok road at about 2 p.m. in the same vehicle. 'She went to the tent. Then she paid me sixty shillings for the campsite and 200 shillings for two people. I charged her for two extra days.'

Etyang entered into evidence the receipt for the Suzuki and asked Nchoko about the logbook. Why did he enter her name himself?

'I realized after she left that she had not printed her own name,' he said through the interpreter.

Aware that Julie had not written her full name in the book when entering Sand River Camp, Etyang asked:

'Where did you get the information that her family name was "Ward"?'

'I got the information from the receipt which she gave me on her arrival.' Etyang produced this receipt, numbered 0099237, in evidence, and ended his examination.

Georgiadis stood up slowly from his table on the right side of the room. Already on his face as he moved his eyes across the court was the look of unalloyed skepticism with which he approached most African witnesses. Nchoko stared back nervously.

'Can we establish that you speak English very well?'

'No, Your Honor,' the clerk replied through his interpreter.

'But you gave three false statements to the police, all in English, did you not?' That was true. Nchoko fell silent.

The lawyer paused.

'How many personnel were assigned to Sand River Gate on September the third?'

'There were five rangers and the constable.'

'That would be Constable Karuri?'

'Karuri, yes, Your Honor.'

Georgiadis picked up the receipt book entered into evidence. 'Why are you trembling?' he asked Nchoko. The young clerk was silent.

'He might not like being in court,' interjected Etyang.

'Isn't it one of the main rules of the Sand River Camp, that if people don't come back for the night you issue an immediate alarm? What action did you take on September the second?' That was the night Julie and Burns had spent in a Guerba tent.

'Nothing.'

'And on September the sixth, you are alleging that you were the last person to see the girl alive and driving out of the camp.'

'Yes, I was the last person, Your Honor.'

Georgiadis pressed him on how he knew to sign 'Ward' on the forged logbook. He attacked Nchoko's assertion that he had drawn it from her entry receipt.

'At that date it was not there, when you were making entries. It was at Sekenani Gate, where she had entered, was it not?'

'No, Your Honor, she had given me a vehicle permit.'

Then Georgiadis brandished the logbook again. He pointed at the forged name of 'Julie Ward.'

'You have maintained, under oath, that this was an innocent act.' Georgiadis waved his arm airily. 'Nothing wrong with it, you say. Now listen very carefully indeed. On Saturday, September the twelfth, 1988, did Mr Ward, Mr Whitford, who is an investigator, and Mr John Ferguson of the British High Commission arrive at the

Sand River Gate, along with Superintendent Wanjau?'

'I don't remember.'

'You have amnesia?'

Nchoko did not answer.

'Do you remember saying to Mr Whitford and the others that she had signed the vehicle book herself?'

'I don't remember.'

'A vital thing like that! Why did you lie, if it was an innocent mistake?'

Nchoko said nothing.

'Well? Can't you answer?' Georgiadis pressed. 'Are you thick?'

At this Mango cut in to stop Georgiadis from getting too insulting. 'How did he get his job if he's so thick?' the magistrate said.

Then Georgiadis asked Nchoko how he knew, when Ward and Weld Dixon reported to Sand River Camp on 13 September, that the remains discovered in the park 'had anything to do with Julie'.

'From the radio, Your Honor.'

'But the radio did not report this for days after that.'

Nchoko had little more information to give. But it was evident the next day that the reporters had taken Georgiadis's hints, for the domestic press and many of the British newspapers henceforth treated Nchoko as a suspected killer. Georgiadis did little to disabuse them of the notion. For in fact, he and Ward were convinced that the clerk was somehow implicated.

The barrister would be even tougher on the next witness the following morning.

Like Nchoko, Gerald Karuri was led gently through his story by Etyang when the inquest reconvened on 12 August. The constable corroborated Nchoko's version that Julie had arrived at Sand River at about 2 p.m. the previous 6 September, hauled down her tents, and left about a half-hour later. But he added the detail that he had helped her with the tents himself.

'I saw a lady at the camping site across the river, pulling down a tent,' he recalled. 'I crossed the river. I greeted her. I asked her if the second tent was hers too.'

'Then what did you do?' prompted Etyang.

'I helped her pull it down. I told her I was a police officer, because I was in jungle uniform. I informed her there was an unpaid bill for camping and she had to report to the revenue clerk,' he added. 'She said she had a problem with the vehicle.'

'Did you see her again?'

'Yes, Your Honor. Later I saw her vehicle passing the road, heading toward Keekorok.'

'What time was that?'

'About two forty-five.'

'Did you hear any more about her?'

'On September the ninth, Your Honor, I was informed that the lady had gone missing. Later on that day, I was informed that the vehicle had been found.' Etyang ignored the discrepancy in dates. The jeep had not been found until 13 September.

'What was she wearing when you saw her?' he went on.

'When last seen, she had a gray pullover with a zip. She had a light green sheet on her lower part, tied around the waist.'

'Any other details?'

'Her hair was pulled back, and she had a ring.' This remark caught Ward's eye when he came across it in the transcript later that night. Who would notice a modest detail like a ring, he asked himself, except someone perhaps intending to steal it? Details like this were what led Ward to believe that Julie must have been kidnapped at or near Sand River Gate, and that the two gate attendants knew more about it than they were letting on.

In the courtroom Georgiadis's expression, as he stood up to take his crack at the constable, suggested that Etyang had scarcely begun to delve into Karuri's role.

When Ward, Whitford, and Ferguson had visited Sand River a week after the remains had been found, he noted, Karuri had been unable, or unwilling, to identify Julie from the large color photograph they had brought with them.

'You didn't want to face the situation, did you?' Georgiadis asked. Karuri was silent.

'Did you or the rangers at Sand River Gate ever discuss her disappearance?'

'I was informed of her disappearance, Your Honor.'

'Did you or the rangers ever discuss her disappearance?' Georgiadis repeated stridently. Karuri shifted uneasily. Mango leaned over his desk.

'Is your nerve going?' he asked Karuri.

Georgiadis continued. 'You have testified that you heard on the ninth of September that the girl had gone missing, and later that day that her vehicle had been found, is that correct?'

'Yes, Your Honor.'

'When were you informed that her remains were found?'

'I was informed of that on September the thirteenth.'

'And what did you do then?'

'Nothing, Your Honor.'

'Wouldn't it have been helpful if you said you had seen the girl and helped her? How come you hid all this?'

Karuri said he had mentioned it to the group of Britons when they visited Sand River Gate a week later. At this Georgiadis exploded. Why had he never mentioned earlier that he had seen the girl, the lawyer demanded.

'Your whole story is a tissue of lies! Why were you hiding the information? You know more about this matter, as does Nchoko, than you are prepared to tell us!'

Now Mango joined in, bluntly asking, 'Did you kill her? Why don't you say it? Is she haunting you?'

Karuri looked terrified. 'No, no, Your Honor.'

'You and a few others killed the woman.' He indicated Georgiadis with his pen. 'That is what this man is saying.'

'No, Your Honor.' Karuri shook his head vehemently.

Georgiadis stepped in again. 'Were you ever asked to identify the Suzuki as the vehicle you had seen?'

'No, Your Honor.'

'Well, are you there at Sand River as an ornament?' the barrister asked sarcastically. 'Don't you look over tourists

238

and the security of the camp? Is it a serious matter if a tourist disappears?'

'Yes.'

'You got no instructions? You had no initiative? You knew, with one or two others, what had happened. Isn't that true?'

Karuri turned toward Mango. 'I did not know, Your Honor.'

Now Georgiadis turned his attention to Karuri's contention that he had helped Julie strike her campsite. 'You say you saw the girl from your post at Sand River Gate and went over to help her with her tents . . .' He paused. 'Do you help other women take down their tents? Is that your job? I suggest this is all a load of rubbish! You are trying just to corroborate the testimony of the revenue clerk that she was there at all.'

'I help people in need,' the constable insisted.

'I suggest you never saw any woman taking down a tent from where you were. There will be evidence to show that about eighty-two people were camping there. What was so extraordinary that you thought you had to go and see the lady taking down the bivouac tent?'

'She was alone.'

'How did you know she was alone?'

No answer.

'I suggest you are trying to say you had a proper reason for going to talk to her.'

Karuri strained for a response. 'I went because I suspected the other tent was not hers.'

Georgiadis dismissed this with a sneer. 'Rubbish! When did you ever have tourists stealing other tents?' Most of the campsite was invisible from the gatehouse, he observed. To see the campers Karuri would have had to hike a fair way downstream along the Sand River. 'From the area of the gate, you would not have seen two low tents on the ground anyway.'

Finally, Georgiadis elicited the detail that shortly after the remains were discovered Karuri had been ordered to report to police headquarters in Nairobi.

'Who called you to report?'

'Superintendent Masika,' Karuri said.

'Did he ask you about Julie Ward?'

'He just told me to report to Nairobi. He asked me no questions.'

'And how long were you in the police commissioner's office?'

'Thirty minutes.'

Georgiadis harumphed. 'You survived a lot longer in there than you would have in my office,' he said.

CHAPTER THIRTY-TWO

Blond and slim, with the colorful logo of his balloon safari firm embroidered on his forest-green sweater, Sebastian Tham could not have made more of a contrast with the two shaking witnesses who had preceded him to the stand. Erect in the box, Tham was the image of the 'Kenya Cowboy', the type of young white native who still strode firmly around Nairobi and upcountry as if he were still divine heir to this land of lush potential.

Under Etyang's questioning, Tham gave a precise chronological version of his and Ward's search and the first view of Julie's Suzuki. He had first heard that the jeep had been spotted 'in general gossip' around Keekorok on 13 September, he said. Then he described how the mud-colored vehicle appeared when they arrived at the gully.

'Of the four wheels, one was off the ground, the others down in the mud. I found a jack near the wheels.'

'What did you do next?' Etyang prompted.

'I took up a rock and broke the left-side window. There was a general jumble of things inside. We had a reasonable look around.'

'Did you see any blood?'

'No, there were no traces.'

'Which way was the vehicle facing?'

'It was pointing east, along the Sand River.'

'And were there any tire marks?'

'No.'

Tham said he and Ward stayed at the site for a little less than an hour, calling for Julie. They kept within about a hundred meters of the jeep for fear of wild animals in the area. Eventually they returned to Keekorok Lodge, arriving about 2 p.m. They were informed two hours later that

241

the remains had been found by Makallah and Othiambo. Tham remembered 'taking an active part' in searching around the fire near the remains and recalled it was he who discovered the can of half-eaten pilchards and the orange towel hanging from the tree.

'Did you see the remains? What did they look like?' Etyang asked.

Tham had a characteristic shrug he employed to suggest he thought the question trifling.

'It had a blue appearance . . .' Apologetically, he added, 'I'm not used to seeing bits of human beings laying about.'

Georgiadis then took over. With Tham he wanted to concentrate on getting more details of the jeep site on to the record, but he had very little time to do so. Not long after he rose to begin his cross-examination, Mango adjourned the inquest for the afternoon. Then he added that because of a vacation coming up, the hearing would not reconvene for three more weeks. The inquest would resume on 4 September, almost a year to the day since Julie's disappearance. As it happened, from the government's standpoint the hiatus would prove to be a masterpiece of bad timing.

When Mango made his announcement the visiting reporters in the gallery groaned in dismay. No matter how exciting or titillating a murder case is, long hours of sitting in a noisy courtroom absorbing testimony on details significant and trivial has a numbing effect. No-one can sustain interest in a case for long under such circumstances, and the dimly uttered testimony of the Ward inquest was already taking its toll. Now the tedious process was to be extended by at least three weeks. No-one was happy.

Georgiadis was unnerved most of all. To him the delay smacked of subterfuge, and he wondered aloud what its real purpose was.

'I think they're looking for ways and means to slide from under,' he said. 'Perhaps soon after we start again the prosecutor will say, as a result of further information we now think there's something in the charges and we're

242

asking for an adjournment *sine die* to conduct an investigation.

'So – they pull the rug from everyone, close matters like this . . .' He slapped his hands together as if to wipe dust from his palms. 'If we get that, I think the father will have won vindication. Although whether justice is done depends on whether the investigation continues.' He looked unconvinced that it would.

Georgiadis believed the evidence thus far clearly suggested a crude conspiracy. 'It may have been to protect a specific person,' he allowed, but it was more likely 'done with a view toward not rocking the boat, not hurting the tourist industry. It's the general malaise of Africa, not wanting to lose face before the world. Now they have to continue the official denial.'

Someone booted the ball horribly, he felt. 'You know, there are murderers and psychopaths all over the place. If the government had just come out immediately and acknowledged it as a murder, everyone would have said, jolly good, Kenya's doing its best. Now I think they're ruing the day they ever went down this road. I think what they're weighing is, will the world press crucify us?'

In truth, to many Kenyans the cross seemed to be already erected. On Sunday, 14 August, just after the inquest was adjourned, the top African news of the day was that Oliver Tambo, head of the antiapartheid African National Congress, had suffered a stroke. In the *Kenya Times* this was relegated to a small box at the bottom of page one with a reference to a story on page eight. The lead headline in the quasi-official newspaper partially owned by KANU (half was owned by Ward's bête noire, Robert Maxwell) was:

KENYA STILL A POPULAR DESTINATION

The newspaper regarded coverage of the inquest as another example of a persistent bias against Kenya in the British press. Only bad things were ever printed about Kenya, or broadcast on the BBC, Kenyan newspapers and

243

officials complained ceaselessly. They often suggested that foreign correspondents were engaged in little less than a conspiracy to dissuade tourists from visiting the country.

In its latest story the *Kenya Times* detailed the sensational coverage of the inquest in the British papers, appending its own interviews with London travelers and tour operators expressing confidence that the country's tourist trade would be undamaged.

'On Friday and Saturday the popular tabloid press – referred to by the intelligentsia as the 'gutter press' – pulled no stops in giving front-page treatment to the inquest. Each tabloid was competing against its rival for better coverage,' the *Kenya Times* wrote.

'The *Daily Mail* had pictures of Julie Ward and David Nchoko, named as the alleged killer, on its front page, with the headline: "I Did Not Kill Julie". The *Daily Mirror* joined the gravy train with the headline, "Safari Girl's 'Killer' Named by Cop" on the front page.

'During his preparations for the inquest, Mr Ward increasingly leaned on the usually sleazy tabloids for support and publicity.

'In Britain, the "gutter press" has a reputation for playing with the grief of its subjects. The "news" in some of the papers, according to surveys, is never believed by many of their readers.

'The reason why British media decided to give so many centimeters of newspaper space and airtime to the inquest is that Britain is in the middle of what, in journalism, is known as the "silly season",' the article explained. 'This is a time when many people go away on holiday and little news is generated . . .'

CHAPTER THIRTY-THREE

Mohammed Maru was the first to hear the gunfire. It was high noon, 20 August. They had sent two guests off not long before to pick up some new visitors landing at the nearest airstrip, and the gunfire seemed to come from that direction. Panicked, Maru ran to the room where his boss was hunched over a typewriter, writing a letter.

'Did you hear the shots?' Maru asked.

Even at the age of eighty-three George Adamson could move fast and decisively. He told Maru to get his rifle and two other men, and tucked a pistol into the belt of his khaki shorts. With Adamson at the wheel of a green Land Rover they sped off toward the airstrip.

A few minutes later they rounded a bend. Maru had time to see the guests' vehicle at the side of the road, one man down, a gang of intruders manhandling the young German woman who had been staying in the camp. He shouted at Adamson to stop but the old man seemed more determined to press on. Maru rolled out of the car, rifle in hand, just before the gang fired a fusillade at the windshield. Three bullets hit George Adamson, one in the chest. He never had a chance to get out his pistol. The two men who stayed in the car died with him.

No naturalist ever looked the part like George Adamson. The bright white hair swept back in a mane over his head, the white moustache and long goatee: He could have been deliberately trying to resemble the lions he raised and trained to re-enter the wild from his Kenyan game reserve at Kora, directly on the equator.

Adamson's move to Kora in 1970 had marked the beginning of his estrangement from his wife and partner, Joy, the author of *Born Free* and other books about their

245

joint projects to reacclimatize orphaned big cats to savage life in the bush. Ten years later, in 1980, Joy herself was murdered at her own reserve by a native worker she had sacked.

And now George. The murder, it seemed, had been the work of *shiftas*, Somali bandits who had ranged this part of central Kenya for years. They toted Soviet-made automatic rifles with which they had been equipped in the Somali army before mustering out or deserting. For years their prey had been elephants, for the ivory market was at its peak. *Shiftas* roamed so freely around parts of Kenya that it was not unusual for a busful of tourists to happen on an elephant carcass even in a carefully secured game reserve. It would have been felled by automatic rifle fire and the tusks lopped off; sometimes a power saw had been wielded unsurgically to do the job, leaving on the road the eerily faceless corpse of a majestic beast.

The economic impact of this poaching was not lost on the Kenyan government. If the big game continued to disappear, its 700,000 tourists a year would also vanish.

In early 1989, amid rising distress over the collapse of the elephant population and increasingly nasty debate in the Kenyan parliament, President Moi had made an important change in the wildlife management department. He fired George Muhoho, an MP whose response to the crisis had been limited to personal slurs against the naturalists making the most noise, and appointed as director of the Kenya Wildlife Service a man Muhoho himself had recently insulted in parliament as a 'cheeky white': Dr Richard Leakey.

Leakey was a brilliant choice. He was the son of the reknowned Louis S. B. Leakey, the white Kenyan paleontologist whose excavations in Tanzania's Olduvai Gorge had helped establish the prehistoric ancestry of man. Richard Leakey was an accomplished paleontologist in his own right, with many groundbreaking discoveries to his credit. He belonged to one of Kenya's most prominent families of white citizens; brother Philip (from whom Richard was estranged) was the parliament's only white member and the government's only white minister. As a white and a prominent scientist Richard Leakey could attract worldwide attention to the crisis of African ivory poaching in a way which, unfortunately, no black African could manage.

With a personal constituency securely insulated from Kenyan politics, Leakey moved fearlessly to wean his force of game rangers from nepotism and corruption. It was an open secret that many of the ill-paid rangers engaged in poaching themselves. The ivory trade was sometimes said to reach into the highest levels of Kenyan society. For rangers to prey on tourists was not unheard of; one domestic newspaper had recently run a letter from an irate American who claimed to have been 'commandeered' by a ranger during a game trip out of Keekorok Lodge. The man had refused to show them any identification, but hauled them to the main ranger office at Keekorok and gruffly ordered them to pay a park fee, which they assumed had already been paid by their tour company. 'We feel like we have been robbed – in the common term "poached" – by park rangers,' the tourist complained.

Leakey fired 2,000 superannuated or incompetent rangers – nearly half the force – and recruited an antipoaching force of professionals from among Kenya's élite military and paramilitary units (keeping them safely segregated in three isolated bivouacs). Moi obliged him by sanctioning a shoot-to-kill policy in the national parks. In July, a few weeks before the Julie Ward inquest convened, Leakey masterminded a world-class publicity stunt to dramatize the fight against the ivory trade. In a Nairobi field he had twelve tons of contraband tusks piled in a towering mound and doused with gasoline. With the world's press and international television crews watching, Moi touched a torch to the pile and it went up in a sheet of flame. The resulting photographs got page-one placement in newspapers all over the globe.

For a time the antipoaching campaign seemed to stem the depredation of the elephant herds. By midyear at least thirty poachers had been killed in confrontations with

Leakey's revitalized army. Ivory was no longer such a good business. Suddenly the *shiftas* were turning to victimizing humans.

At the moment of Adamson's death the tourist toll was rising. Marie Ferraro's death in Tsavo, in July, had been the fourth killing of a tourist in the Kenya parks. Another three visitors had been seriously wounded. Stories of ambushes and robberies in remote quarters of the game reserves began to hit the European and American newspapers, but they were nothing compared to the publicity that followed the murder of George Adamson.

Adamson's death made the front pages just like the ivory-burning. There was even a feature in *People* magazine. This time, however, the context was not Kenya's valiant fight against wildlife poachers, but the country's inability to keep its famed tourist venues safe and secure. Legions of reporters came into the country to document the hazards of game safaris. (KILLERS PROWL PARADISE was one British headline.) If they wanted a news peg it was not hard to find. Adding to the discomfiture of a tourism industry trying to mollify hundreds of thousands of skittish tourists, the inquest into Julie Ward's death in Kenya's most renowned game reserve was about to reconvene.

CHAPTER THIRTY-FOUR

The evening before the inquest recommenced, Caroline Davies got a personal introduction to the investigative capabilities of the Kenya Police. Stepping out of a taxicab in front of a Chinese restaurant in downtown Nairobi, she felt a tug on her shoulder as a car whizzed by behind her. Someone had leaned out from the car and, slashing the leather shoulder strap with a razor, roared away with the handbag in which she kept her money and passport.

When she called the police to report the theft, their response was something Nairobi residents were accustomed to hear: 'Can you send a car over to pick us up?' The next day she walked into a police station to report the theft personally, only to be told that the office did not have the appropriate forms on hand and she would have to return the following morning.

'I'm not coming back tomorrow,' she said. 'I want to report it right now.'

The desk officer reluctantly leaned down, pulled out a drawer, and laid the proper form in front of her after all. Even John Ward chuckled at the anecdote.

Meanwhile, interest in the inquest had intensified dramatically during the three-week hiatus. The murder of George Adamson and the killing of Mrs Ferraro had helped make tourist security in Kenya an issue of international curiosity. As tour operators secretly fretted and publicly expressed serenity, more reporters than ever before were scrambling for the padded gallery seats. Ward gave countless interviews as he paced the concrete corridor outside the courtroom.

'You're not from the Maxwell press, are you?' he could be heard asking every new arrival.

Other than that, no reporter could ask for a more amicable interviewee. 'I don't know how he does it,' remarked Jenny Jenkins one morning, crossing the traffic roundabout on her way into the Law Courts. Jenkins by then had spent considerable time with the entire Ward family, staying at the house in Bury during a home leave with her husband. Ward's unemotional determination amazed her. 'He's not vindictive, he's not angry about it,' she said. 'He just goes on.'

Every morning Ward arrived at the courthouse, sometimes with Georgiadis after an early-hour session, sometimes alone. It was a peculiarity of the proceedings that as a prospective witness he was not permitted inside the room; after all, he was paying for the stenographic transcript and he got a complete copy of the testimony to read every evening, before Georgiadis handed a complimentary text up to the magistrate the next day. Each morning and most afternoons he could be found pacing the hallway, stopping people coming outside for a break to ask: 'How do you think it's going?'

Sebastian Tham was back in the box on the morning of 4 September. Georgiadis took the floor to resume his examination after three weeks off.

Tham described how he and Ward had arrived at the mired Suzuki at about 11.30 a.m. They passed Henri Berney's camp on the way. The Swiss were not there, but Tham could not help noticing the bivouac's surfeit of electrical equipment and its impressive vehicular fleet. A few minutes later they reached the Suzuki, which Tham placed 300 meters from the Swiss camp 'as the crow flies.'

'What was the topography like?' Georgiadis asked.

'The terrain was fairly open, there was a fair amount of bush.' He shrugged. 'Typical Mara.'

'On approaching the Suzuki did you see any footprints?' Georgiadis asked.

'No, even though we were looking pretty hard for them,' Tham answered.

'During the search, did you leave any yourself?'

'Yes, I would have thought so.'

250

'The vehicle had a crude SOS on it,' Georgiadis stated.

'Yes.'

'You saw two tins of food, a bottle of beer, and some chocolate,' Georgiadis said. 'All of this certainly portable. Anyone wanting a walkabout and thought they might need food would have taken them, wouldn't you say?'

Tham shrugged. 'I would have thought so.'

'And fifteen feet from the site was a dry ford.' The lawyer's voice rose to stress the point. 'Perfecly obvious to anyone getting that close!'

'Very obvious. In fact it was crossed by a Ker & Downey vehicle while we watched.'

'So two possibilities suggest themselves. Either this was done in the dark – the jeep getting stuck, that is. Or it was planted there to give the appearance of a vehicle that had stuck.'

'Correct,' Tham agreed.

'To anyone climbing the bank, would the Swiss camp have been perfectly visible?'

Tham demurred at this. 'You would have had to walk a fair way,' he said, uncertainly.

'Now, while you were there, a Land Rover arrived with eight to ten people in civilian clothes, and one police officer – from the Ministry of Environment and Natural Resources, or some such thing.'

'Correct.'

'They milled about the area – leaving hoofprints all over, presumably,' Georgiadis remarked sourly.

'Correct,' Tham said, grinning.

Tham reiterated that he and Ward left the jeep after about an hour and returned to Keekorok Lodge, where Ward arranged to be taken on another aerial search. Late that afternoon he flew the father in his helicopter to see the discovered remains.

'Was there any blood around?' Georgiadis asked.

'No . . . I would say that near the fire were certainly body fluids.'

'But no large patches suggesting carnivores had consumed a person in that area.'

'No.'

'The rangers and police didn't bother to take samples of the fluids, of course,' Georgiadis said resignedly. 'Now, you, having had long experience of Africa and the Mara: Have you ever heard of carnivores cooking their meat before eating it?'

Tham grinned again to the accompaniment of snickers from the gallery. Georgiadis waited, looking off expectantly toward the side windows as if to indicate that his query was not rhetorical.

'No, I haven't,' Tham said.

'No, you haven't,' Georgiadis repeated. 'Now, Mr Ward is going to say that Inspector Othiambo said Julie had somehow set herself on fire and then was eaten by wild animals, possibly hyenas. Also he will say, "At this time the parties seemed ready to leave the scene and I formed the impression they were going to leave the remains there, as if nothing further could be done with them." You, Mr Tham, then offered a plastic seat cover so Mr Ward could take the remains. Inspector Othiambo then wanted to take charge of the bag. Mr Ward will say, "I was reluctant to give the remains to Othiambo, and a minor argument ensued."'

'I don't remember the argument, but I would agree with the rest of that.'

'Ward will say that while at the scene, he asked how the remains were found at such a desolate spot. Makallah said they followed footprints from the jeep, saw vultures circling in the distance, and went directly to the spot.'

Tham seemed amused. 'I was under the impression that it was more luck than anything else,' he said, 'not seeing vultures from eight kilometers away.'

'Later on, Mr Ward gave you the vehicle in gratitude for your help. What did you do with the Suzuki?'

'We just collected it and drove it back to Keekorok.'

'Did anyone from the police tell you the vehicle shouldn't be touched, because we need to investigate it?'

'No.'

'Did the police ever dust it for fingerprints, take photographs, examine its contents?'

'The police did take photos, but by then it had been washed and cleaned out.'

'What sort of photos?'

'Oh, they just came by one day, had us drive it out into a field, and they took some pictures around it.'

Georgiadis signaled he was finished, and Etyang rose to redirect. The short distance from the Swiss camp to the Suzuki might be a serious flaw in the government's case. The prosecutor tried to take Henri Berney's camp out of the landscape.

'Did you ever go there when the Swiss were there?' he asked.

'No.'

'How did you know this was the Swiss camp, then?'

'I assumed it from the talk.'

'Who was talking?'

'The talk around town.'

'Did they tell you the number of people at the camp?'

'No.'

'Did they tell you what they were doing?'

'No.'

'Could you tell from what country?'

'No,' Tham said. But there had been no other large independent camp in that part of the Mara at the time.

The balloon pilot waited patiently as the prosecutor mulled his next question.

'How long were you at the Suzuki before the police arrived?'

Tham shrugged in disinterest. 'I don't know.'

Etyang paused, as if for effect. 'Now,' he said, 'I want you to remember because this is *crucial*!' There was tittering from the gallery at the attempt to lend heft to such a vacuous question. 'Didn't you think it important to wait for the police?'

Tham shrugged again, as if amused at the suggestion. After all, he had been searching for a missing person and time was of the essence.

Etyang repeated his question.

'No, I didn't,' Tham replied.

CHAPTER THIRTY-FIVE

Charles Issika was an outsized caricature of a provincial police chief, a professional cousin of the sheriffs of many a southern American nightmare. He was the former superintendent of police in Narok, the man who had official jurisdiction over law enforcement in the Mara on the day Julie disappeared and for about a month after her remains were found. He fairly spilled over the sides of the witness box, bald head glistening and eyes narrowed in a permanent glare of suspicion.

By now the questioning of the Kenyan witnesses had fallen into a pattern. Etyang would lead them vaguely through their testimony, rarely stopping except to interject some minor question from behind his table, an elbow propped in one hand and the other stroking his chin. When their train of thought ran out he would himself seem a little lost, flipping the white pages of his notebook as if in search of some new point to raise.

Issika's examination began that way as the superintendent sought to portray his response to word of Julie's disappearance in a positive light. He said his first hint that a tourist had gone astray in the game reserve came at 3 p.m. on 12 September, when Paul Weld Dixon found him in his office.

'I immediately did a missing-persons report,' the superintendent said. 'It was felt that the girl might have lost her way and gone into Tanzania. I signaled the Masai Mara police' – that is, Inspector Othiambo at Mara Bridge – 'that if the girl is found she should be assisted.'

'Is it easy to get lost in that area?' Etyang asked.

'No,' replied Issika, 'because there's a gate between the

254

Kenya and Tanzania sides. If you don't turn off the main road, it's hard to get lost.'

At that Issika demonstrated the contrary. Trying to trace on a road map the paved routes out of a game park that had been under his command for ten years, he became hopelessly confused. Three mains road led out of the park in its eastern half, but only two of them went toward Nairobi – one from the Sekenani Gate, through which Julie had entered the park, and a second through the Ole Malepo or Olaimutiek Gate, a few miles east. Issika seemed to believe that Julie had been heading out of the park to Nairobi via the third road, which led off to the west and nowhere near Nairobi. Georgiadis took the opportunity to engage him in a long angry argument about the mistake and the superintendent's native abilities.

At length resuming his testimony, Issika said he ordered his men to open an inquest file on 15 September, when Othiambo reported that the leg found in the Mara was human. But he was transferred to Nairobi on 19 October, he said, before the file had grown much.

To Georgiadis, Issika was a key to one of his principal goals in the inquest: If the proceedings would not generate charges against a suspect, as he doubted it would, he could at least use it to lay open the weeks and months of complacent police inaction that followed the discovery of the remains.

Indolently propping his rear against the witness box, Issika was a heaven-sent exhibit A, a time-serving superintendent preoccupied with the patronage possibilities of his post in KANU. As Georgiadis strolled around to the front of his table, the officer tried to fix him with a glare.

Georgiadis said, 'You testify, Superintendent, that the first time you heard about a missing Julie Ward was on September twelfth, from Paul Weld Dixon. Had you not had any sort of message from any Nairobi police station before then?'

'No, Your Honor.'

'But there was information about a missing person well before the twelfth.'

255

'Could be,' Issika said, grinning carelessly, 'but it had not reached me.'

'Did you express any interest in this case after that? Did you ask to examine the leg yourself, for example?'

'I did not.'

'Why not? You were the senior police officer of the Mara. Weren't you interested?'

'I could tell nothing from the leg. It might have been an animal leg.'

Georgiadis shot him a look of exasperated disbelief. 'You can't tell the difference between a human leg and something that's not a human leg? Come on, Superintendent. Brace up!'

Issika explained that he had assigned the case to a deputy, and left it all to him.

'Can you produce to me a single statement that your officers took, for instance from the rangers at Sand River on the sixth?'

Issika shifted uneasily and admitted to having been preoccupied. 'By then, KANU elections had started.'

'KANU elections started. Indeed. I put it to you that after shrugging off the responsibility, you took no further interest in this matter. And absoutely nothing happened!'

Issika tried to look indignant. His deputy 'had moved in,' he said.

'Well, what sort of briefing did he give you?'

'He told me about the postmortem that Dr Kaviti performed, that the leg and jaw were human.'

Georgiadis smiled indulgently. 'Yes, right. Well, Dr Kaviti was not at the postmortem. Your deputy said the "police pathologist" had done the examination, and you assumed that meant Dr Kaviti. That I can understand, even though it is sloppy. Did you ask the deputy to make a statement regarding the happenings at the mortuary?'

'No.'

'You just shrugged it off.'

'Yah,' Issika said lazily.

'And evidently he did not repeat the pathologist's allegation that the bone was cut and it was murder. I suggest to you, Superintendent, that no proper police procedure was followed after that. And as a result of zero activity by the police, Superintendent Wanjau had to be put in charge of the investigation.'

'No! Wanjau was to assist.'

Georgiadis dismissed the assertion with a wave. 'Now come on, Superintendent. Let's brace up, shall we?'

The next morning the lights failed. As the principals and spectators milled around, Georgiadis's voice sounded off in the chilly gloom. 'We're in our usual Stygian darkness,' he said.

When the lights came back on Dr Perez Malande Olindo took the stand. President of the African Wildlife Federation since the previous May, he had been director of the Kenya National Parks for ten years and director of the wildlife conservation department for two. Professorial and precise, he testified that Paul Weld Dixon, his Langata neighbor, had reached him on 10 September to ask if, as wildlife director, he could extract some information from the posts at the Mara.

'It was after dark and there was no way to get through,' he observed. 'The radio network, even for me as director, closed at 6.30 p.m. I couldn't do much.'

At 8.30 the next morning, as Olindo recalled, he flew Weld Dixon to the park in his own plane. Etyang interrupted to pursue a couple of irrelevancies.

'What type of aircraft was this?'

'This was a Cessna 182.'

'A 182 . . .' Etyang paused as if trying to envision the specifications in his mind's eye. 'And . . . how many seats?'

'It was a four-seater,' Olindo said patiently.

After describing meeting Simon Makallah in Keekorok Lodge upon landing on the gravel airstrip, Olindo resumed, 'I asked the senior warden one question: whether the police had been informed. He said yes. I was satisfied that if the Kenya Police were on the case, the matter would be in good hands.'

Weld Dixon went off to Sand River with Makallah, while Olindo decided to overfly the area. At 300 feet he and two volunteer spotters flew over Keekorok, from Keekorok to Sand River Camp, then along the river, but they saw nothing.

Etyang: 'At what speed where you flying?'

'We were cruising at about a hundred to a hundred and twenty nautical miles per hour.'

'Would you say that was fast or slow?'

'I would say that at that height, and flying at about a hundred and twenty nautical miles per hour, your ability to take in detail is limited.'

'If the car were somewhere in thick bush would you have seen it?'

'I don't think we would have seen it.'

Georgiadis rose. He was holding the first blue page of Olindo's police statement.

'Could you tell us,' he asked, 'when did the police approach you to take this statement?'

'They came to ask me on August twenty-eighth, 1989.'

'Yes. After this very proceeding had begun. And you were one of the people intimately involved, initially, in the search for the car and the girl. And you were never asked for a statement at any other time?'

'No.'

'When you were at the Mara, did you ask what steps Mr Makallah had taken?'

'No.'

'And the reason you didn't ask,' Georgiadis said with a suspicion of sarcasm in his voice, 'was that you had left it in the good hands of the Kenya constabulary.'

As if as an afterthought he raised another issue. 'You say that if the vehicle were in thick bush you would not have been able to see it from the air. You know, of course, that when it was found the vehicle was out in the open. It was not obscured by trees.'

As Georgiadis finished his questioning of Olindo the lunchtime treads of passersby were already echoing in the corridors outside. It was a propitious time to break, for in a way all that had transpired up to now in the inquest was merely a prelude. When the hearing reconvened at 2.30 that afternoon the main course would be on the table: Simon Makallah.

CHAPTER THIRTY-SIX

Ward and Georgiadis had been careful to tell people in Nairobi that they could not be sure who was implicated in Julie's murder. They only indicated their suspicions of person or persons they preferred not to name. It was all a bit disingenuous. Any journalist who could leave an interview with either man unaware that Simon Makallah was a suspect was dim indeed.

But not everyone accepted their scenario at face value. One who tried to dispel Georgiadis's suspicions was Aris Grammaticas, the owner of Governor's Camp.

Grammaticas thought he knew both Makallah and the Masai Mara well enough to consider the chief warden's involvement in such a crime dubious. Makallah might be devious, but the lodge owner could not imagine him cast as a killer. He was particularly doubtful that Makallah could have kept his involvement in a serious crime secret for long. The warden was not an entirely popular figure among the Mara staff, he told Georgiadis, a close friend. There had been continual conflicts between the warden and his rangers. Makallah's suspension over the string of alleged administrative infractions was another indication of the delicacy of his situation. The Mara was in many ways a very small place, Grammaticas cautioned the lawyer. If Makallah had been involved, he was sure someone in the park would have already exposed him.

For his part Georgiadis was intrigued by Grammaticas's story of meeting the chief warden just after the discovery of Julie's body and hearing him dismiss the wild-animal scenario with a remark about the fire having been lit with petrol. The lawyer asked Grammaticas to appear at the inquest. Grammaticas demurred: he did not want to get involved unless it was necessary.

'I'll testify if he lies,' he finally agreed. In the event, Makallah did lie and Grammaticas came to testify about the conversation late in the inquest.

Meanwhile, Ward and Georgiadis had so successfully painted Makallah as the devil incarnate that the court seemed to be taken a little off guard when the witness himself appeared carrying a brown leather briefcase with a jumble of papers, bowed to Magistrate Mango, and stepped into the box.

Makallah was an unlikely-looking demon. He was short and tubby, with smooth glistening skin and a receding hairline. It would be too much to say his face had an angelic glow, but it did wear a permanent half-smile that could be at turns ingenuous, smug, or ignorant, depending on the prevailing conditions. Over the next two days all three qualities would be mustered up as the ex-senior warden of the Masai Mara put up a fight for his life.

Makallah was also an unlikely-looking Masai or outdoorsman. Masai were common sights all over Kenya, even on the busiest sidewalks of Nairobi. They were a distinctive-looking people, tall and lean, with prominent cheekbones and angular, nearly Caucasian features. Among the western-garbed Africans on Nairobi's sidewalks their women stood out with their shaved heads and red-and-white shawls, strings of colored beads and geometrically twisted wires hanging from their distended earlobes. As they went on their business on the modern streets of the city, the Masai in their proud and even haughty demeanor could draw the stares urbanized Africans otherwise reserved for peculiar European behavior.

Makallah's face was nicely filled out, as if he might be more familiar with the lunch buffet at Keekorok Lodge than with the traditional tribal diet of milk and cow's blood. One earlobe was slightly distended, suggesting he was torn between Masai traditions, exemplified by the strikingly looped earlobe, stretched from childhood by progressively larger plugs of wood, and the modern young

261

Masai's repudiation of the practice entirely. He placed his briefcase at his feet, draped one arm indolently over the railing of the stand, leaned back with his half-smile, and looked out over the courtroom with an air of indifference. The place was packed, for Georgiadis and Ward had left no doubt that this was to be an important day.

Alex Etyang went first. He started slowly. Makallah allowed that he had been working in the Mara for fourteen years, the most recent four years as senior warden in charge of the reserve's 154 game rangers. Etyang led him tediously through a statistical resume of the reserve: its 1,690 square kilometers, six entry gates, three posts, and so on. Then he let Makallah reveal that he was at the moment on leave, which had begun 15 July and was to finish at the end of September. To Kenyans and Britons, for whom leave is a synonym for vacation, the statement was unremarkable.

Etyang asked him, 'Have you had any instances of tourists molested by your staff reported to you?'

'No, Your Honor,' Makallah said.

'Have you ever had any instances where tourists were killed in the park?'

'We have never had an instance of people killed by people in the park, Your Honor. But we have had two cases of people killed by wild animals.'

In 1984 at Governor's Camp, the luxury tented camp owned by Grammaticas and William ole Ntimama, he said, a tourist who strayed into the adjacent forest 'met a buffalo which gored and killed him.' At about the same time, at Kichwa Tembo, another camp on the edge of the reserve not far from Governor's, an American woman on a 'walking safari' was also killed by a buffalo. 'The walking safaris were stopped after that time,' the warden said.

Makallah said he had first heard of Julie's disappearance through a message from Langata – evidently Olindo's radio message the morning after the director first heard from Weld Dixon. Olindo instructed Makallah 'to find out whether she did come into the park.'

Makallah's chronology was mysterious. Olindo recalled

being contacted by Weld Dixon on the 10th, too late to send a radio message. That meant that Makallah must have got his message on the 11th – but that was the day Olindo arrived early in the morning. The discrepancy was never elucidated.

Makallah continued to say he checked at all six gates and eventually scored a hit at Sekenani, the likeliest entry place for a tourist driving from Nairobi. The visitors' register showed she had entered at 4 p.m. on 2 September with a companion, headed for Sand River.

He went to Sand River, where he was told by the clerk, David Nchoko, that she had arrived and left on the morning of the 3rd for a game drive. Nchoko also told him that when she failed to reappear, the rangers had queried the lodges in the park and discovered that she had checked into the Mara Serena. Nchoko, curiously, had never mentioned to anyone else this early alert on Julie's whereabouts.

Makallah learned from the Serena that she had left on the 6th to return to Sand River. There he was told, again by Nchoko, that she had left for Nairobi on the 6th after packing her tents. Nchoko showed Makallah the vehicle receipt, but Makallah said he discovered that in filling out the receipt book the clerk had skipped two pages, meaning that two vehicles which left the campsite after Julie had evidently been given receipts with lower serial numbers. Nchoko 'explained it was just a mistake,' Makallah said. 'He was not careful.'

Presently Makallah headed back to his headquarters at Keekorok 'to wait for the director,' who arrived by air with Weld Dixon.

'From that day we started to do a quiet search on the ground,' Makallah said equably.

'What kind of search?' Etyang asked.

'A quiet search. I simply instructed my men to look out as they go out for their normal duties. We just carried out a look around.'

Two days later he was informed by police that the Suzuki had been found on Makindu Stream off the Sand

River. Makallah collected some rangers and policemen and set off in a Land Rover. 'We found a brown Suzuki stuck in the river mud in the bed of the stream. No-one was there when we arrived.'

He described the SOS on the roof, the broken side window, and the sight of two beer bottles, one partially consumed, inside the jeep. 'We found a small track under the vehicle had been dug so as to divert water,' and the ground around the jeep had been heavily trampled.

'You could see that somebody was walking around that vehicle, Your Honor.'

Makallah also claimed to have seen the tire marks of the Suzuki, indicating it had come from the west, that is, from Keekorok or Sand River, and that he followed these tire marks back for about a kilometer until they disappeared.

That was too much for Georgiadis. Tham had already testified that there were no tire marks around, and Ward was going to corroborate it. 'He's telling you a lot of lies and you know it,' he complained aloud to Etyang.

The prosecutor asked Makallah to continue. He said he returned to the jeep, observing that the area 'was a place where tourists normally don't go.' He saw that somebody had evidently tried to dig the mud out from under the tires, as if to give the jeep some traction. Mud caked the exterior of the vehicle from the spinning of the wheels.

But the four wheels were all in the mud, he said, contradicting Tham, who recalled that at least one was suspended in midair. Then Makallah unwisely volunteered an opinion:

'If that vehicle had four-wheel-drive, I think it could have crossed the gully,' he said.

From his table Georgiadis looked curiously at Etyang. 'You don't know your evidence,' he hissed. Within twenty-four hours Georgiadis would use Makallah's last remark to make a damning accusation.

Makallah continued on heedlessly. The rangers managed to find some footprints in the bank of the stream, he said. Following them, the search party climbed the southern bank of the river and continued for a hundred meters until they disappeared. 'Then we got into our vehicles and said, "OK, let's just move out over the area – just drive around." We generally headed south toward Tanzania. We just drove until four-thirty or four forty-five, when we saw vultures. They were sleeping in the tree. We came closer and the others took off from the ground.'

He had considered this significant. Vultures circle over carrion. 'Naturally, we use vultures very much when we are looking for poachers.'

They searched the small clearing where the vultures had been feeding, Makallah continued, and found the two pieces of jawbone. 'We came across the foot, in an old animal track about ten meters away. We also found where there was a fire, where there were some tins and coins and film cassettes, a spoon and knife, cooking stove, saucepan, cup. From what I saw, there was no firewood around.'

Etyang asked, 'Did you know this camp of Swiss photographers?'

Makallah, who had found them their campsite, answered, 'Yes, they were camped on the same tributary as the jeep.'

'How far away?'

'Three or four kilometers,' Makallah said, placing them and Julie well out of each others' range.

'Can you see them from the vehicle?'

'There is a rocky hill between the two,' Makallah said, 'so you cannot see the vehicle from the camp, and you cannot see the camp from where the vehicle was.'

'Did you ever see Julie Ward alive?'

'No, no, Your Honor.'

'Did any of your rangers?'

'Other than Nchoko, no.'

With that Etyang turned Makallah over to Georgiadis.

Georgiadis got up from his seat behind his table and looked over at Makallah. He walked around the table and approached the witness in almost a friendly way. First he asked his age. Makallah said he was born on 24 February, 1950.

'Please speak up,' Georgiadis said. 'You know . . . I'm

265

hard of hearing.' There was an expectant titter from the gallery.

Georgiadis knew that Makallah's authority over park workers, including the forger Nchoko, had already been established. That was point one of the lawyer's three-point profile of the murderer. The second and third points would be to show that Makallah knew the park well and had unhampered entrée within its perimeters.

'You've worked in the Mara for thirteen, fourteen years now, is that correct?' he asked Makallah.

'Yes, Your Honor.' Makallah relaxed back into the witness box.

'So,' the lawyer observed equably, 'you know it pretty well. Every road and byway, every track, and so on.'

Makallah inflated with pride. 'Yes, Your Honor.'

'Could find your way around it in the dark, if necessary,' Georgiadis said amiably.

'Yup,' Makallah grinned.

Point two. Georgiadis looked satisfied. But before he moved to the final point, he aimed to destroy Makallah's credibility.

'While you are on leave, where do you stay?'

'I have a house in Kilgoris,' Makallah said, naming a small village not far from the Mara boundary. 'It consists of my house, my wife, my children, my cattle – everything.'

'I see. And until the fifteenth, when you say you went on leave, where were you?'

'Working at Keekorok.'

'Are you sure?'

'Yes, Your Honor.'

'Were you not interdicted last year or this year?' This was one of Georgiadis's trump cards. For the plot against Makallah begun when the Ntimama clique took over Narok had resulted in his indefinite suspension, or interdiction. As Ward had discovered when he tried to seek the warden out, Makallah had not been inside the park boundaries for almost a year.

Makallah looked concerned at Georgiadis's question. 'No, Your Honor.'

'At no time?'

'No.'

'I submit to you that you have been under interdiction since within a few weeks following this event . . .'

Makallah was shaking his head. 'No!'

'. . . and that another chief warden has taken over from you.'

'No. I have a letter of compulsory leave from the Narok County Council.'

'A letter of compulsory leave? Let's see it. Do you have it with you?'

'Yes, Your Honor.' Makallah lifted his briefcase and rummaged for a couple of minutes in the chaos of papers. At length he looked up and said, 'It is not here. I think it is outside.'

Mango interjected to tell Makallah to get it. The witness left the box and disappeared out the courtroom door. There was a pregnant silence, until Georgiadis broke the tension by articulating what was on everybody's mind.

'I hope he doesn't disappear,' he said. 'I haven't even started.'

Ward was pacing in the hallway when he was startled by Makallah's sudden emergence from the courtroom. He was even more surprised to see the warden take aside a police officer Ward recognized as Wanjau. They conferred for a few minutes under Ward's suspicious gaze, and then Makallah returned to the courtroom.

He stepped into the witness box empty handed. Reaching again into his briefcase, he brought out another page. 'I only have this.'

'And what is that?'

'A charge sheet.'

Georgiadis reached out his hand.

'OK, let's see the charge sheet.'

Makallah hastily replaced the page in his bag. 'No, I don't have it here.'

'You just showed it to us!' The gallery roared with laughter. 'Now, let's have it!'

'No, that was something else.'

In exasperation, Georgiadis turned to Mango. 'He was proffering the charge sheet. I ask he be ordered to produce it.'

'Where is this sheet,' Mango leaned over to ask Makallah.

'It is not here. That was something else.'

Wearily, Mango gave up, ordering Georgiadis to proceed. The lawyer tried to object again, but finally, reluctantly, continued.

'Michael Koikai is now the acting senior warden, is he not? When was he appointed?'

'It must have been earlier this year,' Makallah said.

'So you have not assumed your duties since earlier this year.'

'But so long as I have not been sacked or transferred, I am still there,' Makallah said defiantly.

The lawyer paused.

'When you are at the Mara how do you get around? Do you have vehicles at your disposal?'

'No, Your Honor, I do not drive.'

'You don't drive?'

'No, someone has to drive me. I don't have a licence.'

'But you yourself drove Mr Ward and Mr Ribeiro from Keekorok to the Sand River Gate on September twenty-fifth.'

'No, Your Honor.'

'I see. If Mr Ribeiro or John Ward says you drove them from Keekorok to Sand River, that would be untrue?'

'It would be untrue.'

Georgiadis asked, 'Do you think you're an honorable man and a truthful man?'

'Yes,' Makallah affirmed.

'I see. Good. Let's record that.'

He moved on.

'Were you trained to use the radio at Mweka?' he asked, referring to the Tanzanian wildlife institute were many top wardens had been taught.

'Yes.'

'And you've used it for thirteen years.'

'Yes.'

'And in your radio training you were also trained to utilize distress signals.'

'No, Your Honor.'

'No? But you know what "SOS" means, don't you? "Save our Souls"?' Georgiadis was convinced that a civilian like Julie would have scrawled 'Help' rather than 'SOS' on the jeep. Makallah was of scant assistance on this point.

'I know it, but from novels,' Makallah said.

'I see, novels. With the radios are you daily in touch with Sand River?'

'I think so.'

Georgiadis shot him a look. 'You think so? Why are you so guarded in your answers, Mr Makallah?'

'I'm not guarded.'

'No. Well. Now, there are no vehicles stationed at the gates, is that right?'

'Yes.'

'The gates call on radio for a vehicle if the need arises. Is there a system of logbooks for each vehicle?'

'Yes, Your Honor.'

'Did the police ever ask you to produce any of the work tickets relating to the use of your vehicles?'

'No.'

'Did the police ever come and search the headquarters' sleeping quarters?'

'No.'

'Did they ever ask to search your home in Kilgoris?'

'No.'

'Did the police ever ask you to record a statement of your movements with the vehicles?'

'No.'

'Did they ask to search or inspect any vehicles that you used during the relevant period?'

'No, Your Honor.'

'Did the police ever ask you to produce any of the clothing you wore from the sixth to the thirteenth of September, 1988?'

'No.'

'Is there any occurrence book at the gates which records your entry or exit?'

'No, Your Honor.'

'So is there any corroborative evidence of your movements in the Mara?'

'Yes, Your Honor. A work ticket says what area is visited in the vehicle.'

'A work ticket. Which is really under your own control. So you had complete freedom of movement in the Mara, and other than the work ticket, there was no system of recording your travels.'

Point three. Georgiadis was ready to wrap up the testimony for the day. 'Did you ever conduct inquiries of your own about this incident?'

'No, Your Honor. Once the body was found it became a police case.'

CHAPTER THIRTY-SEVEN

Georgiadis thought he had the right to expect his cross-examination of Makallah on 5 September to create a splash. He had shown him up for lying about his suspension from duties and confronted him with a further lie about his driving. He had established quite clearly, he thought, that the police had shown not the slightest interest in investigating whether the warden or his rangers might have been implicated in the crime. He had shown that Makallah knew his way around the park even at night, when the most sinister crimes could be committed, and that no-one could track his movements.

The next day's Nairobi newspapers ignored all this. Instead they concentrated on Etyang's preceding direct examination, in which Makallah had tediously related his story about searching for Julie, finding the jeep, and following footprints and vultures to the remains. In the *Daily Nation*, normally the best of three domestic English-language newspapers, Georgiadis's three-hour assault on the warden was reduced to one paragraph, incorrect even in its main assertion:

'On being cross-examined by Mr Byron Georgiadis, the game warden denied that he had been interdicted and replaced by another senior game warden for his "inactivity" in the search for the girl.'

Georgiadis was on the warpath when he stalked into the courtroom that day. He paused in front of the jury box, where the Kenyan reporters were clustered, and remarked: 'Got your earplugs in today? You'll need them.'

When Etyang followed him in, Georgiadis went so far as to engage the prosecutor in a brotherly colloquy about the semiliterate domestic press. 'Don't they have editors?' his polished diction rang out, even in its rage, from behind his table. 'Where are they? They couldn't be entirely dim.'

When inspired to be, the Kenyan press could be as accurate and incisive as any in a country with a constitutional right to a free press, as Kenya was. But in modern Kenya the inspiration was more often toward self-censorship.

The three daily newspapers, the *Standard*, *Daily Nation*, and *Kenya Times* (all were published in English and the latter two in Swahili editions as well), harbored some very astute journalists and acute political analysts on their staffs, but they all kept mostly quiet in recognition of the Moi administration's distaste for criticism.

Government pressure on critical publications manifested itself in several ways. A favorite stratagem was to threaten independent printing shops, so a magazine might find itself with no way to get printed and bound. In Kenya's highly controlled business world official permits were needed for thousands of mundane activities (this also contributed to corruption, for a bureaucrat could hold up even a routine permit indefinitely in quest of a bribe); at least one magazine publisher had been charged with the seemingly innocuous crime of failing to register his journal with the registrar of books and newspapers.

The ultimate penalty was to be banned. It was not one from which the government shrank; in the eighteen months preceding the start of the Ward inquest the authorities had put three outspoken publications permanently out of business. The first was *Beyond*, a magazine published by the National Christian Council of Kenya, which had printed accusations of election rigging in a KANU primary. A year later the *Financial Review* ran afoul of the authorities for criticizing government economic policy (and incidentally publishing an article about the two Asian-owned conglomerates through which President Moi made most of his secret investments in Kenyan businesses), and soon after that *Development Agenda*, another business review, was also banned.

These were all small, privately financed publications.

The newspapers were different. The *Standard* was partially owned by Lonrho, the British mining and hotel company run by Tiny Rowland, Moi's friend. A large interest in the *Nation* was held by the Aga Khan, the Ismailite Moslem leader with a large religious and cultural following in Kenya, as in dozens of other heavily Muslim countries.

Since the *Kenya Times* was half-owned by KANU itself, the *Standard* and the *Nation* were really the only legitimate independent dailies in the country. Despite their powerful owners neither was exempt from government pressure and both kept really pointed criticism of the government out of their pages. (To criticize Moi personally, moreover, was strictly out of bounds.) Not long after the Ward inquest ended, several of the *Standard*'s top editors were briefly jailed when the paper published some biting coverage of a government program using bulldozers to raze shanty towns in Nairobi's outskirts.

Just before the inquest started, parliament itself had barred the *Nation* from covering its activities after the newspaper critiqued the puerile quality of debate in the legislature. The MPs threatened stronger action and had begun to wax offensive about the Aga Khan himself. One story making the rounds of Nairobi said that the Aga Khan responded by sending a sealed letter directly to President Moi, warning that unless the newspaper's status was restored forthwith, he would withdraw from all activity in Kenya. Since the philanthropy-minded religious leader financed countless hospitals, schools, and development programs in the country, such a threat would be an important one. Four months after it was ejected from parliament the *Nation* was invited back.

The lesson of this sort of government behavior was absorbed by the newspapers just as it had been by the civil service: Don't rock the boat. The sloppy reporting of each day's events in the Ward inquest – names were wrong, testimony reduced to gibberish, important details overlooked or misconstrued – could have been explained by ineptitude and by the poor working conditions and acoustics in the courtroom. The inquest was not ignored

– in fact it was front-page news almost every day. But that there was no affirmative effort to examine critically what it revealed about the state of Kenya's law-enforcement and legal systems testified to the timidity of the press as an institution. It was easier to treat the proceedings as just another attempt by colonialist whites to denigrate the black government of independent Kenya.

When Mango stepped up to the bench on the second morning of Makallah's testimony Etyang rose to complain about the misinterpretation of the interdiction order, which he pointed out had nothing to do with Julie Ward.

Georgiadis then seized the floor to continue in the same vein. Mango was as aware as anyone else of the way the domestic papers had mishandled much of the testimony. But he was also wary of the foreign press in the room. Georgiadis proceeded to give him an opportunity to deliver to them a firm warning.

'The local newspapers have not been reporting the inquest properly,' the barrister complained. 'It's been a garbled mess most of the time. In fact, my cross-examination yesterday in the *Daily Nation* has been reduced to one idiotic paragraph that doesn't make any sense at all to me.'

Mango was aroused by the epithet. 'What word did you just use?' he asked Georgiadis.

The lawyer this time left out the offending word. 'I said the *Daily Nation* only referred to my cross-examination in only one paragraph in their report.'

Mango then gave the local papers their lead for the next day. 'Mr Georgiadis, I heard what you just said. Refrain from using insulting language in court. I am warning you that this court will not hesitate putting you in the cells if you continue doing so. Now sit down!'

Chastened, Georgiadis mumbled, 'As Your Honor pleases.'

(MAGISTRATE GIVES CELL WARNING TO GEORGIADIS was the headline in the next day's *Standard*.)

Now Mango himself let loose about the poor reporting.

But he directed the bulk of his remarks toward the visiting British press in the gallery. 'Don't think we do not read what the British papers have been writing about this inquest. We also get copies of their newspapers here. I take this chance to warn the concerned newspapers and especially the British press that this court will not hesitate to clear them from the courtroom for misreporting!'

Georgiadis had a good reason for wanting to fire a shot across the press's bow: This was the day intended to bring his cross-examination of Makallah to a spectacular climax. With the warden's credibility in question the lawyer was going to pick apart his story piece by piece.

Makallah testified that after hearing the Suzuki had been found on 13 September, he collected a detachment of rangers and two vehicles at Keekorok and sped to the scene. 'By about eleven a.m. we were there.'

Georgiadis knew this was impossible: Tham had said he and Ward were the first to arrive, at 11.30, and stayed an hour. He did not want to give Makallah so much free time without making him account for it.

'Eleven a.m.? Are you sure?'

'It could have been some minutes past eleven.'

'Not some hours?' the lawyer asked.

'No.'

'I suggest to you that you are mistaken.'

'I am not mistaken, Your Honor.'

Georgiadis let Makallah describe again how he gave the Suzuki a cursory glance while he was at the gully.

'Had you ever seen the Suzuki before?' the lawyer asked.

'No,' Makallah said casually.

'Ever see it again after that day?'

'No.'

'You took no photographs, made no measurements?'

'No.'

'Know anything about cars? Look underneath it?'

'No.'

Georgiadis stopped. Makallah's arm was again propped indolently over the railing. The half smile played over his face.

With a tone of quiet menace Georgiadis said, 'You made a bad mistake yesterday in your evidence.' The room was silent.

'You said it was possible for the Suzuki to cross the Sand River if it had four-wheel-drive.' He read from his notes: "If it had four-wheel-drive, I'm sure it could have crossed." Remember saying that?'

'From my experience you cannot cross that spot without four-wheel-drive,' Makallah said uncertainly.

Georgiadis fixed him with his steely eyes. 'How did you know that this vehicle was not a four-wheel-drive?'

Makallah stammered. 'I didn't know, Your Honor. What I meant was, if any did—'

'How did you know this particular Suzuki did not have four-wheel-drive?' Georgiadis repeated, raising his voice.

'All I meant . . . Your Honor . . . any vehicle with four-wheel-drive would have crossed the stream—'

'You volunteered this statement. Now I'm asking you – how did you know – how did you get this esoteric knowledge—'

'From the way it was stuck . . . It was not badly stuck.'

Georgiadis cut in. 'Mr Tham told the court that this vehicle was stuck irretrievably in the mud of the stream. He had to drag it out, tow it out. What you said doesn't make sense unless you knew about that vehicle, and had driven it before!'

'I am saying based on what I saw,' Makallah replied.

Mango interrupted. 'Had you driven the vehicle?'

'No, Your Honor.'

'I suggest,' said Georgiadis, coming from behind the table to stand directly in front of Makallah in the dock, 'you knew about this vehicle and you had driven it into the Sand River the night before!'

'It's not true! I never saw that vehicle and I never drove it.'

Georgiadis and Makallah faced each other across the rim

of the witness box in a standoff. But the lawyer had more to come.

'Now,' he said. 'About these footprints . . . did anyone measure these footprints you say you followed? Take a photograph? Make a plaster cast?'

'No.'

'So we have to rely on your word?'

'Yes.'

'You followed them a hundred meters, going upstream along the eastern bank, following the Sand River . . . What did they look like? What kind of mark?'

Makallah seemed to search for an answer. 'Whoever walked there had some shoes, they were not barefoot, the toes weren't showing . . .' The warden was getting addled by his own testimony.

Georgiadis could not suppress a chuckle. 'You're making this up as you go along, aren't you?'

A muddled Makallah replied hastily, 'Yes!'

'Yes.' Georgiadis laughed along with the gallery. 'I'm sure you are.'

Then he turned serious again. 'Are you aware that a previous party of persons, Mr Ward and Tham, and others, arrived before you?'

'Yes.'

'Are you aware they scouted around looking for footprints, signs of the girl?'

'I am not aware.'

'Are you surprised to hear that Mr Tham and Mr Ward saw no footprints at all?'

'I was not aware . . .'

'And that the running of sand on the rooftop "SOS" showed it had showered the night before?'

'I was not aware.'

'And that another vehicle got there before you—'

'I am not aware of that.'

'—eight or ten people. These people would all leave footprints, wouldn't they?'

'Yes.'

'So how come,' said Georgiadis, 'you saw only one set of

footprints, in an indeterminate type of shoe, which you followed?'

'Your Honor,' said Makallah, stubbornly, 'I am talking from what I have seen with my own eyes.'

'When you saw Mr Ward at the site of the remains later that afternoon,' Georgiadis asked, 'did he inquire how the remains had come to be found in such a desolate spot?'

'I don't remember,' Makallah replied.

'Didn't you inform him the rangers saw footprints crossing the river a hundred yards from the jeep, and that you followed another hundred yards and then saw the vultures and went to the spot?'

'No – I never discussed anything with him.'

'You've seen many kills and many remains stripped by vultures – you'd consider yourself a bit of an expert, wouldn't you?'

'Not "a bit",' Makallah said. 'I am.'

'If that girl had been lying there for many hours and you haphazardly came across the vultures, would not that leg have been stripped bare?'

'I don't know,' Makallah said. 'I can't tell exactly when the vultures arrived there.'

'So you think the vultures arrived prophetically a few minutes before you did?'

'I can't tell.'

'May I suggest to you,' Georgiadis said evenly, 'that the only reason you mentioned vultures at all was that you had to suggest a reason to head to that area. You put them there to give you a reason to find the remains in bush where you could have passed ten yards away without seeing them . . . to give you a cause and a reason to find them ten kilometers from the jeep.'

'The vultures are wild animals,' Makallah replied. 'I cannot put them there by myself.'

'In fact,' Georgiadis continued, 'the leg would have been consumed by vultures in a matter of minutes.'

'I don't know . . . It depends on what species of vulture . . .'

'Did you think these vultures had come just for a look-see?'

'Of course not.'

'No, they came to feed.'

'Yes, Your Honor.'

'Well, if they came to feed, you would not have seen a leg like this,' Georgiadis said. 'It would have been stripped to the bone.'

Georgiadis's attack on Makallah had to be considered a draw. The warden's reputation was in tatters, but he had not broken down. His denial of having driven Julie's Suzuki had held, and without eliciting this admission Georgiadis still had no firm evidence that Makallah was guilty – just the man's suspect behavior. Before allowing Makallah to step down the lawyer informed the court that he might want to call him later in the inquest. Mango nodded agreement, but it was for nothing. Makallah disappeared. He would not resurface again until many months after the inquest had concluded.

CHAPTER THIRTY-EIGHT

Within minutes of taking the stand in his turn Inspector
George Othiambo contradicted Makallah on a key point. It
was the morning after Makallah was finally dis-missed
after two and a half days as a witness. Characteristically,
the Nairobi papers had ignored Georgiadis's most carefully wrought moments. Only one of the three dailies
made any mention at all of the exchange over the Suzuki.
None focused on the question of what time Makallah
contended he and his party had arrived at the gully, but it
was on that issue that Othiambo undermined the senior
warden's testimony.

He first heard a radio call from Makallah at his post at
about 11 a.m., 13 September that the jeep had been found,
Othiambo testified. By the time Makallah had collected
him and they made their way over the rough terrain to the
gully, he said, it was about two in the afternoon – three
hours later than Makallah had said they arrived.

Yet on all other points Othiambo supported Makallah
steadfastly. Yes, he had seen the footprints, and yes, he
had seen the vultures. These were the claims over which
Georgiadis had tried to better the warden; he would have
no better luck with the modest, ill-trained police inspector
from Mara Bridge, who had been placed in charge of
twelve Masai Mara police constables and one sergeant but
had never been issued a vehicle.

Georgiadis directed Othiambo's attention to the period
between the tenth, when Makallah had evidently heard
from Olindo about the missing tourist, and the thirteenth,
when he collected the inspector at Mara Bridge.

'During those three days did Makallah tell you a tourist
was missing in the Mara?'

'No'.

'Did any radio messages reach you on the tenth?'

'No.'

'Did you get any message from Nairobi?'

'No.'

Georgiadis flipped through his notes.

'On leaving the Suzuki you began your search at three-thirty, heading toward the range of hills near the Tanzania border. You testified you went ten to twelve kilometers, and you found the remains about four-fifteen, four-twenty p.m.'

'Yes.'

'Now, I have visited there,' Georgiadis continued. 'To do ten kilometers across that country meant you were going at horrendous speed, not enabling you to look at anything.' It was a statement, not a question. Othiambo was silent.

'You can't do that journey in an hour and a half because of the terrain,' Georgiadis insisted. Again, Othiambo made no reply.

'Were you given directions by Mr Makallah?'

'No, Your Honor.'

'Who, then, was telling the driver where to go?'

'We had no special direction.'

'You say you saw the vultures in the last fifty meters. But before that you had no reason to head in that particular direction.'

'Yes.'

'Entering the bush, did you see any trails of blood?'

'I saw blood.'

'You did? Did you collect a sample?'

'No.'

'Well, we've got other evidence that persons there did not see any blood. Bodily fluid, yes. But not blood.'

Othiambo did not react.

Georgiadis said, 'You testified that you returned to the gully to arrange to tow the jeep to Keekorok, but found it had already been taken. But that was two days after it was found. Why did you leave it for two days?'

'We had no guard to post there, Your Honor.'

'You made no attempt to obtain fingerprints from the jeep in those two days?'

'No.'

'Right. Well, you were either all deliberately not investigating this case, or I cannot conceive of what sort of investigation you were doing.'

'You were in the mortuary with Mr and Mrs Weld Dixon on the fifteenth when the autopsy was performed,' Georgiadis asked Inspector Anthony Mwaura, Superintendent Issika's deputy, the next day. 'The pathologist showed you the leg and said the cut had been made by a sharp instrument. You heard this?'

'No,' said Mwaura, a twenty-year veteran of the police force.

'Were you taking notes?'

'No.'

Georgiadis sighed at this blunt refutation of Weld Dixon's testimony. 'Did you hear him say the jaw was cut? The leg was burned subsequent to being cut? Did you hear him say this makes it a murder case?'

Mwaura looked up at the ceiling. Defiantly, he said, 'No, I didn't hear it.'

Georgiadis asked, 'You don't do all your inquiries like this, do you?'

'I do,' Mwaura answered.

Assistant Game Warden James Sindiyo had a ready answer when Georgiadis asked him if Makallah drove a vehicle.

'Oh, yes. I have seen him drive many times,' he said, smiling.

'Did he have a recent accident?'

'I think he had one about June last year.'

'Are you surprised that Mr Makallah told us under oath that he doesn't ever drive?'

'It is strange . . .' Sindiyo replied.

CHAPTER THIRTY-NINE

Wilson Kibel arap Sogomo, the police chemist, followed two other forensic experts to the stand on a benumbingly long day. The tedium of the second straight week of testimony had begun to fray the composure of the visiting press, who were showing less and less interest in the testimony in front of the room and more in the glamorous Kenyan law students sitting behind them.

The British press corps in Nairobi was a mixed bag. Unlike the American, German, and Japanese reporters, most of the Britons assigned to cover East Africa from Nairobi were part-time stringers, paid according to the length of the stories they managed to place, deprived of even rudimentary employment benefits like health care and living allowances. It was a peculiar way of covering a region that had once been a web of important British colonies, but if the resulting reportage was wildly uneven it had the virtue of being inexpensive. The system was followed by all the top newspapers, including *The Times* and the *Daily Telegraph*; even the most respected daily in London, the tangerine-hued broadsheet *Financial Times*, kept a stringer on to cover Kenya, manifestly the only real economic power in East Africa.

The stringers regarded the inquest as rather a mixed curse. On the one hand it generated day-rate pay, a significant improvement over their usual income. On the other, they considered being tied down to a daily story a burden in a post where there had always been plenty of time for fishing or golf between trips to Ethiopian war zones or the Ugandan interior. By now tedium was winning out, and some of the stringer copy was deteriorating so much that editors in London were telling staff writers to pack their bags and book passage to Nairobi. One stringer had sent such a disappointing weekend wrap-up to London that the newsroom had completely rewritten it, raiding wire reports and old files, and run it under a fabricated byline.

The London reporters were also showing the strain of long hours spent on a courtroom bench followed by equally long nights on a bar-room stool. Eyes were more strikingly outlined in red, and the air of the courtroom in early morning reeked more piquantly now of last night's alcohol consumption and cigarettes. Nairobi's nightlife is busy but pervaded by rough trade. Many of the visitors were finding scant respite from the routine of nightly hotel videos and an endless circuit of Indian restaurants. They would spend hours in each others' hotel rooms with wastepaper-baskets full of expense receipts, trading invoices to cadge an extra few pounds in expense claims. On weekends John Ward invited a few of them down to a beach hotel in Mombasa where he had worked out a discount so they could sit by the pool on the steamy coast and drain bottles of beer.

The inquest needed some comic relief. So it was fortunate that Wilson Sogomo, the senior forensic analyst of the government chemist's department, turned his testimony into a farce.

The first hint of a break in the tedium came when a troop of police supernumeraries preceded Sogomo into the courtroom carrying enormous plastic bags full of some unidentifiable matter. The men dropped the bags unceremoniously at the side of the magistrate's podium. Leaning over the gallery rails, some people could see what looked like bones and metal objects.

This was the State's forensic haul. Under Etyang's questioning Sogomo provided a curiously complete inventory of the items he had been given to examine. There was a mixture of burned clothes, human bones, hair, grass, and ashes. Burned pieces of bone and flesh, molten pieces of metal. A cork. Burned paper. Dry vegetation taken from around the fire.

Among the clothes, he said, was a tartan jacket with blue, gray, and orange stripes and leather lining. A pink-brown brassière of cloth and nylon, showing some holes, possibly from animal bites. A yellow cloth material, 'which could not be identified as part of a vest or underpants.' Dark blue jeans, long-legged. Two sets of partially melted earrings. Two 'zips'. Some fecal matter 'belonging to a person or persons who ate meals consisting of white starch and fish.'

Sogomo had also been given Julie's skull to examine before her father took it away to London. 'There was some charring of hair. The scalp had canine teeth bites, and showed some scissoring effect, most probably of canine teeth.'

He continued: 'The clothes of the deceased were partially burned through the use of an accelerant. The blood was group four, human.'

Satisfied, Etyang handed his copy of the inventory to Georgiadis, who immediately remarked on the fact that Sogomo's lab had received the haul on 30 September, and produced its report on 12 December, two and a half months later. Having made the point that the lab apparently felt no need for urgency in examining the evidence, he moved on.

'You got no blood sample separate from the stain on the bone, is that right?' he asked. 'How accurate should the blood grouping from a bone be?'

'Generally, fairly accurate,' Sogomo replied.

'But it doesn't compare with grouping from a blood sample?'

'No.'

'Now, I see on this list "two raw eggs, found where the vehicle was stuck." But we haven't had any evidence of eggs or where they were found.'

'I don't know where the eggs were found.'

'I see. "A light green striped wholly cotton shirt." Where is this?'

Sogomo stepped heavily down from the witness box and crossed the room to the pile of plastic bags. He selected one and dumped its contents out on the floor, producing a pile of charred shreds. Seemingly at random, he picked a tatter from the pile and held it up between thumb and forefinger.

'I think this is the one.'

Georgiadis looked skeptical. 'That is a light green cotton shirt?' There was a titter from the audience. 'Well, all right.'

Sogomo regained the stand.

'Now,' said Georgiadis, still reading. 'A tartan jacket, leather lined?'

Sogomo got down again and walked across to the pile. He rummaged through it a second time. He held up a shred that could have been the same as the first. Peals of derisive laughter came from the gallery.

'This is ridiculous,' said Georgiadis. 'Where do you see leather lining?'

The chemist fingered the shred. 'I think some of the parts of this clothing are not here.'

'No doubt.' Again, Sogomo returned to the box and turned a professional gaze on the lawyer.

'Now I want to see the brassière. I warn you, I know what a brassière looks like. I've seen a number of them in the past.'

For the third time Sogomo made his trip to the mound of sooty tatters. This time he came up empty, except for the black stains on his hands. 'I think the bra has been burned by the criminalization section,' he said apologetically.

'Burned?' The gallery was rolling in hilarity. 'For what purpose?'

'Mrs Pamela did a flammability test.'

'You do not use a whole garment for a flammability test!'

Shaking his head, Georgiadis walked back to his table.

'What about the blue jeans?' he asked. 'Can you identify those pieces here, or were they too given to Pamela to put in her incinerator?'

Sogomo came up with a tiny bit of cloth, about one inch square.

'How can you say long trousers?' asked Georgiadis. 'They might have been short jeans or tattered jeans.'

'I might have been mistaken.'

'Actually, I think you let your imagination run riot. Now, this all gives the impression that she was wearing all these things and they were found,' Georgiadis said. 'How do we know?'

'This is what I was given,' Sogomo said.

'Regarding this fecal matter,' Georgiadis went on. 'There is nothing to indicate that it had anything to do with the deceased exclusively. It could equally have been that whoever burned the remains decided to have a little snack and then relieved themselves.'

Sogomo nodded assent.

'For the record. Even if parts of this human being were consumed or eaten by wild animals, this deliberate burning of clothing, effects, and torso took place. Does this show animal, or human, intervention?'

'It is not for me to say,' Sogomo replied.

'Why not? Aren't you a government chemist? Have you had before remains that had deliberately been burned by animals?' The gallery laughed again at this favorite refrain.

'No.'

'The fact that an accelerant like petroleum was used, is that not an important corroborative fact?'

'You are asking me to speculate.'

'You are speculating all the time in your job. You have never heard of animals lighting fires, have you?'

'No, Your Honor,' Sogomo said.

287

CHAPTER FORTY

Balding and moon faced, his gold wire-rimmed glasses slipping annoyingly down his nose, Dr Adel Youssef Shaker stood uneasily in the box, sweating in the hard spotlight of the inquest. After Makallah he was regarded by Ward and Georgiadis as their most crucial witness. Already he had been warned once of his importance to this proceeding, when Mango had cut short an attempt to evade a question with the barked order, 'Try to remember! Everybody has been waiting for you!'

The moments of elation that punctuated the Egyptian's nervous and beleaguered demeanor of earlier months were gone now. He was not the least cognizant person in the room that virtually the whole point of his testimony was to undermine the authority of his own superior, Jason Kaviti. Youssef might by now have perceived with alarm that he had been ill-used by his bosses in this case. Now he would be an instrument again, this time to expose all the manipulations of the past. In his ill-fitting gray suit, his tie partially undone, he was the picture of an uncomfortable man.

'Your whole career has been channeled toward pathology?' Georgiadis began on the afternoon of 12 September.

'Yes.'

'And you have testified that you performed over one hundred post-mortem examinations in Kenya.'

'Yes.'

'Ever had a report corrected? Apart from this case, of course.'

'Once.'

'I believe you are a deeply religious gentleman,' Georgiadis stated.

288

'It is not for me to say,' Youssef mumbled. 'I cannot judge myself.'

'Telling the truth is important, not only in your profession but your religion.'

Youssef assented.

'For pathologists, do you agree that there is no room for generalizations – in the sense that if you cannot say something is a fact that should be made clear in your report and your evidence?'

'Yes,' Youssef said quietly.

'I would rather you did not whisper,' Georgiadis said.

Youssef confirmed that he had identified the case to Weld Dixon as one of murder. He confirmed the words Ferguson recalled, to the effect that suicide was out of the question. To Georgiadis's queries as to whether he had used the words *sharp* and *cleanly cut* in oral reports to the Britons, Youssef assented.

Georgiadis showed him a copy of the altered report. 'On page two, *cracked*. Is this word overtyped, following the erasure of what was there before?'

'Yes.' Reluctantly, in a low voice.

'Item two: *Cut* is deleted and *torn* substituted.'

'Yes.'

'The word *blunt* is also overtyped on the previous deleted word, but quite clearly not on the same line.'

'Yes.'

'Now, Dr Kaviti said he had found your report in the typewriter and decided to make the alterations. Before Dr Kaviti altered your report, did he seek your permission to do so?'

Youssef considered the question for a while.

'He asked me to see the remains.'

'No, no.' Georgiadis said impatiently. 'That's not an answer. Did he ask your permission?'

'He's my superior. He didn't have to ask.'

'Well, you're suggesting that your superior can do anything at all! After all, you are a professional man and your professional integrity is your biggest asset. Did Dr Kaviti ask your permission?'

Youssef turned to appeal to the magistrate: 'Most of Mr Georgiadis's questions are leading questions.'

'He's allowed to do that,' Mango replied. 'Answer the question.'

Reluctantly Youssef did so. On 21 September, he said, 'we re-examined the leg and after that re-examination he convinced me of his findings, and we went back to the typist to alter the report . . . He convinced me.'

'So was Dr Kaviti lying, when he said he chanced into the mortuary and found your report and read it, and changed it, and that you weren't there? That was a downright lie, in your presence? I suggest to you that your story is the only possible way to explain an attempted forgery and an attempted perversion of justice.'

Youssef looked stricken. 'I think Dr Kaviti can answer this question,' he said.

'Is it a habit of Kenya police pathologists to alter each other's reports?'

'No.'

'If you differ, you produce your own report under your own signature and give your reasons, don't you?'

'But only two words are different here,' Youssef said abjectly.

'Only two words make the difference between heaven and hell, my friend,' Georgiadis shot back.

'Now look at this sorry state of affairs,' he continued. 'You had already made a verbal report to the police. If you genuinely changed your opinion as a result of discussion with Dr Kaviti, did you volunteer to the police that you decided to change your report?'

'No.'

'Do you think it's a good practice to not give your reason to the police?'

'I had been convinced—'

'Come on, Dr Youssef, you're not doing justice to yourself. You're a professional man,' Georgiadis said. 'In fact, you were very unhappy with the whole affair, were you not?'

'I'm unhappy with these questions,' Youssef replied.

Georgiadis showed exasperation. 'This is degenerating into a farce now, isn't it? Now, having read Dr Gresham's report that her head was severed with a sharp instrument, doesn't that confirm your original findings?'

'Yes.'

'So are you saying Dr Gresham is mistaken?'

'I don't know Dr Gresham,' Youssef said. 'I do know Dr Kaviti.'

'Is he mistaken?' Georgiadis repeated.

'I can't judge Dr Gresham,' Youssef insisted.

'Who is mistaken?' Georgiadis pressed. 'Gresham, Kaviti, or you?'

Youssef appealed again to Mango. 'Your Honor, please excuse me from answering this question,' he pleaded.

'No,' Mango said.

'Think about it, and tell us the truth,' wheedled Georgiadis. 'Is Dr Gresham mistaken?'

Youssef finally shook his head. 'Answer out loud,' ordered Mango.

'He is *not* mistaken,' Youssef said.

'I'm pleased you didn't perjure yourself,' Georgiadis said.

Youssef concluded his testimony with an affecting indication of how much the case had already cost him in self-respect. When Julie's skull had been found and transferred to Nairobi for examination it had been given not to himself, as the pathologist assigned to the case, but to Dr Kaviti. Was he disturbed at this, Georgiadis asked him.

No, Youssef replied, he was relieved.

CHAPTER FORTY-ONE

Dr Jason Kaviti followed his subordinate to the stand, his snowy white hair crowning the expression of serene complacency fixed on his smooth, unlined face. 'Doctor Youssef Shaker called me on September the fifteenth,' he began in answer to Etyang's question about how he had come to alter the original autopsy report.

'He wanted my opinion. He had examined the leg and his report was being typewritten at that time. So, we went to see the leg. He showed me various injuries, which he had noted. I did not see any evidence of cutting by a sharp object. Where he showed me a cut, I was not convinced. What I saw was – instead of cuts at the superfibular joint, I saw a tear. This indicated a blunt object. Where he showed me that two pieces of the jaw were cut by a sharp object, they'd been cracked into two, not cut. The wounds on the leg were lacerated. In other words, this was a tear and not a cut.'

'Did you talk about anything else in the report?' Etyang asked.

'Those are the only findings we discussed. And we agreed that he should change those parts. The rest of the report was not changed.'

'What could have caused the injuries you saw?'

'What could have caused them was a blunt object, like the teeth of carnivorous animals,' Kaviti thought for a moment. 'Or any other blunt objects.'

'You have experience with wounds by carnivorous animals?'

'Yes. I have experience of hyenas, leopards, lions, jackals, and dogs.'

'And when you examined the skull, did you find any injuries?'

'The skull was completely intact. There were no fractures.'

'And after the submission of the postmortem report, did you have a meeting with John Ward?'

Kaviti let a rueful smile play on his face, as if recalling an unpleasant memory. 'Yes, he came into my office, fuming. Mr Ward wanted to know why I instructed Dr Youssef to change his postmortem findings. My answer was I did not force him. He consulted me as his superior, and when we went through the material we agreed some of the wording in his report should be changed to reflect what the actual findings were.

'Much later I was called to the commissioner of police's office and shown a report on the leg made by – by some medical doctor in the UK.'

'What was the finding of the UK doctor?'

'He said it was impossible to tell the cause of death, but there's no doubt the leg and jaw were cut off the body by an implement.' (In fact Gresham had specified a 'sharp' implement.)

'And what was your opinion on this?'

Kaviti made a generous gesture. 'There is not much difference between us,' he said. 'On the whole we agree, that it's difficult to state the cause of death.'

'And the implement?'

'An "implement" would include the teeth of animals, of course.'

'And the date of the initialed changes? You wrote twenty-second September, not fifteenth.'

'This was the day Mr Ward came and asked about the change in wording. Mr Ward insisted that I initial this and that is what I did. It was the twenty-second of September.'

Etyang signaled that he was finished. Georgiadis approached Kaviti with a bland expression.

'All that you have been telling us this afternoon, Dr Kaviti . . . Did you make a statement to the police about it?'

'I can't remember if I did,' Kaviti answered.

'I suggest to you that you have never made a statement to the police.'

'That may be true.'

'At no time have the police ever asked you for a statement?'

'That may be true.'

'You are the chief pathologist, are you not?'

'That is true.'

'Do you concede the job is a very responsible one?' Georgiadis rolled the *r* in *responsible*, making a sound like a rumbling truck.

'Yes.'

'Were you present at the postmortem conducted by Dr Youssef on the remains of Julie Ward in the city mortuary?'

'No. I was consulted later.'

'Were you around the city mortuary at all?'

'What time?' Kaviti asked.

'Around ten to twelve o'clock. Did you see Mr and Mrs Weld Dixon?'

'I do not recall.'

'Are you surprised to hear that the date you've given, September the fifteenth, does not coincide in any way with the evidence Dr Youssef gave today and yesterday?'

'Yes, I am surprised.'

'According to Dr Youssef, the date of the alterations occurred on the twenty-second and were initialed as such.'

'No!' Kaviti responded emphatically.

'That is the evidence also of Mr Ward and Mr Ferguson.'

'No!' Kaviti insisted again.

'Look at the report!' Georgiadis waved it at Kaviti.

'That is the time I signed for the alterations, while Mr Ward was in my office.'

'So you say,' Georgiadis snapped out. 'You maintain that you and Youssef met at ten-thirty on the fifteenth and the report was then being typed. Did Youssef tell you he had already done the postmortem in front of Mr and Mrs Weld Dixon and the police?'

'He did not.'

'Did he tell you he opined it was murder?'

'No, he had not told me that.'

'Isn't it strange,' Georgiadis asked, 'that Youssef didn't tell you about what he said?'

'It is strange,' Kaviti agreed.

'I believe you,' Georgiadis offered. 'Because I can't conceive of the actions that followed otherwise.'

As Georgiadis pointed out, Kaviti's chronology was contradicted by most of the other evidence. Youssef testified that Kaviti came to him on 21 September, to look at the leg. And Ferguson said that Youssef had reiterated his finding of murder during their conversation on 19 September, or four days after Kaviti claimed to have changed the postmortem finding in consultation with his subordinate. Clearly, Kaviti could not have made the changes until later.

'Are you surprised to hear,' Georgiadis asked Kaviti, 'that Youssef was unhappy with the changes that were made in his report?'

'Yes,' Kaviti said. 'I am surprised, because he had agreed.'

'Are you surprised to hear he would have been happier if it had not been changed?'

'I am very surprised.'

'You're full of surprises, regrettably,' Georgiadis muttered. He jumped ahead. 'On the twenty-third of September, 1988, did Ferguson, Ward, John Lee, and Frank Ribeiro come see you at Kenyatta National Hospital?'

'They came.'

'In front of these persons, when confronted with the changed report, did you say that on the twenty-second, the previous day, you were at the city mortuary and noticed the postmortem in Youssef's typewriter? Did you say this?'

'I didn't.'

Georgiadis looked surprised.

'Did you say you'd made the changes—'

'I'm sticking to what I said,' Kaviti interrupted curtly, wary of Georgiadis's play with the dates.

'Did you say it was Youssef's use of poor English – "cleanly cut" meant "cracked and torn"?'

'Yes . . . I did say that.'

'Were you asked how the leg, if torn, could then be placed on the fire and burnt without there being foul play? Were you asked that?'

'Yes, I was.'

'Mr Ward asked, how could your conclusions be drawn when the leg was burned *after* the dismemberment? You were silent.'

'Yes, I was.'

'Why were you silent?'

'Because I didn't think it was proper for me to be questioned like that in my own office. I was on the point of throwing them all out.'

'Ward asked if you were told to make the changes, and you denied it.'

'Yes.'

'Pausing there a moment . . . look at your alterations that you initialed.'

Kaviti took the pages. 'I put the date twenty-second when I initialed it for Ward.'

'But the meeting was on the twenty-third, not the twenty-second,' Georgiadis said. 'There's plenty of evidence of that.'

Kaviti hesitated. 'I still say that's the date they were in my office.'

Georgiadis sighed. 'How long were you in the city mortuary on the fifteenth, Dr Kaviti?'

'I can't tell. I was not timing myself, you know. Maybe three hours.'

'Did you coincide with Dr Youssef's postmortem at eleven-thirty? Did you see the Weld Dixons, the police officer?'

'I don't remember seeing them.'

'Did you know that a postmortem was going on?'

'No.'

Georgiadis wondered how Kaviti could have been unaware of any other activity in the cramped mortuary. 'I suggest to you, Dr Kaviti, that you are not telling the truth when you say you examined the remains on the fifteenth, and you are not telling the truth deliberately, to give you an opportunity to try to explain the alterations to a post-mortem report belonging to another pathologist.'

'That's not correct.'

'Well, in view of the fact that the alterations made all the difference between wild animals and human intervention in the dismemberment of the deceased's limbs, shouldn't you have signed the report?'

'No.'

'So today we're left with only your word, your say-so.'

'That's correct.'

'You have a very arrogant approach, Dr Kaviti. Assuming that the remains were found near a seat of fire, or in the vicinity, and the leg showed first- and second-degree burns, does that not indicate to you that the words *with subsequent burning* suggest human intervention?'

'Not necessarily.'

Georgiadis shot him a quizzical look. 'The leg could have been flung into the fire by animals, just for a little barbecue?'

Kaviti pondered. 'When they were tearing and gnawing the bones some piece could get into the fire,' he said. 'Something they were fighting over. It depends on how many there were.'

Georgiadis chuckled. 'Come on, Dr Kaviti. You know, and we know, that carnivores do not like fires and they go nowhere near them.' Kaviti shrugged. 'To conclude, Dr Kaviti, I suggest you chanced on this report on the twenty-second, lying in the typewriter—'

'That is untrue!'

'—You read it and, seeing the import of the words *cleanly cut* and *sharp instrument* you obliterated those words and wrote yourself *torn*, *cracked*, and *blunt*.'

'That is wholly untrue.'

'You altered it for no scientific purpose, but to give a totally false view of the findings.'

'No! I did not do such a thing.'

Georgiadis remarked aloud that Kaviti took no notes during his 'consultation' with Youssef. He also took no notes months later, when he examined Julie's skull and concluded it showed no signs of head injuries.

'I suggest to you you've got into these bad habits with postmortem reports, Dr Kaviti, leaving yourself elbow room for coming into court and telling us what you please!'

Kaviti's angry 'No!' echoed off the walls.

'Is not the jaw a part of the skull? If the jaw is anatomically severed by a sharp instrument, that would be a cause of death, no? That would be a head injury?'

'In a way, yes,' said Kaviti.

'So why did you put this rubbish in your report about finding no head injuries?'

'That referred to the main bones of the skull,' Kaviti replied.

A few days later Professor Gresham, ensconced by Ward in a suite down the hall from his own in the Nairobi Safari Club, grimaced as he read the transcript of this exchange in preparation for his own testimony. He applied a match to his metal-shanked pipe and said, 'It's like slogging through mud, isn't it.'

Kaviti's description of his examination provoked the precise Gresham to stride around his suite in frustration. He flipped through his own file of reports for a curious visitor, extracting a set of photographs and X-rays.

'Look at this!' he said, waving a photo of the underside of the skull. His index finger traced five symmetrical wounds on the bone, arranged in a pattern around the point where the spinal column enters the cranium.

'Now, to produce five symmetrical wounds on the base of the skull by separate blows is impossible,' he said. 'An injury like this could only have been produced by one single swipe.' His hand swooped down in a broad karate chop. 'Wham! Like that. With a sharp instrument. This girl,' he said, 'was decapitated from behind.'

Meanwhile Ward had kept his vigil in the hallway outside Courtroom Four. When Kaviti was shown out of the room there remained only one major witness before Ward himself would have his chance to tell his own story to Magistrate Mango. That witness was Inspector Wanjau.

CHAPTER FORTY-TWO

As he presented his evidence to Etyang that afternoon Wanjau seemed like a model police investigator. He spoke distinctly with a clipped air of authority. He talked about 'swinging into action' with 'my team.' He had a time and date, if scanty notes, for every step he described. Like the first time Ward met him, he was dressed in dark colors: a checked brown and pink shirt and brown rep tie, under a black suit coat.

On the day he was assigned to the case, Wanjau said, he and his team came upon a temporary Maasai manyatta, or encampment, about 1.7 kilometers to the north of the fire under the sausage tree. He dropped Othiambo off at the fire site and returned. The manyatta was nothing more than a collection of sorry dung huts with a couple of old men inside who spoke no Swahili.

'I lit a cigarette to test the wind direction,' Wanjau testified. 'We started shouting at the top of our voices. None of us could hear each other properly from the boma to the fire. The shouts were out of range.'

'What were you doing?' Etyang asked.

'Your Honor, I was trying to find out whether the residents would overhear some shouting from that scene of fire.'

Wanjau's remark set up one of the bigger red herrings of the inquest: Did the Masai hear Julie's death screams? The next day's British papers all had similar headlines: TRIBESMEN MAY HAVE HEARD SCREAMING, and so on. ('The editors love stories about "tribesmen" in Africa,' one British reporter remarked sourly.)

In fact, nobody's theory of the case placed the murder scene at the fire; Etyang still cherished the notion that wild

300

animals had got her near there, but he and Georgiadis had established in their questioning of other witnesses that there was no evidence of blood around the site.

But Georgiadis pursued the question intently. What happened to these Masai? he asked. Through the end of the proceedings Georgiadis kept suggesting that Makallah, or someone higher up, had somehow encouraged these nomadic witnesses to migrate over the border to Tanzania. As with many other threads of the case, nothing ever came of it.

Wanjau testified that after consultations in Nairobi, he returned to the manyatta with a Masai interpreter, Simon Makallah.

'As I interviewed the two Masai,' Wanjau said, 'I concluded that they were not connected with the disappearance of the late Julie Ward.'

Wanjau moved on to testify how he questioned Nchoko and Constable Karuri at Sand River Gate, going so far as to search their houses.

'I did not find anything suspicious there, Your Honor.'

He traced Julie's path from Sand River to the Mara Serena, 'where she had been seen with a white man,' and established the story of the broken fuel pump and the tow from Watson. Later he and his team combed the area around the fire and found Julie's skull.

At length Etyang asked Wanjau if he had ever seen the Swiss photographers' camp. He had, the superintendent said.

'How far was it from the gully where the jeep was found?'

'About four kilometers, Your Honor.' Tham had estimated the distance as no more than four hundred meters, but now Wanjau agreed with Makallah's testimony placing it well out of range of Julie's jeep.

Wanjau continued to testify about how he had entered the Makari post, where he found five rangers and their little VHF radio. 'I went into the huts but did not get anything suspicious.'

In all, he testified, after searching through the Mara and

visiting all the places through which Julie had passed, 'I did not come across any suspect.' At the Mara Serena he had learned that 'the last person who had spent the night with the deceased was Mr Stephen Watson.' After questioning Watson in Nairobi much later, 'I did not connect him to the death of Julie Ward.'

In April he submitted his investigatory papers to the attorney general's office to be filed, Wanjau testified. On 18 May the file had been returned to the CID with the instruction that an inquest be held. Four days later it was forwarded to the chief magistrate.

'And,' said Mango, 'here we are.'

Georgiadis prepared to begin his cross-examination. He looked as if he could see his whole case embodied in Wanjau.

'Did you keep an open mind?' he began.

'Yes,' Wanjau replied.

'You would not have ignored a line of inquiry if you thought it showed foul play.'

'I did not.'

'Nor would you ignore it, if it tended to be embarrassing generally.'

'I did not come across any information which tended to be false or embarrassing.'

'Now. These distances which you measured. You never saw the Swiss at their camp. Who told you where the Swiss camp was?'

'Mr Makallah, and the rangers at Makari.' That at least explained why Wanjau's testimony corroborated Makallah's.

Georgiadis produced the statement Henri Berney had made for Ward, which Wanjau had seen earlier. 'In English translation they have placed the distance of the camp from the gully at three hundred to four hundred meters. As superintendent in charge of the investigation, what steps did you take to ascertain, confirm, or refute this report?'

'To me it was not evidence,' Wanjau replied obstinately. 'It was an allegation. Let the father bring the man in here for questioning.'

At this Georgiadis exploded. 'The father! That is the whole point here! Why do you expect the father to conduct an investigation that the Kenya Police should have done? If the father hadn't done what he did, there wouldn't even have been an investigation!'

Wanjau was silent. Georgiadis went on. 'Mr Makallah. Was he excluded as a suspect?'

'No.'

'Then what right did you have to accept his assertions of where the Swiss camp was?'

'It was not just Mr Makallah. The rangers too—'

'Did you exclude the rangers at Makari camp from your suspicions?'

'Your Honor, there was no evidence from the beginning.'

'Can you produce a single statement you took from a ranger?'

'Your Honor, it was not necessary.'

'That's what I was afraid of,' Georgiadis said. 'Who are you to say it was not necessary? I suggest to you that far from doing an investigation you did nothing of the sort. You did nothing but go through the motions unless you were pushed by the father.'

Wanjau responded angrily. 'I did all that was necessary!'

'Did you ever take the names of the rangers at Makari?'

'I did not have any interest in their names. After all, they were involved in the search for this lady. From the very beginning they were not taken as suspects.'

'So today, we have this ludicrous situation where this court does not even know the names of the rangers at Makari post, even though the answer to this murder lies in a very small area, between the rangers at Sand River Gate and the Makari post. It doesn't concern little green men from Mars!'

Georgiadis was just warming up. Through merciless grilling over a day and a half he tried to expose the full extent of what he considered Wanjau's dereliction of duty. In truth, what Wanjau failed to do far overwhelmed the few things he had managed to accomplish. Wanjau seemed to have taken almost no notes during his investigation of what steps he had taken or in what order. He never searched Makallah's quarters. He never checked the work tickets for the rangers' vehicles to determine how they might have been used in the days between Julie's disappearance and her death. He did not take the names of the rangers who accompanied Makallah on the search for the body, so he had no way of questioning them about how the team managed to find Julie's body so quickly after leaving the Suzuki.

'It was not necessary,' Wanjau repeated forlornly to every question. 'They were not suspects.'

'I'm beginning to think you went there to conduct a cover-up!'

'That's not true!'

'You didn't go there to investigate one bit. You went there to appease an anxious and bereaved father. You were there as a bit of window dressing. Did you know that on the sixth of September, when Julie Ward's tents were at Sand River, there were eighty other campers?'

'That I don't know.'

'Didn't the rangers tell you?'

'No, I did not ask them.'

'But Mr Ward pursued it and tendered some fifty names to you for your investigation. Did you try to question them?'

'No, Your Honor. They had already left the country.'

Georgiadis hammered incessantly at Wanjau's failure to consider Makallah a suspect – indeed, his reliance on Makallah as a guide and go-between with the rangers and the local Masai. But he could not shake Wanjau's air of uninterest.

'In light of Makallah's statement about the Suzuki's lack of four-wheel-drive, and in light of Makallah saying he did not drive, is that significant?' Georgiadis pressed.

'No,' said Wanjau.

'Why is that not significant?'

'I was not investigating whether he was a driver or not.'

'Is it not significant?' Georgiadis repeated.

'No, Your Honor.'

'Why not?'

'Because it is not significant!'

Wanjau also displayed a selective memory about the meetings between Ward and Kilonzo at which he was present.

'On October the eighteenth did Commissioner Kilonzo tell Mr Ward he was now taking the matter seriously and if there was a murderer in the Masai Mara he wanted him caught?'

'He said that.'

'But Commissioner Kilonzo said he was awaiting your report.'

'I did not hear that.'

'And Mr Ward said he was getting concerned about police foot-dragging.'

'I did not hear that.'

As the session on 18 September was drawing to a close, Georgiadis turned to the issue of the two white men with whom Julie had been seen in the park. Wanjau agreed that he had questioned Watson about his movements around the time Julie disappeared, 'after which I failed to connect him with the murder offense and subsequently I cleared him and I let him free.'

Then Wanjau testified he had taken a statement from Glen Burns in early October.

'Did you eliminate Dr Burns from complicity?'

'Not yet. I will be investigating.'

Georgiadis turned to Etyang. 'Are these two Europeans going to be called to testify?'

Etyang slowly rose. 'We have asked that they report for the inquest,' Etyang said. 'We have requested that Interpol trace their whereabouts.'

His remarks took a minute of the court's time, inserted at the very end of a long day. The next morning the local newspapers had blown them up into a major development. JULIE LAST SEEN WITH AMERICAN, trumpeted one. JULIE WARD INQUEST: INTERPOL CALLED IN.

Georgiadis entered the courtroom the next day fuming.

'The press this morning excelled itself,' he complained to Mango. 'The last person to see her was the policeman who watched her driving out of Sand River Gate, and yet you have this smokescreen about an American.' (Actually, Watson was British.)

Mango could not help but agree. 'Yes, the newspapers this morning are definitely not accurate,' he said.

By now Wanjau had maintained his obstinate, even officious demeanor for two days of testimony. Georgiadis was winding down his cross-examination.

'The deceased was probably alive up to the night of September the twelfth, is that correct?'

'Yes, Your Honor.'

'Did you consider the possibility that she was kept prisoner in the Mara, locked up somewhere? Did you consider that?'

'I did.'

'You checked the lodges and camps?'

'Yes.'

'Did you not consider it essential to check the rangers' accommodations?'

'I did check them,' Wanjau said. 'I just did not consider it necessary to write it down in my report.'

Georgiadis directed one of his glares of disbelief at the gallery. 'Oh dear,' he said. 'Did you check them alone or with others?'

'With others.'

'Who were these others? Are they in any of the police statements?'

'No.'

'I suggest to you that is an untruth.'

'No, Your Honor.'

'But you didn't check the accommodation of Makallah or the other senior officers?'

'No.'

'What do you think she did for a whole week while missing?' Georgiadis asked. He threw it out as almost a rhetorical question. But Wanjau took it seriously.

'She was a woman who would go out with any man in the park,' he said truculently.

Georgiadis exploded. 'Do you have any evidence or statements for that, other than your bad-mouthing a dead lady?'

'I have no statements.'

Mango cut in. 'Then you should be careful with what you are saying.'

Wanjau retracted his remark. What was left was nothing.

'What do you think she was doing between the sixth and the thirteenth?' Georgiadis asked again.

'I don't know,' Wanjau said.

'She has a plane to catch and yet she blithely turns off the road and disappears in the Mara and you have no idea what happened to her?'

'Your Honor,' Wanjau said, finishing his testimony, 'I have no idea.'

CHAPTER FORTY-THREE

John Ward took the stand in Courtroom Four on 20 September wearing a gray pinstripe suit and a blue shirt and tie. 'You are a most important witness,' Mango assured him from the bench.

It was almost a year to the day since he had begun his own investigation of Julie's death by flying a second time to Nairobi 'to find out what the hell is going on.' In the courtroom the gallery was full and there had been jostling for seats. Toward the rear one could even spot Wanjau in his dark suit jacket, sullenly listening to Ward's testimony about what he thought the police had done wrong.

For the next two days, as Georgiadis gently guided him, Ward described a year of trying to determine what had befallen his eldest child. Sometimes he gripped both sides of the witness box and delivered his testimony over the heads of the gallery, toward the opposite wall. He read painstakingly in a drone from his own extensive diary. This was a program to which Mango occasionally objected, halting Ward when he was about to relate someone else's speech; that was hearsay, Mango said. But in the end almost the whole diary was placed on the record.

Georgiadis occasionally interrupted the flow to clarify a point or stress Ward's view on an issue where he and the other witnesses disagreed.

'Did you specifically look for footprints around the Suzuki when you arrived there?' Georgiadis asked at one point.

'Yes, we searched the area as thoroughly as possible.'

'See any?'

'No, we did not.'

'Did you leave footprints yourself? Or were you treading on air?'

'I'm sure we did leave some.'

In the midst of this testimony Georgiadis interrupted his client to spring a nasty surprise, one he had likely been planning for weeks. He began innocently enough with the words 'on another subject . . .' just as he might have worked up to the exposure of a different witness's untruth. Here, however, he was just trying to elicit a certain reaction.

'On another subject, Mr Ward,' he said, 'Superintendent Wanjau's letter to the director of criminal investigation of the Kenya Police, concerning the Julie Ward inquiry.' The letter was dated 6 April, 1989. Ward had never seen it; in fact, until that moment he was unaware of its existence. Georgiadis held a couple of sheets of paper in his hand and read from them. 'Page two, second paragraph, it says, "On twelve September 1988 word received by police she was missing . . . They swing into action on the thirteenth . . . Ward joined police in searching the Masai Mara . . ."'

He turned to his client. 'Did you recall the police "swinging into action"?'

Ward scowled, envisioning the half-open but idle hangar of the Kenya Police Air Wing at Wilson on the morning he and his little flotilla set off to find Julie. 'There were no police aircraft at all,' he said.

Georgiadis returned to the papers in his hand, reading Wanjau's words. '"On the thirteenth the remains were found burned and eaten by wild animals. After extensive investigation of this death no evidence could be found of foul play. If anything, the deceased committed suicide."'

Ward was thunderstruck. His eyes sought out and found Wanjau sitting in the rear of the room and fixed him with a bitter glare. It was inconceivable that Wanjau could still be spouting this suicide theory in April, when it had been discarded at the very first. Gresham's autopsy was already six months old. Julie's skull had been found, with its evidence of her decapitation. Had Wanjau learned nothing?

Georgiadis interrupted Ward's reverie. 'Did your daughter have any reason to commit suicide, Mr Ward?' he asked quietly.

'No,' Julie's father replied. 'None whatsoever.'

Georgiadis then asked Ward about the physical evidence he had provided to the police, through Wanjau: Julie's handwriting, a sample of the orange towel from home, the Macleans toothpaste tube.

'Are you surprised to hear Superintendent Wanjau threw that away?'

Ward gave a sigh. 'I should not be surprised by now, but I am.'

Ward finished his testimony not long after that. The Wanjau letter created a sensation, and he was besieged outside the Law Courts by the British press.

'It's just disgraceful,' he said into a BBC microphone. 'It's obviously absolutely outrageous. I can't believe Wanjau is suggesting suicide at that time, when he knew my daughter had been murdered. This continual assertion of suicide and animals – it simply goes to show there's a considerable cover-up here, and I hope the magistrate will expose it.'

In the final days of the inquest, as Ward was giving his testimony on the stand, he was grappling with another conundrum.

Paul Molinaro was in his early twenties, the son of an expatriate manager at the Hotel Inter-Continental in Nairobi. He had been out of the country until recently, he told Ward one day, and had only just heard about Julie's disappearance and death, as well as the reward posted for information and the missing camera. He thought he had something to add because at the beginning of September 1988, he and a few friends had been camping in the Masai Mara. On 6 September, he remembered, they had seen Julie three times in three different places in the park. One was Sand River Camp.

Here at last was an independent witness to Julie's movements. Molinaro told him the first time he saw Julie had been in the morning at the Mara Serena, when he and his friends noticed an attractive blonde loading her Suzuki and getting ready to leave. A little while later they passed her on the road to Keekorok and waved. Molinaro specifically remembered seeing Julie's expensive camera lying on the vacant front seat next to her.

The third time he recalled as being late in the afternoon at Sand River. The boys watched Julie pulling down the tents and then leaving the camp. Did they see anyone helping her – a policeman, perhaps? No, Molinaro recalled, she struck the tents by herself. He said it was already getting late in the day. He could not be sure, but the time must have been around 4 p.m.

Molinaro thus flatly contradicted the story given by Nchoko and Karuri, the revenue clerk and constable at Sand River. By placing her departure an hour and a half later than Nchoko's record at the gate, he cast doubt on the clerk's entire testimony. And he seemed to confirm Georgiadis's doubts about the constable's story of wandering over from the gatehouse to help Julie strike camp.

Ward was elated to have someone finally come forward, after so many months of fruitless searching, with a sighting of Julie on that important last day. Yet he was a little doubtful about putting Paul Molinaro on the stand. In appearance Molinaro did not come off as entirely credible. He dressed in ragged student garb, and his face often took on a glazed, inattentive expression. It was a toss-up.

'It's never easy, is it,' Ward sighed to an acquaintance. Instead of deciding right away, he embarked on a frenetic search for Molinaro's companions; perhaps one of them would project a more upstanding look. But they were dispersed all over the world. One was a student in Germany, another in the United States. Eventually, Ward managed to track down the latter, a young Korean-American studying in Los Angeles. But he was even less help. He'd been sleeping in the back of their car for most of the morning, he said. He hadn't seen anybody. His recollections of the rest of the day were even foggier than Molinaro's. Somewhat reluctantly, Ward decided to ask Molinaro to testify.

This he did on one of the final days of the inquest. On the stand Molinaro looked a little more believable than when he first approached Ward. He was dressed in a suit-jacket and tie, although his head was topped by an unkempt mop of hair. He looked like someone who had been specifically cleaned up to come to court.

But he was polite and lucid enough. Ward could only hope that his testimony might have some impact.

CHAPTER FORTY-FOUR

Byron Georgiadis started with the only uncontroverted fact. 'That Julie Ward died is beyond question,' he said.

It was 5 October, thirteen months after Julie had driven up to Sand River Gate in the mid-afternoon and driven off to oblivion. Now, after two months of the inquest, the volume of what was known beyond doubt about her death was overwhelmed by what still remained a mystery. All Georgiadis could do with his cultivated voice and systematic mind was try to arrange a mass of speculation into a rational pattern. This he was about to try in his summation. Before he finished, he was also going to point the finger of guilt.

The barrister gave a brief character sketch of each of the actors, concentrating on those on the other side. He opened with Kaviti. What he contended to be the pathologist's manifest dishonesty seemed to rankle him the most.

'Can one possibly accept any of his evidence? I submit not. If he said his name was Jason Kaviti I would want to see his original birth certificate, and I may even be constrained to check with the registrar of births.' There was laughter in the courtroom. 'His evidence and activities are totally incompatible with the professionalism and ethics of the medical profession.'

Dr Youssef was viewed by the lawyer as an honest man made into a puppet by his superiors. At least he was a sound pathologist. Georgiadis said, 'He merely lacks a backbone.'

He was surprisingly easy on Kilonzo, as if he pitied the commissioner his incompetent underlings and the burden of Kenyan politics. 'He was doing his best to allay the

313

anxieties of Mr Ward. But by his refusal to order the launching of a proper and full murder inquiry and investigation in this matter it seems he was not fed, perhaps, by the full facts or proper information. Perhaps Mr Kilonzo was being as helpful as he possibly could within the limits of knowledge imparted to him by his investigative officers. More than that he could not do.'

Yet at the same time he suggested that Wanjau, who after all was Kilonzo's hand-picked representative, deliberately underinvestigated the case. He paid Wanjau the compliment of assuming he knew how to conduct a proper investigation. But to him that only made it manifest that he must have been purposely covering up. 'The noninvestigation of Superintendent Wanjau! If he had been a recently promoted corporal in the CID, then perhaps there might be gross negligence in the investigation. But having a senior official specially chosen by the commissioner is a most unlikely reason for the number and size of the lacunae in the investigation.'

Nchoko and Karuri he treated together as pathetic figures, like clownish gravediggers in a Shakespearean tragedy. 'Of course they told untruths at this inquest. They were, and are, probably terrified out of their wits. They dare not tell us what they really know. Nchoko went as far as forging the deceased's entry in the visitors' book and maintained the lie until confronted. The police should have charged him long ago – not trotted him into court as a truthful witness.

'PC Karuri was another tongue-tied policeman in the witness box. Why was he tongue-tied? I submit because the poor fellow is basically an honest, but not a very brilliant, policeman, and he was having to maintain a cock-and-bull story against the true facts. He was trying to corroborate Mr Nchoko about her departure. However, he too knew something fishy had occurred and couldn't say without letting the side down. Can anyone in their right senses ever imagine Police Constable Karuri being able to do anything spectacular or unusual or criminal, except perhaps to try to lie, painfully, and with the greatest difficulty?'

314

Finally Simon Makallah, the slick evil genius of the case in the view of Georgiadis and Ward. 'Mr Makallah, of course, had and has a sizeable problem. I have already alluded to his untruths in court. They are inexplicable by any analysis one chooses to employ. He certainly enjoys a charmed life and appears to be immune from all the normal investigations one would expect to be conducted – even to try to clear him. That he should have been a principal suspect appears to have escaped the eagle eye of Mr Wanjau.'

Having painted this gallery of characters, Georgiadis moved on. 'Let us review shortly the theory propounded by the police,' he said.

'The police will have you believe that the only possibility is that having gone back to Sand River Gate on the sixth of September, and having allegedly dismantled the tents and gone through the gate at two forty-seven p.m., allegedly on her way to catch an airplane out of Kenya, Julie Ward suddenly, for no apparent reason, branches right off the main road across country for several kilometers and gets stuck in the Makindu tributary of the Sand River.

'There she got out of the security and warmth of the Suzuki car, which contained food and beer, and leaving her two maps, binoculars, and gym shoes, but carrying tins of food, a pan, stove, bag, sunglasses, camera, cassettes, knife, mug and spoon, plus twenty liters of petrol, flip-flopped across the Mara wilderness from the sixth to the twelfth of September clanking like a Christmas tree, purposefully in the direction of the Tanzanian border after crossing the Barakitabu Road, which incidentally was nearly opposite to the direction she is alleged to have driven until the Suzuki became stuck. And then on the night of twelfth September, after consuming half a tin of pilchards, decided life was not worth living and hacked off her left leg with a nonexistent sharp implement like a panga, then lopped off her head and finally decided to douse her mortal remains with petrol and set fire to herself. Thus committing suttee after committing suicide!'

The lawyer's refined tones echoed in the harsh acoustics of the chamber. 'For anyone to believe that he must indeed be gullible, or worse. For Superintendent Wanjau to have advanced that theory of suicide to the DCI on the sixth of April 1989, seven months after starting his investigations, can only be described as deliberate mis-information for purposes of convincing the DCI that all possibilities had been explored to no avail. That, in my book of heinous offenses, suggests incontrovertibly a cover-up and, moreover, such an obvious one that far from allaying anxiety, has fueled it to the point that the father of the deceased said, "Hang the expense, I shall find out what happened to my daughter whatever the cost or whatever the Kenyan police say about it."

'The Kenyan police, I am certain, do not believe or subscribe one moment to this absurd theory of suicide.'

Georgiadis paused to draw breath. Then he gave his own version.

'What are the basic facts? Dr Youssef Shaker was convinced that she met her death by foul play, and said so. The "subsequent burning" in his postmortem report clinched it. This was corroborated to the hilt by Professor Gresham, only he did it in a much more scientific and precise manner than ever appears before these courts. And – it is no use taking the attitude that his way is not our way, and that we do things here "Kenya style." Scientific facts and results are immutable and cannot be changed to suit the circumstances.

'Superintendent Wanjau had two possibilities to con-sider when her Suzuki was found. Either she got stuck – the facile, obvious one. Or it was planted. If it was, then clearly whoever planted it had to have an accomplice or accomplices. No-one in their right mind would plant it and chance walking to safetly alone on his flat feet in the Mara – especially in the dark.

'To distribute and burn her remains he had to have the time and the opportunity as well as a very good knowledge of the park.

'He also had to have the authority to drive during the

316

hours of darkness anywhere unchallenged and to give orders for the doing or undoing of anything without question from subordinates, and to pass through the park gates unchallenged.

'Mr Makallah, of all persons, had the mobility, the intimate knowledge of his kingdom, and the authority.'

There Georgiadis had it: the three ingredients of the case, and the direction they pointed. He took a moment to address Makallah's discovery of the remains.

'In that bushy, featureless country, in a Land Rover you could pass ten metres from her remains and never see them in the grass. Thus our resourceful Mr Makallah invents some overfed "vultures" sitting in a tree to give verisimilitude to his story of how he came to find out where her remains were.'

He gave his characteristic glare of disbelief. 'As a cynical old lawyer,' he said, 'I don't believe in fairy tales. Mr Makallah knew where her remains were and was going there to make sure nothing was left. But he was with others, so when he saw that some still remained he had to "find" them. What a coincidence! Clearly, Mr Makallah knows more about this sad affair than he admitted to the Inquest Court. He is indeed a privileged person. Instead of being a suspect we find him being used as an interpreter at the Masai manyatta to take statements!'

Having disposed of the murder and identified, to his own satisfaction, the culprit, Georgiadis turned to the cover-up. He dealt only glancingly with the idea it might have been a conspiracy to protect someone very high up. Instead he focused on the notion that it was a blundering attempt to protect the tourist industry.

'What is so sad is that so many are trying so hard to entice our visitors to see for themselves the many marvels and beauties of this country. To have their efforts undermined by this sort of incompetence is inexcusable.' He shook his head. 'Can it seriously be considered that tourists will feel happier suspecting that there is a psychopathic killer loose in the Mara, rather than accepting that murders occur in all countries, but at least in

317

Kenya we try our best to catch them and deal with them according to the law?'

Only John Ward pursued the evidence, Georgiadis stressed. 'Effectively he was given the runaround, but they never expected him to have the dedication and the resolve to continue to try to find out what really happened to his daughter, and certainly they never expected him to have the money to do so. What Wanjau expected was that he would burn himself out after a couple of abortive trips to Kenya. Instead, he kept on coming for thirteen or more trips with new evidence, which causes Wanjau to go through the motions in order not to appear supine or static. Fantastic! Is this the way we treat murder in Kenya? Are we really so unmotivated when a visitor to our country gets chopped up and burned?'

There now remained only one last issue to address: the assault on Julie's character. Georgiadis did it quickly and simply at the very end of his address.

'The attempts to besmirch this girl's character are inexcusable. Assuming she did have an affair with Watson one night several days before she drove on the sixth of September to Sand River – so what? Even a common prostitute is entitled to her life. This is all a smokescreen – don't let's play charades.

'Let's face it,' he concluded. 'Our police, if left unimpeded, are perfectly capable of solving this crime, if they want to.'

CHAPTER FORTY-FIVE

Etyang did not have Georgiadis's flourish and certainly not his air of passionate indignation. On the afternoon of 6 October he rose to make his case. Like Georgiadis's it had remained almost unchanged from the version he had presented on the first day of hearings before Magistrate Mango.

Etyang's opening was almost identical to Georgiadis's, stating the only stipulated fact in the whole proceeding. 'There is sufficient medical evidence to establish that Julie Anne Ward is dead,' he said.

From there Etyang embarked on an attempt to salvage the State's theories of suicide or animal attack. 'From the facts disclosed in the investigator's file the cause of death was uncertain,' he said. 'She could have committed suicide, she could have been killed by wild animals, or she could have been killed by person or persons unknown. As far as the investigating officer was concerned, as far as the evidence disclosed, it was not clear whether the deceased's remains were burned before or after she had died.'

This was untrue, of course. Youssef's original language that the bone was burned 'subsequent' to dismemberment was never changed, even during Kaviti's surgical operation on the report. Etyang was suggesting Julie could have been alive for a considerable time after her limbs were hacked apart, something that Gresham and Kaviti had agreed was not likely.

Etyang continued. 'Who was Julie Ward?' He ran through the elements of her life story as narrated by her father at the outset of his testimony. But along the way he made some odd detours, as if trying to inject some new mystery into the case.

'She was taken to Mr Weld Dixon's place by a man called Mr David Tree. We never heard of Mr Tree again after Julie had been given permission by Mr Dixon to camp in his garden.' As it happened, the government could have assuaged its curiosity about Tree without difficulty; since depositing the Ho-Bo tour group at Weld Dixon's he had spent the year pottering around the workshop area of the same estate, preparing a truck for his own overland group. He had not been called to testify by either side. But Etyang was really not interested in Dave Tree. Having mentioned his name, Etyang just as abruptly dropped it for good. He now went on to resurrect the issue of Burns's and Watson's failures to appear before the inquest.

'I cannot tell how Julie met Dr Burns because he elected not to come to give evidence. After she left Sand River Gate, we shall never know whom Julie met. Dr Burns may well have been at Nairobi, having had an argument with her before he left her at the Mara. He never came to this inquest. He decided to stay away. We shall never know why.

'Mr Stephen Watson, the last person who was with her at the Mara, again never came up to testify. Did Julie meet Mr Watson after she left Sand River Gate? We shall never know because Julie is dead and Watson will not be coming to testify.' Here Etyang ignored all the evidence acknowledged by Wanjau that Watson could not be a suspect.

Etyang let drop another vague hint about Julie's private life. 'That was Julie – a twenty-eight-year-old, adventurous woman with three men in her life at the Masai Mara (he included David Weston in the triumvirate). I do not think we will ever know who Julie really was,' he said, as if a metaphysical inquiry had been confounded.

Etyang continued to treat the Youssef-Kaviti affair as a routine consultation between two equally respectable pathologists. 'They both agreed that injuries had not been caused by a sharp instrument,' he said. Gresham's report he tried to undermine by noting the Cambridge pathologist had examined preserved remains, not the fresh remains seen by Youssef and, supposedly, Kaviti. 'Their conditions had considerably changed,' he said. He went further. 'Are we even talking about the same remains? Could Professor Gresham have made a mistake? Just because he is a professor of medicine in Cambridge doesn't make his reports and findings unquestionable.'

The prosecutor maintained the position that the Kenya police had a full-scale search on for Julie after her disappearance. 'There was an aerial search including several planes. There was nothing wrong with Mr Ward getting involved in this search, to supplement the police work,' he said as if Ward had hitched a ride on a police search, not conducted his own. 'The Kenya authorities,' he insisted, 'were as much concerned about Julie's disappearance and subsequent death as Mr Ward. Kenya authorities carried out a search in the difficult circumstances of this case. In return they have been subjected to abuses and insults by Mr Georgiadis.'

At that point Etyang, oddly, questioned Ward's and Tham's motives on the very day of the jeep's discovery.

'Mr Ward and Mr Tham broke into this vehicle and carried out a search inside, looking for a note or clue to Julie's disappearance. They did not wait for the police. Was a note found? We shall never know. What happened to the keys to the jeep? Tham did not tell us about them. (Why the keys to a locked and abandoned jeep should be an issue Etyang did not explain.) The search inside the jeep may have been carried out innocently, but one thing is clear: It was materially interfered with and all clues lost or taken away.' Here Etyang ignored the fact that when Tham and Ward found the jeep, there was no reason to suspect that Julie's disappearance was the outcome of foul play.

'Tham and Ward cannot escape blame for interfering with this vehicle before the police arrived,' he continued. 'After all, throughout this inquest they are in a group of people who have been associated with intelligence and sound judgment. Where had their natural intelligence suddenly gone to? For game viewing?' There was a perplexed murmur in the courtroom at the prosecutor's attempt at sarcasm.

In the last, Etyang tried to clear Makallah. 'From the mass of evidence in this inquest it has not been established at all that Mr Makallah ever came into contact with the deceased when she was alive. He may have lied about his driving,' Etyang conceded. 'What other evidence is there to incriminate this man? Nothing other than speculation. It is claimed that a man who has free movement in the park, has ultimate knowledge of the park, killed Julie. Is that man Simon Makallah? Where is the evidence?'

He wound up his presentation by trying to write finis to the entire case. 'No offense was committed by anybody, if the evidence of Dr Kaviti is accepted,' he said. 'Taking into account the absence of motive, any possible motive, why anybody would have wanted Julie dead, then the other possible verdict is that this was death by misadventure. Apart from her camera, which was not in her jeep and which she probably took along, nothing valuable seems to have been taken from her. What is the motive in this case? I don't see any.

'The police have exhausted their investigations. Mr Whitford, private eye of Mr Ward, he too has hit a dead end. It would be futile,' Etyang concluded, 'to carry out any further investigations.'

CHAPTER FORTY-SIX

No-one knew what to expect when Judge Mango stepped up to his podium on 27 October to deliver his verdict. The two sides in this adversarial proceeding had begun and ended so far apart: the Ward family accusing the police of malfeasance and seeking a verdict of murder, and the State defending the government investigation as complete and asking for a finding of misadventure. One Kenya news-weekly speculated that Mango would split the difference by issuing a harsh verdict on police ineptitude and finding the question of murder inconclusive.

Mango took one and a quarter hours to give the audience his answer. First and at length he recapitulated the weeks of proceedings in the courtroom. Mango reviewed the long story of Julie's arrival in Kenya and last trip to the Masai Mara. The faulty fuel pump made another appearance. Ward's search of the park was rehashed. Here and there Mango allowed himself a touch of wry humor, familiar to those who had read his ruling in the Karanja inquest, as when he recalled how Julie had shrugged off David Weston's concerns about her driving alone in the park.

'She would not yield,' Mango said. 'She said she would manage. As we now know, she did not manage!'

Mango continued to narrate the discovery of Julie's remains and the history of the several postmortem reports. Here, twenty minutes into the judge's recitation, Ward seemed to have won his first skirmish.

'Mr Georgiadis asserts that Dr Youssef was leaned on and made to say that the changes in the report were made after he and Dr Kaviti both re-examined the leg and the lower jaw. For my part, I would say that I found Dr Youssef extremely unsatisfactory in this regard. Mr Georgiadis described Dr Youssef as a man without a backbone. I do not consider this to be too far off the mark. He is a man who can't stand by his word, as he is said to have promised Mr Weld Dixon and Mr Ferguson he would.'

So Mango appeared to have accepted the Gresham-Youssef version. But while chiding Youssef, the refugee Egyptian, for his lack of backbone in standing up to, among others, Kaviti, he never took Kaviti himself to task for his role in altering the evidence. Instead he continued on, reviewing the course of the police investigation in the first days after the discovery of the remains and Wanjau's assignment a week later. Eventually, Mango's meanderings brought him to the sausage tree and the fire set beneath it.

'The ash was found to contain pieces of flesh, burnt clothing, hair, and so forth,' he said. 'My view is that the burning of these items was a deliberate act, possibly closely guarded, carefully organized, for otherwise some piece or pieces of unburnt cloth would have been blown out of the fire. No unburnt dress nor piece thereof was found.

'Looking at the scene, this is the picture that emerges: that Julie Ward, to take leave from her flip-flopping across the Masai Mara, settled at this spot. She lit a fire either to warm herself, or to keep away the animals. She then sat down by the fire to let the night pass. She was then suddenly surprised by wild animals and in the course of the struggle she was flung on to the fire where the animals continued to chew her until they had their fill.'

Then he said, 'This theory does not seem plausible or realistic. In that case some of her clothing would have escaped the fire. Pools of blood would have been left behind. No expert was called to tell us how wild animals relate to fire, but I often read and hear that fire and the wild game are not the best of friends!'

Taking a leaf from the father's book, he observed, 'Unless she was mentally sick, it is hard to believe that she would have chosen to go across country in a direction she did not know. By the Kenyan law,' he added, 'everyone is presumed sane until the contrary is shown, and this presumption should apply with equal force to Julie Ward.'

Now Mango showed his aptitude at walking a tightrope. Having disposed of part of the Kenya Police scenario of Julie's death, he remarked, 'When Superintendent Wanjau took over the investigation, some good and fast progress was made. Some very good quality investigations were carried out, although it is quite clear that Mr Ward refused to give them time to breathe. Places were visited, various and relevant places in the Masai Mara.' The judge was working up to his first mention of Simon Makallah, and here Ward and Georgiadis suffered a crushing blow.

'It is suggested that Simon Makallah should have been thoroughly interviewed, his house searched, and his vehicles' work tickets carefully scrutinized. It is obvious that the prime suspect by the family's standards is Mr Makallah. It is true, as Mr Georgiadis says, that in a murder case anyone connected with the death is a suspect until cleared. Of course this is so, but one must first of all be connected with the death. Makallah never had seen this woman while she lived.'

Mango decided that Makallah's discovery of the remains was not enough to implicate him. He agreed that the warden lied on the stand about knowing how to drive, but he dismissed the point as unimportant. 'From the time Makallah came to the witness box,' Mango said, 'I could see that it never occurred to him that anyone was suspecting him of being connected with the murder. And I see no reason why they should have.'

After that, moving along rapidly, Mango said he agreed that the Suzuki had been planted, but disagreed that the discovery of a toothpaste tube at Makari post made the rangers there suspect. He found Nchoko's story of filling in Julie's name to cover an error in the receipt book 'implausible, and still mysterious,' but accepted it nonetheless, finding that it proved 'the important thing – that Julie has been confirmed to have passed through the gate on the day in question.' Ward had reason to squirm in his seat: Of course the forgery meant that Julie's passage was not confirmed at all.

Yet Mango continued to move closer to Ward's ultimate conclusion: 'From the totality of the evidence I can only conclude that those sharp cuts on the remains were manmade and not animal-made. It is reasonable to conclude that they were made by him who had something to do with the death of the young woman. The killer would have all the reason to carve her up and to burn the pieces to prevent their being found.'

Now Mango addressed the question of the two white men seen with Julie in her last days. Like Etyang he had left it for last, and like the prosecutor he drew adverse conclusions from their absence.

'The obvious suspects were kept at bay by the family lawyer, who does not even want them to be mentioned. I am not saying they had anything to do with the death of this poor girl, but they should have been the first and the obvious suspects. Makallah may have had intimate knowledge of the Mara – but was he the only one? What about Weston, Burns, and Watson? How much did they know of the Mara?'

Finally, he let it pass. An hour and fifteen minutes after starting, he delivered his verdict. 'I agree with Mr Georgiadis,' he said. 'There is ample and circumstantial evidence to show that Julie Ward died as a result of foul play by a person or persons unknown.' Mango directed that the file be sent on to the attorney general, but it was clear that, like Etyang, he considered the case at a dead end. 'Mr Ward has done a lot, but this does not change the fact that his investigations, like that of the police, have come up with nothing. I would see no point in directing the police or anyone else through the attorney general to conduct further investigations.'

Before he rose from the bench, leaving Ward with this half-loaf, Mango cleared one last group of suspects.

'I think the animals are innocent,' he said.

Judge Mango's ability to step on exceedingly few toes was

not lost on many observers. The *Weekly Review*, the most reliable Kenyan news publication, remarked the next week, 'The favorable comments on police activities were all the more interesting in view of the fact that Mango rejected virtually all of the police case.'

It was true, of course. Wanjau's 'high-quality' investigation had resulted in a conclusion of suicide, which Mango thought too little of even to mention. The police theory of Julie's cross-Mara trek he considered 'implausible.' Still, he accepted Makallah's story about following footprints and vultures to the site of the remains, which would have been impossible if Julie had not walked away from the jeep and toward the site.

Ward and Georgiadis seemed torn between elation and depression when they met for impromptu press conferences outside the Law Courts.

'It's a mixed bag,' the lawyer said, frowning. 'I am naturally delighted to have got the decision the Ward family has pursued, from the beginning.'

'Do you think this is a vindication for Mr Ward?' someone asked.

'Well, principally he's been maintaining that she was killed by a man, not wild animals. In that respect he's been vindicated fully. That was the principal hurdle to clear, and Mr Ward has done it. In effect, he won.'

What about Burns and Watson, someone asked, and Mango's complaint that Georgiadis had sheltered them?

'That suggestion is nonsense,' he snapped, 'and not in accordance with the facts. I did not keep them "at bay." I merely argued that they at least seemed to have been cleared by the police while thirty-five others who might also have been cleared had not even been questioned. They were cleared and Makallah wasn't. That's the difference.'

In another corner of the plaza Ward tried to get his feelings in order.

'Well, my opinion of Kenyan justice is a little better than it was a half hour ago,' he said.

'Are you happy with the result?'

Ward hesitated. 'One cannot be happy to have it confirmed that your daughter was murdered, but I'm happy it wasn't ruled that wild animals did it.' He said that now he would seek another meeting with Kilonzo to 'mend fences' and try to launch another investigation.

'Is it a good day for you, Mr Ward?'

'At least some sense has come out of this, I suppose. It's a good day for Kenya, not just for me.'

'Where should the investigation go now, Mr Georgiadis?' someone asked the lawyer.

'There's a number of people they could investigate further. The Kenya police have solved much more difficult cases than this in the past. No doubt,' he said, echoing his closing statement, 'they can solve this one.'

CHAPTER FORTY-SEVEN

The year 1989 was coming to its end, but in the weeks following Judge Mango's ruling in October there had been no new investigation by the Kenya Police. The Julie Ward murder file disappeared into the office of Attorney General Matthew Muli, with its handful of witnesses' statements and Wanjau's eccentric conclusion of suicide. If John Ward wanted a further investigation, it appeared, he was again on his own.

He kept Whitford on the payroll and instructed him to field any evidence that came in. Occasionally someone would show up with a clue, more often just a wild story, and on Ward's instructions Whitford would give the person traveling money and pay a few expenses. Most were dead ends.

'All sorts of chaps would come in here with various theories,' Whitford wearily recounted later. 'I would tell them we don't want theories, we want evidence. But they were just trying to get the reward.'

One November day in Bury St Edmunds, Ward received an anonymous letter. It had been posted from Blackpool, England, although its unsure hand and grammar suggested the writer might be Kenyan. Ward presumed it had been carried to the UK by a tourist at someone's request.

The writer said he could identify Julie's killer. As bait he gave the first name of his suspect.

Ward quickly sent a copy to Whitford in Nairobi, with instructions to trace the source, if possible. Meanwhile he set out to have the paper and the handwriting tested. The results were disappointing: The paper was indeed from Kenya, it seemed, torn from a writing pad. But an expert

329

examination indicated that someone had been practicing writing, probably with his left hand. Reluctantly, Ward had to accept that the letter was a hoax.

Not long after that a more promising lead developed. Ward got a call from a man who identified himself as a Kenyan safari operator. He was in London and Ward arranged to meet him.

But the safari operator was nothing of the kind. His name was Bernard Otieno and his job was running supplies to the lodges in the Mara. Otieno spun an implausible story about his daughter having been kidnapped by poachers. He used the Kenyan term referring to roving Somali bandits, *shiftas*. The daughter's body had been found in the Mara and disposed of by Simon Makallah, Otieno told Ward, adding that some sort of incriminating tapes and photographs existed. He gave Ward the name of a Maasai ranger who had information about the case, cautioning that the ranger had since been transferred to a game park in Meru, in central Kenya.

Whitford was sent tramping up to Meru, only to find that Otieno's story seemed, as he reported later, 'a load of baloney.' No Masai ranger was working at the park, he learned. Eventually he returned to Nairobi, feeling deeply the waste of his time. Like the others Otieno faded away.

Still, the occasional leads kept Ward and his efforts in the news. Every time an anonymous letter or mysterious clue emerged, the British press would jump on it optimistically. Then an odd thing happened one day in December when President Moi himself was visiting London. At a meeting with British Foreign Secretary Douglas Hurd, the president of Kenya remarked that solving the murder of this young British tourist in a Kenya game park had proved to be beyond the capability of his own police, and he asked Hurd for the investigatory assistance of the world's premier detective force, Scotland Yard.

330

Part Three

The Jeep in the Gully

CHAPTER FORTY-EIGHT

Ken Thompson, a superintendent in the International and Organized Crime section of Scotland Yard, was the first British detective to take a look at the case after Moi's request to Hurd. Thompson spent two weeks in Kenya around the beginning of January simply to determine if there was enough left of the case for the Yard to investigate. When he got back to London to submit his report, he called Ward as a courtesy.

'I think there's something we can do here,' he said. Thompson thought it was clear that there had been huge gaps in the investigation – Georgiadis's 'lacunae' – which could be filled in if the Yard started at square one. He also seemed determined that if Scotland Yard committed itself some action would have to be taken. 'I don't want this report gathering dust,' Ward, elated, heard him say.

After more than a year of fighting the Kenyan government all alone, finally he felt he might have someone on his side. Scotland Yard would not stand for the kind of runaround he had put up with, he thought happily.

Graham Searle and David Shipperlee complemented each other physically, in the best Hollywood tradition of police partnerships. Searle, the senior man, was of average height and stocky, with broad shoulders that emphasized his seriousness of purpose and a shock of straight dark hair that fell over his forehead. Shipperlee was tall and solidly built, light haired, and with a fair complexion that would take on a ruddy burn the instant he set foot under the powerful equatorial sun of Kenya.

They had just been teamed together in the International and Organized Crime section when Ken Thompson asked them to interview John Ward in Bury St Edmunds as a first step toward reinvestigating Julie Ward's death in Kenya.

They spent two hours with Ward on that first visit, hearing the same story Julie's father had told countless times to countless people. That afternoon, as they were driving home to London, heading south down the M-11 motorway, Searle turned to Shipperlee and said, 'You know, Dave, I don't really relish this job, if we get it.'

The reasons for wariness were obvious to both. It had been nearly eighteen months since Julie's death. Witnesses were dispersed all over the world. Forensic evidence, if any existed, might long since have been destroyed by time and the elements. Investigating a crime that had already been investigated once, however ineptly, by the Kenya Police was not an inviting prospect.

A month later, after a second, much longer interview with John Ward, the two of them were on a flight to Nairobi. They were still not looking forward to the task.

Searle would later say that he and Shipperlee expected to do 'nothing more than a cosmetic exercise on the investigation that had already been done.' It was hard, particularly with such a time lag, to strike out in completely new directions when you were reinvestigating something. You always tended to be guided by the first investigators' path. On the other hand, as they recollected later, they had no idea how little had actually been done.

As their plane made its way over the Mediterranean and into African airspace, they indulged in some professional speculation over what might have happened to Julie Ward. 'You know, it might even be one of the rangers,' one of them remarked to the other.

They arrived in Nairobi on the morning of 25 February and checked into the Hotel Inter-Continental. Their first appointment was with Commissioner Kilonzo. Kilonzo was engagingly cooperative, seemingly ready to put his force at their disposal. In picking a liaison officer they made the most obvious choice, the man who had conducted the initial investigation: Superintendent Wanjau.

Kilonzo agreed immediately, barking the order into the telephone as the British detectives sat in his office. 'Get him here at once,' he said. Kilonzo even offered to have Wanjau conveniently installed with them in a room at the Inter-Continental.

'That would be great,' Searle said. Later the detectives thought it a lucky break that Wanjau had refused the offer. 'Otherwise,' one remarked, 'we would have had him around all the time.'

Meanwhile, the Inter-Continental was coming to resemble a home away from home for Scotland Yard detectives. Shortly after Searle and Shipperlee arrived they were joined there by a second team of officers from London. Under Detective Superintendent John Troon the new team had been requested by the Kenya government to investigate a killing whose domestic political ramifacations made the death of Julie Ward pale in comparison.

The victim was Robert J. Ouko, Kenya's minister of foreign affairs. At the beginning of the year Ouko had accompanied President Moi on a semi-official visit to Washington. No-one was ever entirely sure what happened during this journey, but it seemed that in the US capital Ouko's rise to prominence in Kenyan politics had met its abrupt end.

The whispering was that it had something to do with the esteem the polished and educated Ouko won from American officials who considered Moi unsophisticated. The flashpoint may have been a discussion about the so-called *Kenya Times* tower. This was a planned sixty-story skyscraper to be situated on a Nairobi site carved out of Uhuru Park, the most accessible patch of greensward in the increasingly congested Kenyan capital. The idea was to create a grandiose new headquarters for the KANU-Maxwell newspaper, but many people saw the project as largely a tribute to President Moi. It would include a convention hall presumably designed to supplant the Jomo Kenyatta Conference Centre, whose cylindrical tower dominated the Nairobi skyline, with a newer one identified with the current president. Its front entrance would be adorned by a six-story statue of Moi himself.

The tower had become a political issue when a grass-roots environmentalist named Wangari Maathai publicly criticized it for appropriating such valuable parkland. Since the tower was to be partially owned by the ruling party, Mrs Maathai found herself subjected to the familiar hoots of derision in parliament. KANU's minions stooped to calling her a man-hating divorcée, and the government office space she had been granted as headquarters for her nonprofit reforestation program was withdrawn.

When parliament voted to put the government's own credit behind the bonds needed to build the skyscraper, the international banks keeping Kenya fiscally afloat had added their own objection: The new debt could destroy the entire country's credit rating. Privately the government was backing off from the tower plan. But in Washington, it was said, Ouko unwisely took it upon himself to blurt out the news of the project's cancellation, embarrassing and upstaging an enraged Moi.

On their return to Kenya, Ouko was sent to Coventry, as it were, instructed to return to his hometown on Lake Victoria and wait there for instructions. Family and friends observed that the urbane minister was preoccupied and nervous. Very late one night a mysterious white limousine came for him. Three days later his family disclosed that he had not been seen since. A day after that his body, charred almost beyond recognition, was found in the woods a few miles away.

The discovery created an agonizing crisis for Moi. It was true that his regime had never been known for using assassination as a political tool. This was in stark contrast to Kenyatta's days, when one prominent opponent had been gunned down in public and another kidnapped and murdered. Yet some government ministers had a reputation for teeming with political thugs, and there was a feeling that it was possible that Ouko's death had been the result of a cautionary beating gotten out of hand.

In any event, the Kenyan public was keeping a watch on

how the investigation progressed. One day soon after the discovery of Ouko's body the Kenya Police made its first statement. A pathological examination of the remains indicated that death had been caused by a gunshot wound to the right side of the head, and as it happened Ouko seemed to have been holding a revolver in his right hand. The examination had been done in the police pathology section, Dr Jason Kaviti, chief. In short, the conclusion was: suicide.

With that announcement it was as if all of the Kenya Police Department's residual credibility evaporated. Riots erupted in Nairobi and Kisumu, Ouko's home city on Lake Victoria. Students marched through the streets carrying placards reading, NO COVER-UP! During a Nairobi memorial service for the slain minister hundreds of thousands of people gathered on the boulevard fronting the church. When mourners emerged with spectacular expressions of grief, having viewed Ouko's burned body through a port in his coffin lid, the crowd went wild, pelting police with stones and rampaging through Nairobi's downtown amid clouds of tear gas. Clearly, a credible investigation of Ouko's killing was beyond the capacity of the Kenya Police, and a second appeal for Scotland Yard went out to Douglas Hurd.

Meanwhile, Searle and Shipperlee were finding their new Kenyan colleague a puzzle. At first they tried to welcome him as a new member of their team, but like many Africans with limited experience dealing with Europeans as equals, Wanjau was edgy and uncomfortable. With one or two exceptions he refused their invitations to join them for meals. He refused even to eat the same Western food, preferring the greens and *ugali*, or cornmeal, with which rural Africans made their light meals.

Wanjau struck them as irritating and amusing at turns. It was soon clear that the sullen Kenyan was a thin reed indeed to lean on for any reliable assistance or even information. Nothing would annoy Searle and Shipperlee more than to be ready to start a full day of tightly scheduled meetings and interviews at 8 a.m., only to have their liaison officer wander into the hotel at 10.15 with some lame excuse, insensitive to their requirements and thoroughly ruining their plans as they waited, seething, in the hotel's musty lobby.

But to a certain extent Searle and Shipperlee had sympathy for the Kenyan officer, who volunteered the complaint that he had seemed entirely unable to escape the Ward case. Every time some new shred of evidence emerged his superiors detached him from his post in up-country Meru and sent him chasing all over the country to track it down. He had been dressed down by Ward, grilled at length by Georgiadis on the witness stand, and hauled in from a comfortable sinecure in Meru to second for Thompson and again for themselves. Whatever tiny nugget of enthusiasm he was ever able to muster for the investigation had long since vanished. He made no secret of his detestation of busy, congested Nairobi. Shipperlee later described him as 'a fish out of water everywhere.'

He seemed to make no effort to absorb the evidence. From time to time he suggested to the detectives that Julie might indeed have been eaten by animals. Once, to their surprise, he even repeated the old discredited theory that she had committed suicide.

One day, not long after their arrival in Nairobi, Searle and Shipperlee had Wanjau show them the Masai Mara.

The two Britons were impressed with the desolation of the place. As they drove off the Keekorok–Sand River road on to open land to find the gully, they were surprised at how quickly the terrain deteriorated. Leaving the main road, it was evident, one would never know what hard country lay ahead.

The terrain was so harsh that by land vehicle they were unable to get to within a quarter mile of the gully. They had to turn back and take a helicopter to the site. There, they were surprised to see how deep the gully was. When Shipperlee lowered his more than six-foot frame into it Searle, standing on the edge, could not see the top of his head.

The two detectives' first couple of weeks in the country did little to change their minds about the unlikelihood of solving the case. Working conditions in Kenya were worse than either of them had ever experienced before, even on cases outside the British Isles. One problem was the location of the Masai Mara itself, 'a real ball-acher,' as Searle bluntly described it. To get to the scene of the crime from Nairobi necessitated either an hour's flight or a six-hour drive over terrible roads. So if something occurred to one of them to check out, they could not simply run down to the scene. From the park there was almost no telephone communication with headquarters in Nairobi – just radio-telephones operating between the tourist lodges and the capital. Those were worse than useless, so heavy with static that most conversations were incomprehensible. On the other hand, they could not just move their head-quarters to the Mara, because most of the important witnesses were in Nairobi.

Searle and Shipperlee found themselves shuttling back and forth between the capital and the game reserve. From the old camping receipt books kept at Sand River Gate Shipperlee determined that 183 campers had stayed at Sand River camp between 2 and 13 September, 1988. The books showed local Kenya addresses for most of them, but of course this represented a lost opportunity. All these tourists would since have left the lodges and hotels represented by these postal box numbers and dispersed to their home countries. In the weeks after Julie's death, they reflected, Wanjau could have extracted full home addresses for all of them, had he tried, from the guest records maintained by their lodges. Now, eighteen months on, the lodges would have thrown away most of the records.

In Nairobi things were not much better. The formal statements Wanjau had collected from witnesses were almost useless. They were incomplete, confused, filled with Wanjau's own speculations and conclusions mas-querading as facts. Searle pulled out a statement taken from Paul Weld Dixon more than a year earlier. It was two paragraphs long. Later, he would interview the retired filmmaker himself; when he was finished, the statement was seven pages. Almost every witness had to be reinterviewed in this way.

Quickly they recognized how Wanjau's uncaring attitude had made a complete hash of the case. A major mistake, it was immediately clear, was that none of the rangers had been interviewed or even identified. When Searle asked Wanjau for a list of the rangers on duty in and around Keekorok and Sand River in September 1988, he replied, 'No records are kept.'

In fact, Shipperlee promptly discovered, records were kept and they were very good. At the game reserve he had put the same question to Michael Koikai, who had taken over as chief warden from Simon Makallah. Koikai produced the names of thirty-four rangers, and within a day managed to summon twenty-one of them for sessions with the Scotland Yard detectives. Most of the others followed later.

It was obvious to the detectives that none of these men had ever been interviewed before. Not a single one even remarked in passing, for example, 'As I told Superintendent Wanjau . . .' Most of them had nothing to contribute. But as the detectives worked their way through the men on the list, something struck them as very important.

It involved Makari, the isolated ranger post nearest to Julie's stranded jeep. This was the place John Ward had fetched up on the day he found the jeep, from where he radioed for Sebastian Tham's helicopter to take him to Julie's remains. At Makari he had found the little button battery placed atop the Kenyan coin in the sun, and at the same place Frank Ribeiro had unearthed the Macleans toothpaste tube that Wanjau had uncaringly discarded.

Searle and Shipperlee had been told that five rangers were assigned to Makari post at any one time. That was true. But as they collected their interviews, they realized that at the time of Julie's arrival, three of the rangers were on leave.

That left two, both local Masai. One was named Jonah

Magiroi and the other was Peter Kippeen, the very man who had come upon the stranded *Sunday Times* correspondent in the bush near the gulley a week after Julie's death.

Both men's statements, Searle and Shipperlee agreed, were suspicious. Among other things they had insisted that they never patrolled far from the post – not farther than 500 meters or so. But that was demonstrably untrue: the *Sunday Times* crew was much farther away than that when they were found by Peter Kippeen. They hinted they were unfamiliar with the area – also untrue. They were local boys who knew it like the backs of their hands.

With this and other evidence in hand, after two weeks in country, eighteen months after the Kenya Police had supposedly investigated the disappearance and death of Julie Ward, Searle and Shipperlee were able to form their own opinion of what had happened to Julie. When John Ward heard it, he was not pleased.

CHAPTER FORTY-NINE

They started with the jeep.

'I won't accept,' Searle would say later, 'that a person who has just killed, dismembered, and burned a girl will then drive her jeep away, write SOS on the roof, and dig a pair of furrows to make it look like she tried to get it out. I've never known of a guy in a panic doing these things.'

It was simple, really. Julie Ward did get her own jeep stuck in the gully. Searle and Shipperlee were sure that she had spent a night, or a night and a day, in or around the vehicle. With stray shreds of plastic she lit the fire that Ward had found on the ridge near the gully, they figured. She painted the SOS on the roof with mud. And she had tried to dig the jeep out of the gully, all by herself. The detectives had discovered that the Suzuki's battery was dead when Tham and his crew arrived at the gully to take it to Keekorok; it had to be towed out and then bump-started twice to get it to Keekorok under its own power. They presumed Julie had been hooting the horn or keeping the headlights on to attract human attention or ward off animals.

The two detectives found some support for this scenario from an unexpected source: Bob Whitford. The Welsh investigator, who occasionally helped them man a private phone line for tips in the Inter-Continental, proved an eager revisionist. 'The SOS was always in the back of my mind,' he said later. 'If someone is dumping the jeep, why take the time?'

The only genuine problem with the theory, they realized, was Henri Berney. His insistence that his crew would have seen Julie, or that she would have heard his camp, raised a real question. Before they were done, they

342

would need to see Mr Berney about all that.

But for now, the detectives' theory put a new light on things. It tended to absolve David Nchoko, the revenue clerk at Sand River, and Constable Karuri. Searle was already confident that Nchoko's forgery of Julie's name had been an innocent attempt to straighten out his books before an audit caught a discrepancy. Now his theory of Julie's path put her more than six kilometers from the gate when she might have been abducted.

Who, then, was responsible? Burns or Watson? The detectives were satisfied that Burns had been out of the country at the time of the crime. They made plans to interview the zoologist in Australia, but it was a formality.

The suspicion of Steve Watson was even more risible, considering the evidence, most of which had been lying unappreciated in Kenyan hands. On the night Julie was thought to have been murdered, Watson was with John Ward himself, having dinner on the Norfolk Hotel verandah and planning the next day's search with Morey.

For 6 September, the day Julie disappeared, Watson also had an ironclad alibi: He was at Lake Naivasha, hundreds of miles away, in the custody of none other than the Kenya Police. When Watson and his tour party had arrived at the lake and entered the national park on its shores they had been stopped by the authorities, who charged them with lacking the proper tour permits. This was the product of a dispute between the government and foreign tour companies that had recently flared up as the Kenyans tried to protect Kenyan-owned tour firms from competition.

A squad of police officers took Watson off to see a local magistrate, where he paid a few thousand shillings in fees and got a dated and signed receipt in return. The whole affair had escaped the notice of both sides at the inquest. This was largely Wanjau's fault: his failure to corroborate Watson's alibi exemplified the sloppy way he went about investigating.

Some other minor leads had come in through the investigators' hot line at the hotel, but nothing useful. One of the first calls was an anonymous tip about a politician's son occupying a farm near to Masa. Searle dismissed the tip out of hand.

Finally, the detectives thought again of the two rangers from Makari post.

Magiroi and Kippeen had clearly lied during their interrogations by Searle and Shipperlee. They claimed they never patrolled as far as the gully, which was untrue, and never patrolled at all except in groups of five, also untrue. The detectives were now convinced that Julie had spent all or part of her last week on Earth at Makari post. The two rangers might well have happened upon Julie at her disabled jeep, possibly having heard the engine revving. Perhaps they brought her to Makari post, even with a view to helping her, offering the use of their radio. Makari was an isolated spot even for this portion of the park; it was unlikely that anybody, tourist or otherwise, would come by under normal circumstances. Then it would have got late and dark. At some point, the detectives theorized, the rangers could have raped the girl, imprisoned her, and finally killed her and dismembered her body to destroy the evidence.

One day Searle and Shipperlee got a crew to join them at the little post to sweep out the squat tin huts. It was a disgusting job. With pounds of debris cooking inside under the hot sun, the huts were repositories of overpowering stench and filth. 'These places haven't been cleaned in years,' one of the crew moaned.

In a few hours they had filled five or six good-sized garbage bags with loads of debris, sealed and tagged for shipment to the police laboratory in London. This was their only real chance at getting physical evidence, the detectives knew. But they were pessimistic about the odds of finding in the accretion of dust and dirt a stray blond hair or the residue of blood, or even a discarded cigarette butt that could be DNA-tested for a trace of Julie's saliva. Searching for a needle in a haystack, compared to this, was child's play.

About three weeks after their arrival the two detectives

had enough to call a preliminary press conference. It was held one bright March morning in a conference room in the back of the Inter-Continental, where John Ward had called his own first press conference one and a half years before. Jenny Jenkins, who was acting as their liaison with the High Commission, ushered a crowd of foreign and local reporters into the narrow room.

Searle, Shipperlee, and Wanjau entered and made their way through a forest of television cameras to take their seats at a long table. Wanjau directed his characteristic sullen glare at the cluster of microphones in front of them.

Searle had several items on his agenda. He wanted to clear the reputations of two persons: David Nchoko and Julie Ward. First he read a short statement.

'Ladies and gentlemen, if I may start by introducing myself. I am Detective Superintendent Graham Searle from the International and Organized Crime Branch at New Scotland Yard. I'm accompanied by Detective Inspector David Shipperlee of the same branch, and Detective Superintendent Muchiri Wanjau of the Kenya Police, who has been carrying out this joint reinvestigation with me.

'Two men, who were interviewed by us last week, were interviewed for a second time yesterday. As a result of these interviews both men have been detained by the Kenya Police here in Nairobi and are assisting with inquiries into the disappearance and death of Julie Anne Ward in the Masai Mara Game Reserve in September 1988.

'I am not prepared at this stage to say anything more on that subject. There are, however, two or three matters I do wish to raise, and the first of those is Julie Ward's character.

'There have been some media publications who have attempted to paint a rather sordid picture of this young lady. Can I say during my investigation I have obtained statements from several people in Kenya, and England, to the effect that Julie was not promiscuous in any way. She was a normal twenty-eight-year-old English girl, and from

345

time to time had regular boyfriends and enjoyed life to the full. To suggest other than that is, in my view, quite wrong.

'The second matter concerns the accounts clerk at Sand River Gate, one David Nchoko. He was subjected to a glare of publicity, particularly during the inquest, to the point of its being suggested that he was a suspect. David Nchoko admits forging Julie's signature in the visitors' register, but simply for the purposes of audit. Detective Superintendent Wanjau and I have interviewed him again, and as a result of that and other inquiries made in England, relative to his possible involvement, I wish to publicly state on his behalf that he was not, in my view, involved in Julie's disappearance and death.'

Searle then mentioned the cash rewards still outstanding, of 300,000 Kenyan shillings – $15,000 – for information leading to arrest and conviction of the killers, and 30,000 shillings for information about Julie's missing camera. He repeated a telephone number for confidential tips – for security it did not go through the hotel switchboard – and got ready to take questions.

'Are they game rangers in the Masai Mara?'

'I will confirm that one point. They are game rangers.'

'Is this the first time they've been questioned?'

'As far as I am aware,' Searle said, not looking at Wanjau, 'this is the first time they have been questioned.'

'Can we ask Mr Wanjau that?'

Wanjau looked up, truculently. 'No, this is not their first time to be questioned,' he said, to the British detectives' surprise.

'Have all thirty-four rangers been questioned in the past?'

'We questioned . . . a good number of them,' Wanjau said.

'But the two held have definitely been questioned in the past?'

'Yes,' he insisted.

'How many times?'

'Well, I don't remember how many times.'

One reporter asked about efforts to trace the tourists who had stayed at Sand River. Wanjau evidently thought he was referring to Burns and Watson and responded, 'We appealed to the Interpol police for them to come back to Nairobi. It was a request, during the inquest.'

Someone corrected his misimpression and asked again about the Sand River campers.

'Yes, we tried to trace them,' he said sharply, 'but unfortunately they are tourists, they come and go back to their country.'

Searle interrupted to say, 'That is a matter that we have taken on board.' He said he would try to trace as many tourists as possible. 'But as Superintendent Wanjau quite rightly says, it is not an easy task.'

Wanjau, uncharacteristically loquacious, took the floor again. 'One thing I would rather like to clarify to you is that those people' – he meant the two detained rangers – 'came to us voluntarily and they are with us, helping us with the investigations.' But he acknowledged that under Kenyan law they could be held without charges for up to 14 days.

'So are they under arrest?'

'They are not under arrest at all!' he said defensively.

'Then where are they?'

'They are in Kenya!' Wanjau shouted. At this point Shipperlee made to interject something, but Searle stopped him. 'Don't get involved,' the senior man said in an undertone. Aloud, he said, 'Right, then, ladies and gentlemen, I'm going to draw it to a close.'

CHAPTER FIFTY

Since the New Year John Ward had spent much of his time pursuing publicity for his story. An article in the *Los Angeles Times* about the inquest had mobilized a battalion of Hollywood agents and fringe-level movie producers into expressing interest. 'This has everything,' remarked one, overtaken by enthusiasm, to the father. 'Mystery, corruption, a cover-up, a beautiful girl, sex, wild animals, and African landscapes!' Ward was intrigued by the notion of having Julie portrayed on screen as he remembered her, rather than in the approved Kenyan government or *Sunday Mirror* version. He also liked the idea of getting his own back at the Kenyan government through a Hollywood portrayal of his efforts. A movie deal might also defray the expense of his campaign for justice. He hired a London agent to field offers.

In early March he was in the United States to tape a TV show called *Hard Copy*. This was a syndicated tabloid program which, like its newsprint counterparts, sprayed out a potent stream of sensationalism for its viewers. It had done a piece on a tourist who vanished in the Far East, and now John Ward was going to tell his story about a tourist whose death went almost unremarked by the Kenyan authorities. While in New York for the taping he got in touch with Margaret Beale, the sister of Marie Ferraro, the American tourist shot to death by the poachers in Tsavo a month before the inquest. Mrs Beale had read an article somewhere about Ward and had written him to commiserate and to complain about how hard it had been for her to get information out of the Kenyan government.

Ward invited her to meet him in New York while he was in town for the taping. Mrs Beale came down with Allen

348

Sullivan, the retired schoolteacher who had been wounded across the face in the same burst of gunfire that had felled Marie Ferraro. Sullivan still bore the facial scar from the poacher's bullet as well as a reserve of deep bitterness over the performance of the American Embassy in Nairobi in the attack's aftermath.

He had been shocked at the embassy's indifference upon the group's return from the bush with their passports and money stolen and an American corpse on their hands, Sullivan told Ward. A consular official had met them at the Inter-Continental with tactless words about how 'Americans get killed overseas all the time.' He was armed with an illustrative anecdote about an American citizen's recent skiing death in the Alps.

'Look, buster,' one of the group interrupted angrily. 'This isn't any skiing accident! It's a murder case!'

Sullivan said he and his wife got their passports replaced at the embassy only to be presented with a bill for eighty-four dollars cash on the spot. Their money had been stolen, too, so a friend paid the bill.

Aside from its hint that Kenya's bureaucratic indolence could infect even a First World stronghold like the US embassy, this narrative interested Ward because he nurtured a grievance of his own against the American diplomats. For months he had been trying to enlist the embassy's aid in reaching an American family who had been hijacked and abandoned overnight in the Mara the previous September. Word of the attack had emerged during the inquest. The family's money and shoes had been stolen along with their vehicle. Man and wife and seven-year-old boy, they had spent much of the night walking terrified and barefooted through the park to their lodge. By the time the story was out the family had left the country and their identities shrouded by the embassy. Ward now wished to show them his sheaf of photographs of rangers and others in the Mara, in the hope they might identify some of them as their assailants. But the American consul steadfastly refused to cooperate, on grounds that the family had requested privacy. Ward had even offered to turn the photographs over to the embassy so its personnel could contact the family themselves, but this request was also refused.

Sullivan also entertained Ward with the story of what had happened when an embassy official escorted him to a police station to report the theft of his currency form, which tourists had to turn over to customs officers on their departure from Kenya. 'The police kept asking us, in amazement, how we lost the form,' he recalled. 'I couldn't believe it. The story of our shooting was in all the papers. Didn't they even pay attention? I figured they'd know all about it.'

By now Ward was scarcely making much effort to disguise his bitterness and anger at the performance of the Kenya authorities. As Sullivan later recalled the conversation, Ward told him that 'the Kenya Police were corrupt right to the top.' Sullivan regarded this as the hyperbole of a bereaved and frustrated father, but he listened carefully as Ward delivered a succinct lesson in Sullivan's rights under Kenya law as a victim and an interested party to a felony. Sullivan was entitled to a copy of each of the six or seven depositions he had given at Tsavo and in Nairobi after the shooting, Ward instructed him, as well as the formal reports made about the incident by the police and wildlife officials. Later, as Sullivan tried fruitlessly to extract these documents from the authorities via the American embassy, he came around to Ward's view of the Kenya Police. The only report he was able to get of the violent murder of an American tourist in a national park was a two-paragraph police report from the police post nearest Amboseli. 'The police combed the area where the bandits were headed,' the report stated, 'but unfortunately they were not traced.'

Shortly after his visit to New York Ward returned again to Nairobi. It was his seventeenth trip. On this journey, for the first time, he brought his wife, Janet.

Ward had made the plans months earlier, counting on a quiet visit. Janet wanted to see the Masai Mara scenery her daughter had so prized, and he had a lead he wanted to pursue in Narok, the town midway between Nairobi and the park. But in arriving within days of Searle's announcement about the two rangers he found himself again at the center of news. The Wards even granted an interview to the *Daily Nation*, probably the best of the three Kenyan English-language dailies. A photograph of the two of them ran on its front page, Janet fingering a necklace of beads, under a headline that read, CLUES GIVE JULIE'S PARENTS NEW HOPE.

'We might be coming to the bottom of the matter,' Ward was quoted as saying.

The coincidental arrival of the Wards and the two Scotland Yard teams brought to Kenya another wave of unwelcome publicity. Reporters flying in to cover the police investigations had time on their hands, and they passed it by writing articles about crime waves in Nairobi and deteriorating conditions in the countryside. One London paper, the *Daily Mail*, reported that AIDS was so serious a menace that 'whole villages have been wiped out', a fantastic exaggeration. The domestic Kenyan press fretted about having these nonresident correspondents at large. One compared the *Mail* article unfavorably with a long feature that had run at about the same time in the *Telegraph*, one of Britain's more creditable newspapers. This one was about the salubrious life-style of Kenya's remaining colonial-era whites, quoting them talking about how things had never been better.

Meanwhile Searle got ready to interrogate Simon Makallah. Makallah's house was unlocked and opened for the first time since the end of the inquest and a British forensic expert, borrowed from Troon's team working on the Ouko case, went over it. It was clean, he said. No clues, no evidence.

When Searle escorted the suspended chief warden to Keekorok he was surprised to see the reception Ward's principal suspect elicited from the rangers gathered around. If Makallah had been the object of animosity among the ranger force, there was no sign of it here. The rangers ran up to greet Makallah and shake his hand, genuinely happy to see him back on the grounds for the first time in almost two years.

Searle had prepared himself for this important session by interviewing George Othiambo, the Mara Bridge police officer who had been with Makallah and the other rangers on the drive to find Julie's remains. Othiambo had acquitted himself poorly on the stand under Georgiadis's browbeating. Reading the transcript, Searle had been certain he was hiding something. But in person Searle rather took a liking to the tall, thin officer. He was a simple, unsophisticated person, but off the stand and safe from the lawyer's badgering he showed the British detective that he knew how to do his job. It was Othiambo, after all, who had had the presence of mind to mark the spots where each object was found around the fire under the sausage tree. He had discovered the leg by following the trail of something dragged off from the fire. And now Searle discovered that Othiambo, not Makallah, had directed the search for the remains, starting from the gully.

Othiambo repeated that they had found footprints, on the far side of the Sand River from the gully. They proceeded by doing a sweep search around the prints, a kilometer on each side, he said. Then he added a detail that lent rhyme and reason to the search party's suspicious route: He and Makallah had agreed on a plan to finish work early and go home by heading from the gully toward the Tanzanian border, a direction they all knew. They expected to find nothing, and from there they could just go back to base at Keekorok. They reached the border without seeing anything but on the way back, by sheer chance, they spotted a clutch of vultures and found the remains.

The interrogation of Simon Makallah lasted eight hours and five minutes. After twenty-three years of active police work Searle prided himself on being able to take a man's measure during the course of an interrogation, and he had no doubts about Makallah. The chief warden lied to him about whether he drove, as he had lied on the stand. He told the same story as Othiambo about following footprints from the jeep and eventually spotting vultures in the distance. The broken four-wheel drive? It was commonly known all over the park by the time of the inquest, he indicated. As chief ranger, why wouldn't he know?

Searle also discovered something Wanjau should have found out: For most of the week between Julie's disappearance and murder, Makallah had an alibi. On 7, 8 and 9 September, the days Julie was probably in the worst trouble, he was in Narok, acting as Masai interpreter for a farming seminar sponsored by the European Commission, and checked into a Narok hotel. Wanjau had had no clue of this. By the time Makallah returned to the Mara it was the night of 10 September, and the next day searches were under way. Searle was able to establish Makallah's movements for the remainder of the week, and he was convinced that the warden was innocent.

Meanwhile Dave Shipperlee interviewed Paul Molinaro. The young man's story about seeing Julie at Sand River at 4 p.m. was another obstacle to the Scotland Yard theory, if not a major one. At first the detectives suspected that Molinaro's entire story had been a fake, a subterfuge intended to gain a piece of the reward. Eventually they came to believe the young man was telling the truth, but that he was making an important mistake.

Under Shipperlee's careful questioning it turned out that Molinaro had never had a firm idea of the time he and his companions had arrived at Sand River. None of them wore watches and they had the foggy feel for time's passage of any young people without a firm agenda. They thought it was late, Molinaro remembered, because they were about to start gathering firewood for the evening chill.

Yet Molinaro remembered that he and his companions had left the Mara Serena Lodge at noon, hoping to make Keekorok Lodge in time to have lunch. That traverse would take between sixty and ninety minutes. At

Keekorok they were turned away from the dining room because they looked too scruffy. From there, Molinaro said, they headed directly to Sand River. That was a drive of fifteen to twenty minutes. It all put their arrival at Sand River Camp, and the last spotting of Julie Ward, closer to 2.30 than 4 o'clock. And that tended to confirm Nchoko's story that she passed through the gate at 2.37 p.m.

The two detectives were now close to the end of their stay in Kenya. Searle and Shipperlee were virtually convinced they had figured out how Julie Ward died and who killed her. Now they were ready to try to persuade John Ward of the likelihood of their scenario. In a sort of dry run, they first spent two hours trying to change the mind of Byron Georgiadis.

The two detectives admired the silver-haired lawyer, but after having read the inquest transcripts they were less than convinced that his method of browbeating witnesses was the best way to elicit the truth. The process worked well if one was trying to confirm a pre-existing theory, Searle reasoned. But it worked not so well if one was genuinely on a fact-finding mission.

Searle always took care never to go beyond what could be proven. To accuse somebody of a capital crime, you need evidence, not gut feelings and assumptions. The more time he had spent on this case, the more he felt that people had been accused of heinous crimes without a shred of evidence.

Searle acknowledged to Georgiadis that Makallah had lied on the stand. The warden had even repeated to the Scotland Yard detective his lie about driving, which had taken Searle aback. But did it point to his complicity in murder? The answer, Searle said firmly, was no. Makallah, after all, had already been charged with misusing park vehicles – it was part of the notice of interdiction the lawyer had made so much of at the inquest. Of course he was afraid of admitting he drove, because that would only help strengthen the malfeasance case against him. 'I don't believe him either,' Searle said. 'But there's no big beer in it.'

What about the issue of the Suzuki's four-wheel-drive? Searle and Shipperlee saw nothing in Makallah's confused testimony on that issue to inculpate him either. He was chief warden of the Masai Mara. By the time of the inquest, certainly, everybody knew about the broken drive linkage. And as for the story of the footprints and the vultures, Searle believed it. Makallah was supported by Othiambo, and no-one had given any testimony to contradict it. In short, Searle repeated, 'There is not one shred of evidence that Makallah was involved in the death and disappearance of Julie.'

The detectives left their meeting with Georgiadis feeling that they might have changed the lawyer's mind, or at least slightly redirected his convictions. John Ward, however, would be a tougher nut to crack.

That night Searle and Shipperlee had dinner with Ward, who chose to leave Janet back at the hotel. Just as they anticipated, it was an awkward and difficult affair. They were presenting Ward with what Searle later described as a 'bitter pill': Not only were they convinced that Julie had driven herself into the gully, but they had dispelled the clouds over three of her father's favorite suspects; Makallah, Nchoko, and Karuri.

The detectives were sure that she had spent at least a night in the jeep in the gully, alone and unmolested long enough to write SOS on its roof in mud. That was what suggested she had gone in under her own steam. Her father was still sure she had not.

John Ward could not forget his view of that spot on the Keekorok–Sand River road where Makallah had gestured off into the distance, and how he had been struck by the foolishness of turning off a main road, late in the afternoon, into unmarked and rough terrain. The detectives left the restaurant hoping that Ward would eventually come around to their point of view, but his position remained firm. The next afternoon, as he dressed for a dinner with Byron Georgiadis, he told a couple of visitors that he flatly rejected the Yard's scenario.

'No way,' he said. 'There's just no way she drove off

that road. It isn't logical. It makes no sense at all. And they should know that.'

But clearly he was in something of a box. For the first time the people positing an alternative scenario about Julie's last days were able to muster logical arguments of their own. This was not a case of Kenyan authorities suggesting his daughter had hacked herself to pieces and flung her own remains on a fire. He was dealing with two professional detectives with forty years' experience between them, seconded from one of the world's legendary investigatory bodies. Searle and Shipperlee were precisely the kind of investigators Ward had spent nearly two years trying to get assigned to the case, and to challenge their conclusions in public could cost him a lot of credibility.

Instead he suggested that their findings were just an interesting working theory. 'Their investigation, of course, is just at a preliminary stage,' he remarked. Ward was already thinking in terms of what would happen if the forensic evidence – all those bags of trash from the huts – turned up negative. He commiserated out loud with the detectives' consequent need to come back to Nairobi and start at square one.

That did not seem to be Searle's and Shipperlee's attitude as they packed up for the regular Thursday-night Kenya Airways flight to London. Given the modest expectations with which they had alighted in Nairobi a month earlier they plainly felt that, incomplete as it still might be, their investigation was closer to the end than the beginning.

Ward looked weary that afternoon in the hotel. He had just endured a ten-hour round-trip drive to Narok, over the usual decrepit roads, on his own evidentiary quest. The two detained rangers had been provisionally released to await the forensic examination of the Makari trash. Now, stunned by the Yard's emerging conclusions and deprived of the privileged public attention he had attracted at the crest of the inquest nine months earlier, Ward contemplated the course ahead without enthusiasm.

To his visitors he repeated his familiar vow to 'get the bastards', but if Scotland Yard was going to stick to its disagreeable theory, then once again, eighteen months on, he was going to be on his own.

He had come a long way in just a couple of months, from the time of his first elated realization that Scotland Yard was going to investigate. Later there had been a twinge of dismay at learning that Wanjau would be involved in the new investigation, but that could be written off as just the price one had to pay to have the professionals come in. He had recognized then that as much as Scotland Yard wanted a free hand, they were operating in a sovereign country as foreigners, and that the Kenyan authorities would want to stay close – maybe in order to grab the credit for any solution. But he was confident the Yard would start from square one and fill in the huge gaps in the case. 'These fellows won't take any messing about,' he had remarked when the new investigation was announced. 'They're not there to waste their time.'

Now, in his hotel room, he could not hide his disappointment.

'Do you think you're obsessed?' he was asked.

Ward had always bristled at this description of his motivation to find Julie's killers. Once again he rejected it. 'I don't think so,' he said. 'If I were ever to run out of leads, I would stop coming to this godforsaken place. If it dried up, I'd stop. But as long as there are leads, I'll come. I think that's the difference.'

CHAPTER FIFTY-ONE

Searle and Shipperlee were wrong about Byron Georgiadis: He was no more convinced than John Ward by their hypothesis.

'It's a convenient theory,' he told people after they departed for London, 'but I don't think it's plausible at all. In a hundred years I don't think it's plausible.'

Georgiadis had as much at stake as Ward himself in the portrait of a girl too bright to go jouncing off across country in a failing vehicle. 'A girl who knows her vehicle is clapped out, leaves late one afternoon for Nairobi, suddenly deviates on no apparent path through the bush and goes downhill several kilometers and gets stuck. I found it totally implausible.'

He seemed disappointed in the Scotland Yard detectives. 'I think they ran into a cold trail and a lot of frustration and they were ready to throw up their hands and go home.'

Meanwhile Dave Shipperlee was making the drive from Geneva to Montreux to call on Henri Berney. He found the Swiss documentarian rather less dogmatic than he had been with Ward. Berney was unable to place his Navstar coordinates on the ordinance map Shipperlee had brought, which had precise locational coordinates overlaying the entire Mara on a large scale. *Impossible* was no longer part of Berney's vocabulary. Now he was telling Shipperlee that he 'believed' he would have seen the jeep if it had been there for six days. He finally placed the location of his camp visually on the map on the east side of the 'V' formed by a branching tributary of the Sand River. That put it about two kilometers north of the spot indicated by the coordinates Berney had given Ward to enter into evidence at the inquest, but the difference was not as important as all that: Both sites were roughly 1.5 kilometers from the resting place of Julie's jeep. That was much less than the three or four kilometers testified to by Makallah and Wanjau, but it was not the 300 to 400 meters recalled by Sebastian Tham either.

Shipperlee went on to interview several of the crew members. None of them could place the camp in relation to Julie's jeep because none except Berney had been told where the jeep was stuck. But one point on which they all agreed was interesting: The camp was located in a hollow, heavily shrouded by trees, they remembered. Any direction you left the camp, you had to head uphill. Very little of the camp's noise and activity escaped from the heavy envelope of wood and brush.

'If you got fifty meters away from it,' one of the crew remarked, 'you would lose it.'

Magiroi and Kippeen had spent only a few days in custody in Nairobi before being released, with the acquiescence of Searle and Shipperlee. It was assumed that the Kenya Police would keep an eye on the two rangers so they could be swiftly hauled back in if and when the forensic evidence came in.

Months passed and the forensic haul continued to be a disappointment. The only results were negative, as the police laboratory in Great Britain sifted the accumulated trash and found nothing linking it to Julie Ward.

Still, Searle and Shipperlee felt the circumstantial evidence placing the two rangers near the scene of Julie's jeep was enough to warrant their prosecution for her killing. In June they submitted a report on their investigation and suggested the Kenyan authorities put the two men on trial.

In Bury St Edmunds, John Ward had returned more or less full time to the business of running his hotels. The business had begun to suffer from his single-minded devotion to his quest in Kenya, and some expansion plans had been held up.

He greeted word of the detectives' report to the government with mixed emotions. On the one hand it was clearly progress to have defendants finally brought before the bar of justice. But Ward still gripped his cherished idea that higher-ups – particularly Makallah – were going scot free.

'I'm just afraid they'll put these two blokes on trial and then say, "That's it," and none of the others will be prosecuted,' he remarked one day. The Yard's inability to find any incontrovertible evidence against the rangers seemed to have emboldened him to question their results, and he still talked of having leads to pursue.

But new leads came only rarely now, and their quality suffered a sharp falling-off. Ward had not been back to Kenya since his visit with Janet early in 1990, the trip that had coincided with Searle's and Shipperlee's investigation. Byron Georgiadis was preparing to retire, and Whitford was spending less time fielding tips about Julie's death.

One day that spring a cheap Kenyan magazine named *True Love* ran a feature about Julie's death, illustrated with a handful of mislabeled photographs of people like her father and David Weston and Simon Makallah. It was even more salacious and fantastic than the old *Sunday Mirror* article, as if Julie had ceased to be a real person and now was just fodder for cheesecake fantasies.

The Kenyan authorities resisted bringing Magiroi and Kippeen to trial. During the summer of 1990 Attorney General Matthew Muli appealed for the Scotland Yard detectives to come back to Kenya to continue their work, because the forensic evidence was still nonexistent. The prosecutors were alarmed at the prospect of bringing two rangers to trial and having them acquitted. In any case, the Julie Ward murder had been pushed to the back burner by more pressing events in Kenya. The Ouko killing – Troon's Scotland Yard report on that case was still sealed – had indirectly stimulated a nascent opposition movement in the country. Increasingly, prominent people were calling for a return to the multiparty democracy existent in Kenya until a postcoup constitutional amendment outlawed all parties except KANU.

One week in July, seventeen of these critics were rounded up and jailed without charges. Riots spread from Nairobi through all the old Kikuyu strongholds of the highlands and took five days for the police to contain. The government might have feared that to act on the Yard's recommendations in the Ward case would inspire more questions about what had happened to the Ouko report, and that might be political dynamite. So the rangers remained at large, uncharged.

Late that summer Attorney General Muli began complaining about Scotland Yard's Julie Ward investigation. The physical evidence was inadequate, he said, to charge the two rangers – who had still never been identified in public – with a crime. He asked that Searle and Shipperlee come back and do more work. In mid-September, in part because there were a few minor loose ends they wanted to clear up, the two detectives returned.

The weather in the Masai Mara was much better than it had been during their first appearance the previous March, dry and clear. With Michael Koikai, who had replaced Makallah as chief warden, guiding them, they got their first look at the old fire site. When they arrived Searle and Shipperlee were impressed by the remoteness of the place. Just as Ward had thought a year and a half before, they regarded it as somewhere that only a person deeply familiar with the area would go. Koikai's driver had taken a roundabout route from the gully to the fire in order to negotiate the rough terrain, but the warden gave them an excellent idea of its location. To reach here from the Makari post by foot, he said, would take a pair of experienced Masai rangers less than an hour.

EPILOGUE: A Night Alone in the Masai Mara

Two years after Julie Ward's disappearance and death on her way home from Sand River Gate it was as if some great spirit in the Masai Mara had moved to shroud her case in historical mist.

The entire quadrant east of Keekorok and Sand River had been closed to visitors. This is the area that held Makari Post, the gully, and the resting place of Julie's remains. That side of the Keekorok–Sand River Road, and the southern side of the road leading from Keekorok out to Olaimutiek Gate, were marked by black rectangular signs warning tourists away, on orders of Chief Warden Michael Koikai. Ask around at Sand River, and one would be told that the warden had concluded that overuse had seriously damaged the ecosystem. 'It was getting like a desert in there,' a ranger would say.

Most of those involved in the events of September 1988 were gone. Constable Karuri had been transferred from Sand River. Inspector George Othiambo had left Mara Bridge to take up new duties at Nakuru.

Simon ole Makallah, after an eight-month ordeal, cleared himself of the Narok County Council's charges against him. He won a transfer – a promotion, in effect – to the giant Tsavo West Game Reserve, where he was named chief warden.

Only Magiroi and Kippeen the two rangers who occupied Makari post when Julie's jeep became mired in the gully nearby, were still on duty, although at diferent posts.

Sand River Camp, where thirty or forty tents had been pitched at the time that Julie and Glen Burns arrived to see the wildebeest migration, looked deserted two years later.

Two or three tents occupied the rocky high ground on the northern bank of the river, and there was none on the far side, where they had stayed. Game drivers remarked that this year's migrating wildebeest herd seemed thinner than usual. This they ascribed to wetter weather conditions in the Serengeti, which allowed the animals to stay south, and to a bush fire that had blackened much of the southern Mara. Nevertheless the evidence of nature's savage glory, the skeletons and rotting carcassses of the ridiculous-looking beasts, still dotted the wide plains.

The Kenya government was still enormously concerned about the tourist business. The crackdown on dissent and a week of attendant riots in Nairobi the previous spring had taken a certain toll: Among other things, an international bar association conference scheduled to bring thousands of lawyers and their families to Kenya at the beginning of September was canceled, leaving an immense vacuum in park bookings for that period. Tour operators said business was generally down, although the reasons were unclear and likely varied. The government invited parties of foreign travel writers to come into the country to hear ministers talk about a new, higher level of security in the parks and praise the country's famous political stability.

The Masai Mara remained the country's premier tourist attraction. Doug Morey flew to the park regularly for AirKenya, which was so busy it sometimes had two planes full for every scheduled flight. He had not heard from John Ward in months, since Ward had written to tell him about the barbecue and slide-show he had scheduled in Bury St Edmunds for Julie's companions on the Ho-Bo overland tour.

What was unknown about Julie's last days in the Masai Mara was likely to remain that way forever. But there was enough to posit a reasonable scenario.

Sand River Gate, 6 September 1988. 2.37 p.m.

The sun still burns with a noontime glare as Julie pays her fee at the gatehouse and moves through it north on to the road to Keekorok. She might not be concerned about arriving in Nairobi after dark, as she is now certain to do, but she is likely to be in somewhat of a hurry in order to reach at least the outskirts of the city by nightfall.

With her in the front seat of the car is a map of the Masai Mara. There are at least three maps commonly available in Nairobi bookstores and in the gift shops of the park's lodges, but they are all very different and in varying ways misleading. Julie's is printed on glossy paper, with a photograph of a cheetah and her cub on the cover and the name of the park printed in bright red. The map stresses brightness of display more than accuracy of scale.

Importantly, it shows what appears to be a shortcut out of the park. A dotted red-and-white line extends off to the east from the Keekorok main road, reconnecting a few kilometers farther to a main road heading out of the park via the Olaimutiek Gate, past the Mara Sopa Lodge. It appears to be a shorter route to Narok and thence Nairobi than the way she and Burns had come in via the Sekenani Gate. From Olaimutiek the road to Narok is twenty kilometers longer than from Sekenani, but it is unlikely she knows that because the only indication of the comparative distance is a faded signboard at the junction of the Sekenani and Olaimutiek roads near the Keekorok airstrip, some five kilometers farther up the road than from where she turns off.

The ostensible shortcut to Olaimutiek is given much more prominence on her map than on any other. On one it does not appear at all, and on another, the most authoritative, it is dismissively designated only as a 'motorable track.' As it happens, it is a bad road, hard to follow and easy to stray from. Confident of her ability to handle unexpected eventualities, perhaps even a little complacent amid the sundrenched expanse of the Masai Mara, she steers her little Suzuki off the graded dirt road to Keekorok and heads east. Perhaps thirty or forty minutes later her new route crosses a tributary of the Sand River, just near the place where it branches off. Nearby is an easy ford, but it might be hard to distinguish from the front seat of the jouncing car. She drives straight ahead. Given the proper momentum and a lucky flick of the steering wheel she might have got through, but she does not. The car spins and rocks and finally settles in the mud, immobilized.

She spins the tires in the muck. From the bank she pulls a couple of stray pieces of wood and wedges them under the wheels, then tries to manipulate the jack so as to lift the undercarriage free of the quagmire. These are found later by the search parties. Perhaps she hoots the Suzuki's horn, but this is an out-of-the-way place where people rarely cross. At some point she smears mud on the roof in the form of a squarish SOS. By now it is close to nightfall, and Julie is resigned to staying the night. She pulls a few shreds of plastic from inside the car and lights a fire on the high bank of the gully. She keeps the headlights burning, torn between the need to conserve battery power and the desire to keep animals away or attract human attention.

The next day dawns, and at length the figures of a couple of men appear on the rim of the gully. They might have been uniformed which Julie would have greeted with great relief. They encourage her confidence by remarking that their post is not very far away, and equipped with a radio with which she can summon help.

It's an easy walk, they say. She figures there's no need to pull on her sneakers, her red flip-flops will do just as well. She shoulders her valuable camera and lens but leaves most everything else inside the jeep: a pair of binoculars, her map, beers, and cans of food. She will be coming back shortly anyway. She locks up the jeep and pads off with the men. At their post she finds herself alone with the men, and she is never heard from again. She remains incommunicado for five days, from 7 September until the 11th. By then the search is on. Her panicking abductors kill her, dismember the body, and then strew it over the inaccessible landscape lying between the scene of their crime and the Tanzanian border.

Is this reasonable? Her father considered it ridiculous, insisting that Julie would never have left the road herself.

Why, with a familiar straight and good road ahead of her, would she turn off on to an uncertain and poor route? He believed she was held, shamelessly misused and violated, and perhaps slaughtered at the Makari ranger post, but he was sure that the Suzuki must have been planted by her killers, or that she was lured to the spot by someone – perhaps a ranger or policeman who waved her down and cadged a lift, a common enough event in the Mara where rangers and police officers alike are deprived of official transport. He thought it was likely that she did not even leave Sand River Gate under her own steam.

But Scotland Yard's objections to those theories make considerable sense. What individual, trying to cache evidence of guilt like a car, runs it into a secluded gully and then draws attention to it with an SOS on the roof? This after wasting time trying to spin it out of the muck?

Moreover, if Julie had been accompanied by someone when she drove off the road, she would not have had the time or opportunity to write the SOS. More items of value would probably have been missing from the car, and it would probably not have been left locked. Is it that unlikely for Julie to have driven off the main road? Perhaps not. She was a young woman of great confidence, proud of her growing ability to face the unexpected with equanimity. In the Masai Mara it is no great thing to drive off a main road into bush; often it is the only way to get close to game. To the Scotland Yard detectives the condition of the vehicle indicated these things: She drove into the gully herself, and she left the car voluntarily.

What of the subsequent cover-up of a crime?

Through the prism of subjectivity it is not hard to envision a grand conspiracy like the one John Ward believed himself to be confronting. In any country it might have happened this way: first the alteration of the autopsy report, substituting the activity of animals for that of men, followed by a police investigation obscuring important facts and ignoring others even more essential. High officials demur endlessly, awaiting official reports that never come, offering minuscule shreds of progress in an infinite succession that gets nowhere, smearing the victim's reputation to suggest she was an important contributor to her own demise.

John Ward saw these things: a postmortem counterfeited with such arrogance that verisimilitude was not even attempted. A police commissioner unwilling to let the facts lead to their logical conclusion. An investigator who discarded evidence without examining it and who interviewed almost no witnesses. A park warden whose very demeanor was that of a guilty man. A formal inquest at which obvious red herrings were given more attention than documented evidence. Finally there was a professional investigation that led to two new suspects. In Kenya as in Great Britian and the United States, they are entitled by law to be presumed innocent until judged and to face the evidence against them.

On 12 February 1991, the Government finally moved against the men Scotland Yard had suspected as the killers. Attorney General Muli ordered Kippeen and Magiroi arrested and charged with murder. A trial would follow shortly, he promised.

With the rangers likely to face trial, the events of Julie's last days in the Masai Mara might finally come to light. But even before trial, there was enough to posit a reasonable scenario.

Of course there was a cover-up. But it was not necessarily a conspiracy. It is not necessary to believe that all these agents – Kilonzo, Wanjau, Makallah, Kaviti, Etyang – acted together, because each was capable of doing what he did to cover up the murder of Julie Ward or neglect the investigation on his own, without consultation with anyone.

The ethos of officialdom in Kenya was the converse of sticking one's neck out. And to proclaim that the death of Julie Ward was the outcome of murder committed by a person or persons in public trust would be just that. To anyone with a First World sense of justice and decency, the official handling of Julie's death is appalling. John

Ward reacted in an understandable manner. He pressed, he complained, he proclaimed his determination to force out the truth. In Great Britain his dynamism would be admired and perhaps feared and a public outcry to bring the miscreants to justice might acquire an implacable force. In Kenya, sensitive about its colonial heritage and proud of its successful fight for independence, vexed at outsiders who never cease to suggest that its best efforts are wasted or incompetent, every quantum of force Ward applied provoked an equal and opposite force of Newtonian ineluctability. His determination provoked resentment and his own investigatory efforts only resistance.

Deprived of the official assistance that is crucial in a Western country and indispensable in a closed and unfamiliar society like Kenya's, he turned himself into an investigator. But his lack of training led him astray. A professional detective begins with the evidence, amasses it without prejudice, and follows where and to whom it leads. John Ward found his suspect early, on a dispiriting drive along the road from Sand River to Keekorok, and then looked mostly for evidence to fit the man.

It was a valiant and moving campaign, whatever its outcome. The Kenyan government thought he would go away but he never did, and the result was all the more embarrassing for a country that deserves better. Julie Ward deserved better too: to live or at least to have her killers brought to book. She was a lovely, kind, quiet woman who got out of life all that it had to offer, and would have in generosity given back even more.

ACKNOWLEDGMENTS

It is the usual thing to begin notes of this kind by thanking one's family members for their support, but the debt I owe my wife, Deborah, could not be discharged by formalities. Her contribution to this book went well beyond the customary chore of seeing her husband through the numerous periods of self-doubt inevitable in a project of this scope. Her insights as a journalist with a professional interest in the affair of Julie Ward were indispensable and often expressed persuasively enough to make me change my own mind about key elements of the case. She conducted many crucial interviews that I was unable to undertake, including several that required charm and graciousness to bring off, qualities of which her reserves far outstrip my own, to say the least. In the most real sense this book would not exist but for her.

Many people assisted me in overcoming an important obstacle to telling the story of the inquest: the absence of a formal court record. Those who loaned me their notes and contributed their recollections and impressions of the inquest, which I used to supplement my own and Deborah's, include Todd Shields of the *Independent* and Colin Blane and Peter Biles of the British Broadcasting Corporation. Key contributions to my work on this book were made by my friends Ann and Tony Turner, whose long experience of Kenya and whose inexhaustible supply of friends and contacts around the country opened many doors, including some I would otherwise never have known to exist. In this project as in all my other endeavors in Africa I have benefited from the support of my superiors at the *Los Angeles Times*, including Foreign Editor Alvin Shuster, who gave me the opportunity in

1988 to move to Nairobi to cover the continent, and Assistant Foreign Editor Simon Li, who did his usual superb job of editing my article about the inquest for the newspaper.